CAMBRIDGE LIBRARY COLLECTION

Books of enduring scholarly value

Women's Writing

The later twentieth century saw a huge wave of academic interest in women's writing, which led to the rediscovery of neglected works from a wide range of genres, periods and languages. Many books that were immensely popular and influential in their own day are now studied again, both for their own sake and for what they reveal about the social, political and cultural conditions of their time. A pioneering resource in this area is Orlando: Women's Writing in the British Isles from the Beginnings to the Present (http://orlando.cambridge.org), which provides entries on authors' lives and writing careers, contextual material, timelines, sets of internal links, and bibliographies. Its editors have made a major contribution to the selection of the works reissued in this series within the Cambridge Library Collection, which focuses on non-fiction publications by women on a wide range of subjects from astronomy to biography, music to political economy, and education to prison reform.

Conversations on Political Economy

Published at a pivotal moment in the economic development of Britain, *Conversations on Political Economy* (1816) influenced a generation of economists, politicians and intellectuals. Employing her trademark format of dialogues between Mrs Bryan and her pupil Caroline, Marcet introduces readers to theories surrounding property, population, and the 'condition of the poor'. Despite a target audience of young women, there is little evidence of feminine sentimentality, nor does the author's commitment to female education prevent her from propounding challenging, often controversial arguments: an approach which won her admiration. As one of her avid readers, Anne Romilly, wrote, 'those, who like me know very little … are delighted with the knowledge they have acquired'. In fact, the first edition was so well received that a second was called for before the author had time to make corrections. Marcet had become, as one of her obituarists later put it, the 'instructress of a generation'. For more information on this author, see http://orlando.cambridge.org/public/svPeople?person_id=marcja

Cambridge University Press has long been a pioneer in the reissuing of out-of-print titles from its own backlist, producing digital reprints of books that are still sought after by scholars and students but could not be reprinted economically using traditional technology. The Cambridge Library Collection extends this activity to a wider range of books which are still of importance to researchers and professionals, either for the source material they contain, or as landmarks in the history of their academic discipline.

Drawing from the world-renowned collections in the Cambridge University Library, and guided by the advice of experts in each subject area, Cambridge University Press is using state-of-the-art scanning machines in its own Printing House to capture the content of each book selected for inclusion. The files are processed to give a consistently clear, crisp image, and the books finished to the high quality standard for which the Press is recognised around the world. The latest print-on-demand technology ensures that the books will remain available indefinitely, and that orders for single or multiple copies can quickly be supplied.

The Cambridge Library Collection will bring back to life books of enduring scholarly value (including out-of-copyright works originally issued by other publishers) across a wide range of disciplines in the humanities and social sciences and in science and technology.

Conversations on Political Economy

In Which the Elements of that Science are Familiarly Explained

Jane Haldimand Marcet

CAMBRIDGE UNIVERSITY PRESS

Cambridge, New York, Melbourne, Madrid, Cape Town, Singapore,
São Paolo, Delhi, Dubai, Tokyo

Published in the United States of America by Cambridge University Press, New York

www.cambridge.org
Information on this title: www.cambridge.org/9781108019101

© in this compilation Cambridge University Press 2010

This edition first published 1816
This digitally printed version 2010

ISBN 978-1-108-01910-1 Paperback

This book reproduces the text of the original edition. The content and language reflect
the beliefs, practices and terminology of their time, and have not been updated.

Cambridge University Press wishes to make clear that the book, unless originally published
by Cambridge, is not being republished by, in association or collaboration with, or
with the endorsement or approval of, the original publisher or its successors in title.

CONVERSATIONS

ON

POLITICAL ECONOMY;

IN WHICH

THE ELEMENTS OF THAT SCIENCE

ARE

FAMILIARLY EXPLAINED.

BY THE AUTHOR OF

" CONVERSATIONS ON CHEMISTRY."

LONDON:

PRINTED FOR LONGMAN, HURST, REES, ORME, AND BROWN,
PATERNOSTER-ROW,

1816.

PREFACE.

IN offering to the Public this small work, in which it is attempted to bring within the reach of young persons a science which no English writer has yet presented in an easy and familiar form, the author is far from inferring from the unexpected success of a former elementary work, on the subject of Chemistry, that the present attempt is likely to be received with equal favor. Political Economy, though so immediately connected with the happiness and improvement of mankind, and the object of so much controversy and speculation among men of knowledge,

vi   PREFACE.

is not yet become a popular science, and
is not generally considered as a study
essential to early education. This work,
therefore, independently of all its defects,
will have to contend against the novelty
of the pursuit with young persons of either
sex, for the instruction of whom it is especially intended. If, however, it should
be found useful, and if, upon the whole,
the doctrines it contains should appear
sound and sufficiently well explained, the
author flatters herself that this attempt
will not be too severely judged. She
hopes it will be remembered that in de-
vising the plan of this work, she was in
a great degree obliged to form the path
she has pursued, and had scarcely any
other guide in this popular mode of viewing
the subject, than the recollection of the
impressions she herself experienced when
she first turned her attention to this study;
though she has subsequently derived great
assistance from the kindness of a few

PREFACE. vii

friends, who revised her sheets as she advanced in the undertaking.

As to the principles and materials of the work, it is so obvious that they have been obtained from the writings of the great masters who have treated this subject, and more particularly from those of Dr. Adam Smith, of Mr. Malthus, M. Say, and M. Sismondi, that the author has not thought it necessary to load these pages with repeated acknowledgments and incessant references.

It will immediately be perceived by those to whom the subject is not new, that a few of the most abstruse questions and controversies in Political Economy have been entirely omitted, and that others have been stated and discussed without any positive conclusion being deduced. This is a defect unavoidably attached not only to the Author's limited knowledge,

viii   PREFACE.

but also to the real difficulty of the
science. In general, however, when the
soundness of a doctrine has appeared well
established, it has been stated conscien-
tiously, without any excess of caution or
reserve, and with the sole object of dif-
fusing useful truths.

It has often been a matter of doubt
among the author's literary advisers, whether the form of dialogues, which was
adopted in the Conversations on Chemistry, should be preserved in this Essay.
She has, however, ultimately decided for
the affirmative; not that she particularly
studied to introduce strict consistency of
character, or uniformity of intellect, in the
remarks of her pupil, an attempt which
might have often impeded the elucidation
of the subject; but because it gave her an
opportunity of introducing objections, and
placing in various points of view questions
and answers as they had actually occurred

PREFACE. ix

to her own mind, a plan which would not have suited a more didactic composition. It will be observed accordingly, that the colloquial form is not here confined to the mere intersection of the argument by questions and answers, as in common school-books : but that the questions are generally the vehicle of some collateral remarks contributing to illustrate the subject ; and that they are in fact such as would be likely to arise in the mind of an intelligent young person, fluctuating between the impulse of her heart and the progress of her reason, and naturally imbued with all the prejudices and popular feelings of uninformed benevolence.

TABLE

OF

CONTENTS.

CONVERSATION I. INTRODUCTION *Page* 16
——————— II. INTRODUCTION—*continued* 28
——————— III. ON PROPERTY 46
——————— IV. PROPERTY—*continued* 61
——————— V. ON THE DIVISION OF LABOUR 81
——————— VI. ON CAPITAL - - 99
——————— VII. CAPITAL—*continued* 113
———————VIII. ON WAGES AND POPU-
LATION - - 134
——————— IX. WAGES AND POPULA-
TION—*continued* - 151
——————— X. ON THE CONDITION OF
THE POOR - 171

xii CONTENTS.

CONVERSATION XI. ON REVENUE *Page* 188

———————— XII. REVENUE FROM LANDED
PROPERTY - - 212

———————— XIII. REVENUE FROM THE CUL-
TIVATION OF LAND - 244

———————— XIV. REVENUE FROM CAPITAL
LENT - - - 268

———————— XV. ON VALUE AND PRICE 292

———————— XVI. ON MONEY - - 317

———————— XVII. MONEY—*continued* - 341

———————— XVIII. COMMERCE - - 361

———————— XIX. ON FOREIGN TRADE 382

———————— XX. FOREIGN TRADE —*cont.* 397

———————— XXI ON EXPENDITURE - 419

CONVERSATION I.

INTRODUCTION.

ERRORS ARISING FROM TOTAL IGNORANCE OF PO-
LITICAL ECONOMY. — ADVANTAGES RESULTING
FROM THE KNOWLEDGE OF ITS PRINCIPLES. —
DIFFICULTIES TO BE SURMOUNTED IN THIS STUDY.

MRS. B.

W E differ so much respecting the merit of the passage you mentioned this morning, that I cannot help suspecting some inaccuracy in the quotation.

CAROLINE.

Then pray allow me to read it to you; it is immediately after the return of Telemachus to Salentum, when he expresses his astonishment to Mentor at the change that has taken place since his former visit; he says, " Has any misfortune happened to Salentum in my absence ? the magnificence and splendour in which I left it have dis-

2 INTRODUCTION.

appeared. I see neither silver, nor gold, nor jewels, the habits of the people are plain, the buildings are smaller and more simple, the arts languish, and the city is become a desert." — " Have you observed," replied Mentor with a smile, " the state of the country that lies round it?" — " Yes," said Telemachus, " I perceive that agriculture is become an honourable profession, and that there is not a field uncultivated." — " And which is best," replied Mentor, " a superb city, abounding with marble, gold, and silver, with a steril and neglected country; or a country in a state of high cultivation, and fruitful as a garden, with a city where decency has taken place of pomp? A great city full of artificers, who are employed only to effeminate the manners, by furnishing the superfluities of luxury, surrounded by a poor and uncultivated country, resembles a monster with a head of enormous size, and a withered, enervated body, without beauty, vigour, or proportion. The genuine strength and true riches of a kingdom consist in the number of people, and the plenty of provisions; and innumerable people now cover the whole territory of Idomeneus, which they cultivate with unwearied diligence and assiduity. His dominions may be considered as one town, of which Salentum is the centre; for the people that were wanting in the fields, and superfluous in the city, we have removed from the city to the fields."

INTRODUCTION. 3

Well, must I proceed, or have I read enough to convince you that Mentor is right?

MRS. B.

I still persist in my opinion; for though some of the sentiments in this passage are perfectly just, yet the general principle on which they are founded, that town and country thrive at the expence of each other, I believe to be quite erroneous; I am convinced, on the contrary, that flourishing cities are the means of fertilizing the fields around them. Do you see any want of cultivation in the neighbourhood of London? or can you name any highly improved country which does not abound with wealthy and populous cities? On the other hand, what is more common than to observe decayed cities environed by barren and ill cultivated lands? The purple and gold of Tyre during the prosperity of the Phœnicians, far from depriving the fields of their labourers, obliged that nation to colonize new countries as a provision for its excess of population.

CAROLINE.

That is going very far back for an example.

MRS. B.

If you wish to come down to a later period, compare the ancient flourishing state of Phœnicia,

B 2

4 INTRODUCTION.

with its present wretchedness, so forcibly described by Volney in his travels.

CAROLINE.

Has not this wretchedness been produced by violent revolutions, which during a course of ages have impoverished that devoted country, and does it not continue in consequence of the detestable policy of its present masters? But in the natural and undisturbed order of things, is it not clear that the greater number of labourers a sovereign should, after the example of Idomeneus, compel to quit the town in order to work in the country, the better that country would be cultivated?

MRS. B.

I do not think so; I am of opinion on the contrary, that the people thus compelled to quit the town, would not find work in the country.

CAROLINE.

And why not?

MRS. B.

Because there would already be as many labourers in the country as could find employment.

CAROLINE.

In England that might possibly be the case, but would it be so in badly cultivated countries?

16

INTRODUCTION. 5

MRS. B.

I think it would.

CAROLINE.

Do you mean to say that if a country which is ill-cultivated were provided with a greater number of labourers it would not be improved? You must allow that this requires some explanation.

MRS. B.

It does so, and perhaps even more than you imagine; for you cannot well understand this question without some knowledge of the principles of political economy.

CAROLINE.

I am very sorry to hear that, for I confess that I have a sort of antipathy to political economy.

MRS. B.

Are you sure that you understand what is meant by political economy?

CAROLINE.

I believe so, as it is so often the subject of conversation at home; but it appears to me the most uninteresting of all subjects. It is about custom-houses, and trade, and taxes, and bounties, and smuggling, and paper money, and the bullion committee, &c. which I cannot hear named without

6 INTRODUCTION.

yawning. Then there is a perpetual reference to the works of Adam Smith, whose name is never uttered without such a respectful, and almost religious veneration, that I was induced one day to look into his work on Political Economy to gain some information on the subject of corn, but what with forestalling, regrating, duties, drawbacks, and limiting prices, I was so overwhelmed by a jargon of unintelligible terms, that after running over a few pages I threw the book away in despair, and resolved to eat my bread in humble ignorance. So if our argument respecting town and country relates to political economy, I fancy that I must be contented to yield the point in dispute without understanding it.

MRS. B.

Well then, if you can remain satisfied with your ignorance of political economy you should at least make up your mind to forbear from talking of it, since you cannot do it to any purpose.

CAROLINE.

Oh! that, I assure you, requires very little effort; I only wish that I was as certain of never hearing the subject mentioned, as I am of never talking upon it myself.

MRS. B.

Do you recollect how heartily you laughed at

INTRODUCTION. 7

poor Mr. Jourdain in the Bourgeois Gentilhomme, when he discovered that he had been speaking in prose all his life without knowing it? — Well, my dear, you frequently talk of political economy without knowing it. But a few days since I heard you deciding on the very question of the scarcity of corn; and it must be confessed that your verdict was in perfect unison with your present profession of ignorance.

CAROLINE.

Indeed I only repeated what I had heard from very sensible people, that the farmers had a great deal of corn; that if they were compelled to bring it to market there would be no scarcity, and that they kept it back with a view to their own interest, in order to raise the price. Surely it does not require a knowledge of political economy to speak on so common, so interesting a subject as this first necessary of life.

MRS. B.

The very circumstance of its general interest renders it one of the most important branches of political economy. Unfortunately for your resolution, this science spreads into so many ramifications that you will seldom hear a conversation amongst liberal-minded people without some reference to it. It was but yesterday that you accused the Birming-

B 4

8 INTRODUCTION.

ham manufacturers of cruelty and injustice towards their workmen, and asserted that the rate of wages should be proportioned by law to that of provisions; so that the poor might not be sufferers by a rise in the price of bread. I dare say you thought that you had made a very rational speech when you so decided?

CAROLINE.

And was I mistaken? You begin to excite my curiosity, Mrs. B.; do you think I shall ever be tempted to study this science?

MRS. B.

I do not know; but I have no doubt that I shall convince you of your incapacity to enter on most subjects of general conversation, whilst you remain in total ignorance of it; and that however guarded you may be, that ignorance will be betrayed, and may frequently expose you to ridicule. During the riots at Nottingham I recollect hearing you condemn the invention of machines, which, by abridging labour, throw a number of workmen out of employment. Your opinion was founded upon mistaken principles of benevolence. In short, my dear, so many things are more or less connected with the science of political economy, that if you persevere in your resolution, you might almost as well condemn yourself to perpetual silence.

INTRODUCTION.   9

CAROLINE.

I should at least be privileged to talk about dress, amusements, and such lady-like topics.

MRS. B.

I have heard no trifling degree of ignorance of political economy betrayed in talking on dress. " What a pity," said one lady, " that French lace should be so dear; for my part I make no scruple of smuggling it; there is really a great satisfaction in cheating the custom-house." Another wondered she could so easily reconcile smuggling to her conscience; that she thought French laces and silks, and all French goods should be totally prohibited; that she was determined never to wear any thing from foreign countries, let it be ever so beautiful; and that it was shameful to encourage foreign manufactures whilst our own poor were starving.

CAROLINE.

What fault can you find with the latter opinion? It appears to me to be replete with humanity and patriotism.

MRS. B.

The benevolence of the lady I do not question; but without knowledge to guide and sense to regulate the feelings, the best intentions will be frustrated. The science of political economy is

B 5

10 INTRODUCTION.

intimately connected with the daily occurrences of life, and in this respect differs materially from that of chemistry, astronomy, or electricity; the mistakes we may fall into in the latter sciences can have little sensible effect upon our conduct, whilst our ignorance of the former may lead us into serious practical errors.

There is scarcely any history or any account of voyages or travels that does not abound with facts and opinions, the bearings of which cannot be understood without some previous acquaintance with the principles of political economy: besides, should the author himself be deficient in this knowledge, you will be continually liable to adopt his errors from inability to detect them. This was your case in reading Telemachus. Ignorance of the principles of political economy is to be discovered in some of the most elegant and sensible of our writers, especially amongst the poets. That beautiful composition of Goldsmith, the Deserted Village, is full of errors of this description, which, from its great popularity, are very liable to mislead the ill-informed.

CAROLINE.

I should almost regret to learn any thing which would lower that beautiful poem in my estimation.

MRS. B.

Its intrinsic merit as a poem is quite sufficient to

INTRODUCTION. 11

atone for any errors in scientific principles. Truth
is not, you know, essential to poetic beauty; but it
is essential that we should be able to distinguish
between truth and fiction.

CAROLINE.

Well, after all, Mrs. B., ignorance of political
economy is a very excusable deficiency in women.
It is the business of Government to reform the
prejudices and errors which prevail respecting it;
and as we are never likely to become legislators,
is it not just as well that we should remain in
happy ignorance of evils which we have no power
to remedy?

MRS. B.

When you plead in favour of ignorance, there
is a strong presumption that you are in the wrong.
If a more general knowledge of political economy
prevented women from propagating errors respecting it, no trifling good would ensue. Childhood
is spent in acquiring ideas, adolescence in discri-
minating and rejecting those which are false; how
greatly we should facilitate this labour by diminishing the number of errors imbibed in early youth,
and by inculcating such ideas only as are founded
in truth.

B 6

12   INTRODUCTION.

CAROLINE.

Surely you would not teach political economy
to children?

MRS. B.

I would wish that mothers were so far competent to teach it, that their children should not have
any thing to unlearn; and if they could convey
such lessons of political economy as Miss Edge-
worth gives in her story of the Cherry Orchard,
no one I should think would esteem such information beyond the capacity of a child.

CAROLINE.

I thought I remembered that story perfectly, but
I do not recollect in it a single word relative to political economy.

MRS. B.

The author has judiciously avoided naming the
science, but that little tale contains a simple and
beautiful exposition of the division of labour, the
merit of which you would more highly appreciate
if you were acquainted with its application to political economy. You would perhaps also allow children to hear the story of King Midas, whose
touch converted every thing into gold.

CAROLINE.

Is that also a lesson of political economy? I

INTRODUCTION. 13

think, Mrs. B., you have the art of converting
every thing you touch into that science.

MRS. B.

It is not art, but the real nature of things. The
story of King Midas shews, that gold alone does
not constitute wealth, and that it is valuable only
as it bears a due proportion to the more immediately useful productions of the earth.

CAROLINE.

But children will not be the wiser for such
stories unless you explain their application to political economy. You must give them the *moral* of
the fable.

MRS. B.

The *moral* is the only part of a fable which children never read; and in this they are perfectly
right, for a principle abstractedly laid down is beyond their comprehension. The application will
be made as they advance in life. Childhood is the
period for sowing the seed, not for forcing the
fruit; you must wait the due season if you mean to
gather a ripe and plentiful harvest.

CAROLINE.

Well, my dear Mrs. B., what must I do? You
know that I am fond of instruction, and that I am
not afraid of application. You may recollect what

14 INTRODUCTION.

pleasure I took in the study of chemistry. If you could persuade me that political economy would be as interesting, and not more difficult, I would beg of you to put me in the way of learning it. Are there any lectures given on this subject? or could one take lessons of a master? for as to studying scientific books, I am discouraged from the difficulty of the terms; when the language as well as the subject is new, there are too many obstacles to contend with at first setting out.

MRS. B.

The language of a science is frequently its most difficult part, but in political economy there are but few technical terms, and those you will easily comprehend. Indeed, you have already a considerable stock of information on this subject, but your notions are so confused and irregular, such a mixture of truth and error, that your business will rather be to select, separate, and methodize what you already know, than to acquire new ideas. It is not in my power to recommend you a master on this subject, for there are none—perhaps because there are no pupils. Those who seek for instruction on political economy, read the works written on that science, particularly the treatise of Adam Smith. Lectures on political economy have occasionally been given at the universities, especially at Edinburgh, and many of the students there are

INTRODUCTION. 15

well versed in this science, as they turn their attention to it at an age when the mind is not yet strongly biassed by prejudice.

CAROLINE.

But what then am I to do, Mrs. B.? I cannot attend those lectures, and I fear I shall never have courage to undertake the study of treatises which appear to me so difficult.

MRS. B.

Perhaps I may be able to smooth the way for you. It has been my good fortune to have passed a great part of my life in a society where this science has been a frequent topic of discussion, and the interest I took in it has induced me to study its principles in the works of the best writers on the subject; but I must tell you fairly, that I did not commence my studies by opening these works at random, or by consulting Adam Smith on an insulated point, before I had examined his plan, or understood his object. I knew that in order to learn I must begin at the beginning, and if you are of opinion that my experience can be of any service to you, and will be content to receive an explanation in a familiar manner of what has been discussed or investigated by men of acknowledged talent and learning, I will attempt to guide you through the first elements of the science, without, however, presuming to penetrate into its abstruse parts.

16INTRODUCTION.

CAROLINE.

Well then, I am quite decided to make the attempt; you are but too good to me, Mrs. B., to allow me again to become your pupil. You have so much indulgence however that I am never afraid of exposing my ignorance by my inquiries, though I fear I shall put your patience to a severe trial.

CONVERSATION II.

INTRODUCTION — *continued.*

DEFINITION OF POLITICAL FCONOMY. — RISE AND PROGRESS OF SOCIETY. — CONNEXION BETWEEN POLITICAL ECONOMY AND MORALITY. — DEFINITION OF WEALTH.

CAROLINE.

I HAVE been thinking a great deal of political economy since yesterday, my dear Mrs. B., but I fear not to much purpose; at least I am no farther advanced than the discovery of a great confusion of ideas which prevails in my mind on the subject. That science seems to comprehend every thing, and yet I own, that I am still at a loss to understand what it is. Cannot you give me a short explanation of the nature of the science, that I may have some clear idea of it to begin with?

MRS. B.

I once heard a lady ask a philosopher to tell her in a few words what is meant by political economy. Madam, replied he, you understand perfectly what is meant by *household economy;* you need only ex-

18   INTRODUCTION.

tend your idea of the economy of a family to that
of a whole people — of a nation, and you will have
some comprehension of the nature of political economy.

CAROLINE.

Considering that he was limited to a few words,
do you not think that he acquitted himself extremely well? But as I have a little more patience
than this lady, I hope you will indulge me with a
more detailed explanation of this universal science.

MRS. B.

I would call it the science which teaches us to
investigate the causes of the wealth and prosperity
of nations.

In a country of savages, you find a small number
of inhabitants spread over a vast tract of land.
Depending on the precarious subsistence afforded
by fishing and hunting, they are frequently subject
to dearths and famines, which cut them off in great
numbers: they rear but few children, for want destroys them in their early years: the aged and infirm are often put to death, but rather from motives
of humanity than of cruelty; for the hunter's life
requiring a great extent of country, and long and
perilous excursions in quest of food, they would be
wholly incapable of following the young and robust,
and would die of hunger, or become a prey to wild
beasts.

INTRODUCTION. 19

As soon as these savages begin to apply themselves to pasturage, their means of subsistence are brought within narrower limits, requiring only that degree of wandering necessary to provide fresh pasturage for their cattle. Their flocks ensuring them a more easy subsistence, their families begin to increase; they lose in a great measure their ferocity, and a considerable improvement takes place in their character.

By degrees the art of tillage is discovered, a small tract of ground becomes capable of feeding a greater relative number of people; the necessity of wandering in search of food is superseded; families begin to settle in fixed habitations, and the arts of social life are introduced and cultivated.

In the savage state, scarcely any form of government is established; the people seem to be under no controul but that of their military chiefs in time of warfare.

The possession of flocks and herds in the pastoral state introduces property, and laws are necessary for its security; the elders and leaders therefore of these wandering tribes begin to establish laws, to violate which is to commit a crime, and to incur a punishment. This is the origin of social order; and when in the third state the people settle in fixed habitations, the laws gradually assume the more regular form of a monarchical or republican government. Every thing now wears

20 INTRODUCTION.

a new aspect; industry flourishes, the arts are invented, the use of the metals is discovered; labour is subdivided, every one applies himself more particularly to a distinct employment, in which he becomes skilful. Thus, by slow degrees, this people of savages, whose origin was so rude and miserable, becomes a civilized people, who occupy a highly cultivated country, crossed by fine roads, leading to wealthy and populous cities, and carrying on an extensive trade with other countries.

CAROLINE.

This is a very pleasing outline of the history of the rise and progress of civilization: but I should like to see it a little more filled up.

MRS. B.

The subject you will find hereafter sufficiently developed; for the whole business of political economy is to study the causes which have thus co-operated to enrich and civilize a nation. This science is, therefore, essentially founded upon history, — not the history of sovereigns, of wars, and of intrigues; but the history of the arts, of trade, of discoveries, and of civilization. We see some countries like America increase rapidly in wealth and prosperity, whilst others like Egypt and Syria are impoverished, depopulated, and falling to decay; when the causes which produce these

INTRODUCTION. 21

various effects are well understood, some judgment may be formed of the measures which governments have adopted to contribute to the welfare of their people; whether such or such a branch of commerce 'should be encouraged in preference to others; whether it be proper to prohibit this or that kind of merchandize; whether any peculiar encouragement should be given to agriculture; whether it be right to establish by law the price of provisions or the price of labour, or whether they should be left without controul; and so on.

You see, therefore, that political economy consists of two parts, — theory and practice; the science and the art. The science comprehends a knowledge of the facts which we have enumerated; the art relates more particularly to legislation, and consists in doing whatever is requisite to contribute to the increase of national wealth, and avoiding whatever would be prejudicial to it. Mistakes in theory lead to errors in practice. When we enter into details we shall have occasion to observe that governments, misled by false ideas of political economy, have frequently arrested the natural progress of wealth when it was in their power to have accelerated it.

CAROLINE.

But since the world was originally a rude wilderness, and yet has arrived at the improved state

22 INTRODUCTION.

of civilization in which we now find it, the errors of governments cannot have been very prejudicial.

MRS. B.

The natural causes which tend to develop the wealth and prosperity of nations are more powerful than the faults of administration which operate in a contrary direction. But it is nevertheless true that these errors are productive of a great deal of mischief; that they check industry and retard the progress of improvement. Under bad governments particular classes of people are favoured, others discouraged and oppressed: prosperity is thus unequally shared, and riches unfairly distributed. You look very grave, Caroline; do you begin to grow tired of the subject?

CAROLINE.

Oh no; I think thus far I have understood you: but before we proceed you must allow me to mention an objection which I confess distresses me; if it is well founded I shall be quite at variance with the maxims of political economy, and that science will no longer retain any interest for me. I find that you are constantly talking of wealth; of the causes which produce it; of the means of augmenting it. To be *rich, very rich, richer* than other people, seems to be the great aim of political economy. Whilst religion and morality teach us that we

INTRODUCTION. 23

should moderate the thirst of gain, that inordinate love of wealth is the source of all crimes. Besides that, it is very evident that the richest people are not always the happiest. Now, if wealth does not conduce to the happiness of individuals, how can it constitute that of nations? A poor but virtuous people is surely happier than a rich and vicious one. What remarkable examples do we not see of this in history. We are taught to admire the Greek republics, who despised the pomp and luxury of wealth. And then the Romans; during the early part of their history they were poor and virtuous, but the acquisition of wealth depraved their character, and rendered them the slaves of tyrants. Now political economy appears to me to induce the love of riches, and to consider it as the only end to be attained by government.

MRS. B.

This is a most alarming attack upon political economy! When, however, you understand it better, you will find that your censure is unfounded. At present you must take my word for it, as I cannot shew you the benefits arising .from just principles of political economy, before you are acquainted with the principles themselves: but I can assure you that they all tend to promote the happiness of nations, and the purest morality. Far from

24　　　INTRODUCTION.

exciting an inordinate desire of wealth or power, it tends to moderate all unjustifiable ambition, by shewing that the surest means of increasing national prosperity are peace, security, and justice; that jealousy between nations is as prejudicial as between individuals; that each finds its advantage in reciprocal benefits; and that far from growing rich at each other's expence, they mutually assist each other by a liberal system of commerce. Political economy is particularly inimical to the envious, jealous, and malignant passions; and if ever peace and moderation should flourish in the world, it is to enlightened views of this science that we should be indebted for the miracle.

But, my dear Caroline, I suspect that there is some error in your idea of riches. What do you call riches?

CAROLINE.

Of course to be rich is to have a great income; to be able to spend a great deal more than other people.

MRS. B.

You speak of the riches of individuals; of comparative wealth. A rich man in one class of society might be poor in another. But this is not the definition that I asked for—what do you understand by riches in general—in what does wealth consist?

INTRODUCTION. 25

CAROLINE.

Oh, I suppose you mean money?—I should say wealth consists in gold and silver.

MRS. B.

Consider what would be the situation of a country which possessed no other wealth than money. Do you recollect in what estimation Robinson Crusoe held his bag of gold when he was wrecked upon a deserted island?

CAROLINE.

True: but in an island which is not desert, money will purchase whatever you want.

MRS. B.

Then I should rather say that the things which we are desirous to procure with our money, such as land, houses, furniture, clothes, food, &c. constitute riches; and not the money by which they are obtained.

CAROLINE.

Certainly: these are clearly the things which constitute real wealth; for unless we could procure the necessaries of life with gold and silver, they would be of no use to us.

MRS. B.

We may therefore say that wealth comprehends every article of utility, convenience, or luxury.

c

26 INTRODUCTION.

This includes every object of our wishes which can become an article of commerce; such as landed estates, houses, the products of agriculture, those of manufactures, provisions, domestic animals, in a word, whatever can contribute to the welfare and enjoyment of men.

CAROLINE.

Why should you confine your definition of wealth to things that can become articles of commerce?

MRS. B.

Because there are many countries where the earth spontaneously produces things which can neither be consumed nor sold; and however valuable such things would be to us, could we obtain them, they cannot, under those circumstances, be considered as wealth. The herds of wild cattle, for instance, which feed on the rich pastures called the Pampas, in South America, are of this description. Many of those large tracts of land are uninhabited, and the cattle that range at large over them is of no value. Parties of hunters occasionally make incursions, and destroy some of them for the sake of their hides and fat, whilst the flesh, which we should esteem most valuable, is either left to putrify, or is used as fuel to melt the fat for the purposes of tallow, which being transported to places where it can be sold and consumed, it acquires value and becomes wealth.

INTRODUCTION. 27

In other parts of America the grass of rich pastures is burnt on the ground, there being no cattle to consume it.

CAROLINE.

This may be the case in wild and uncultivated countries: but in those which are civilized, any land yielding unsaleable produce would be converted by the proprietor to some other use.

MRS. B.

I have heard that the fruit of many of the vineyards in France was not gathered a few years ago, the grapes being so much reduced in value in consequence of a decree prohibiting the exportation of French wines, that the price at which they could be sold would not pay the expence of gathering them. In England, also, when all kinds of colonial produce were excluded from the continent of Europe, coffee is said to have been thrown into the sea, because it would not pay the charges on being landed. You see, therefore, that the effects of war, or other circumstances, may for a a time, in any country, destroy the value of commodities.

CAROLINE.

How very much you have already extended my conception of the meaning of wealth! And yet I can perceive that all these ideas were floating confusedly in my mind before. In speaking of wealth we ought

c 2

INTRODUCTION.

not to confine ourselves to the consideration of the relative wealth of individuals, but extend our views to whatever constitutes riches in general, without any reference to the inequality of the division.

All this is perfectly clear : no one can be really ignorant of it; it requires only reflection; and yet at first I was quite at a loss to explain the nature of wealth.

MRS. B.

The confusion has arisen from the common practice of estimating riches by money, instead of observing that wealth consists in such commodities as are useful or agreeable to mankind, of which gold and silver constitute but a very small portion.

CONVERSATION III.

ON PROPERTY.

LABOUR THE ORIGIN OF WEALTH. — LEGAL INSTI-
TUTION OF PROPERTY. — OF LANDED PROPERTY.
— SECURITY THE RESULT OF PROPERTY. — OB-
JECTIONS TO LANDED PROPERTY ANSWERED. —
ORIGIN OF NATIONS IN A SAVAGE OR PASTORAL
LIFE. — THEIR PROGRESS IN AGRICULTURE. —
CULTIVATION OF CORN. — RECAPITULATION.

CAROLINE.

WELL, my dear Mrs. B., since you have recon-
ciled me to wealth, and convinced me how
essential it is to the happiness and prosperity of
nations, I begin to grow impatient to learn what
are the best means of obtaining this desirable
object.

MRS. B.

Do not leave every thing to me, Caroline,
I have told you that you were not without some

30 ON PROPERTY.

general notions of political economy, though they are but ill arranged in your mind. Endeavour, therefore, to unravel the entangled thread, and discover yourself what are the principal causes of the production of wealth in a nation.

CAROLINE.

I assure you that I have been reflecting a great deal upon the subject. I do not know whether I am right, but I think it is *labour* which is the cause of wealth. Without labour the earth would yield but very little for our subsistence. How insignificant are its spontaneous productions compared with those derived from agriculture! The crab with the apple; the barren heath with the rich pasture of the meadow!

MRS. B.

It is very true that labour is a most essential requisite to the creation of wealth, and yet it does not necessarily insure its production. The labour of the savage who possesses no wealth is often more severe than that of our common ploughman, whose furrows team with riches. The long and perilous excursions of savages in search of prey, the difficulty which, from want of skill, they must encounter in every process of industry, in constructing the simplest habitations, fabricating the rudest implements; — all concur to increase their

ON PROPERTY. 31

toil. Labour is the lot of man; whether in a barbarous or a civilized state he is destined to earn his bread by the sweat of his brow. But how is it that in the one case labour is productive of great wealth, whilst in the other it affords barely the necessaries of life?

CAROLINE.

You have observed that the labour of the savage is less advantageous on account of his ignorance and want of skill; besides he works neither with the activity and the zeal, nor with the perseverance of men in civilized society. Savages, you know, are proverbial for their idleness.

MRS. B.

Inducements must then be found to rouse them from that idleness; motives to awaken their industry and habituate them to regular labour. Men are naturally disposed to indolence; all exertion requires effort, and efforts are not made without an adequate stimulus. The activity we behold in civilized life is the effect of education; it results from a strong and general desire to share not only in the necessaries of life, but in the various comforts and enjoyments with which we are surrounded. The man who has reaped the reward, as well as undergone the fatigues of daily exertion, willingly renews his efforts, as he thus renews his enjoyments. But the ignorance of a savage precludes all desires

c 4

32 ON PROPERTY.

which do not lead to the immediate gratification of his wants; he sees no possessions which tempt his ambition — no enjoyments which inflame his desires; nothing less than the strong impulse of want rouses him to exertion; and, having satisfied the cravings of hunger, he lies down to rest without a thought of the future.

CAROLINE.

But if the desires of savages are so few and so easily satisfied, may not their state be happier than that of the labouring classes in civilized countries, who wish for so much, and obtain so little?

MRS. B.

The brutish apathy which results from gross ignorance can scarcely deserve the name of content, and is utterly unworthy that of happiness. Goldsmith, in his Traveller, justly as well as beautifully observes, that

> " Every want that stimulates the breast
> Becomes a source of pleasure when redress'd."

Besides, it is only occasionally that a savage can indulge in this state of torpid indifference. If you consult any account of travels in a savage country, you will be satisfied that our peasantry enjoy a comparative state of affluence and even of luxury,

ON PROPERTY. 33

But let us suppose a civilized being to come among a tribe of savages, and succeed in teaching some of them the arts of life — he instructs one how to render his hut more commodious, another to collect a little store of provisions for the winter, a third to improve the construction of his bows and arrows; what would be the consequences?

CAROLINE.

One might expect that the enjoyment derived from these improvements would lead their countrymen to adopt them, and would introduce a general spirit of industry.

MRS. B.

Is it not more probable that the idle savages would, either by force or fraud, wrest from the industrious their hard-earned possessions; that the one would be driven from the hut he had constructed with so much care, another robbed of the provisions he had stored, and a third would see his well pointed arrows aimed at his own breast. Here then is a fatal termination to all improvement. Who will work to procure such precarious possessions, which expose him to danger, instead of ensuring his enjoyment?

CAROLINE.

But all this would be prevented if laws were made for the protection of property.

c 5

ON PROPERTY.

MRS. B.

True; but the *right* of property must be legally established, before it can be protected. For Nature has given mankind every thing in common, and property is of human institution. It takes place in such early stages of society that one is apt to imagine it of natural origin; but until it has been established by law, no man has a right to call any thing his own.

CAROLINE.

What, not the game he has killed, the hut he has built, or the implements he has constructed? These may be wrested from him by force; but he who thus obtains them acquires no right to them.

MRS. B.

When a man has produced any thing by his labour, he has, no doubt, in equity the fairest claim to it; but his right to separate it from the common stock of nature, and appropriate it to his own use, depends entirely upon the law of the land.

In the case of property in land, for instance, it is the law which decrees that such a piece of ground shall belong to Thomas, such another to John, and a third to James; that these men shall have an exclusive right to the possession of the land and of its produce; that they may keep, sell, or exchange it; give it away during their lives or bequeath it

ON PROPERTY. 35

after their deaths. And, in order that this law should be respected, punishments are enacted for those who should transgress it. It is not until such laws have been made for the establishment and protection of property, of whatever description it be, that the right of property is established.

CAROLINE.

You astonish me! I thought that property in land had always existed; I had no idea that it was a legal institution, but imagined that it had originated from the earliest period of the world. We read that in the time of the ancient patriarchs, when families became too numerous, they separated; and that those who went to settle elsewhere, fed their flocks, and occupied the land without molestation. There was no one to dispute their right to it; and after their deaths the children inhabited and cultivated the land of their fathers.

If we were to found a colony in a desert island, every man would cultivate as much ground as he wanted for his own use, and each having an equal interest in the preservation of his possessions, property would thus be established by general agreement, without any legal institution.

MRS. B.

This general agreement is a kind of law, a very imperfect one it is true, and which was perhaps

c 6

ON PROPERTY.

originally founded on the relative strength of individuals. If one man attempts to carry off the cattle or the fruits of another, the latter opposes force to force; if he is stronger or better armed, he either kills his antagonist or drives him away; if weaker, he is despoiled, or he calls in his neighbours to his succour, shews them the common danger, and may induce them to unite with him in taking vengeance on the aggressor.

Many incidents of this nature must occur before regular laws are instituted; that is to say, before a public authority is established, which shall protect individuals against those who attack them, and punish the offenders. It is then only that a man may say, " This is my field; this is my house; this seed which I cast into the ground will bring forth an abundant harvest, which will be all my own; these trees, which I plant, will every year yield fruit, which I alone shall have a right to gather."

CAROLINE.

I now comprehend perfectly the advantage of such laws — it is *security* — before they were established, the strong might wrest every thing from the weak; and old men, women, and children who had no means of defence, were exposed to their rapine and violence. The idle and improvident, when in want of subsistence, became the natural enemies of the laborious and industrious. So that without this

ON PROPERTY. 37

law the men who had toiled hardest would be most likely to fall victims to those who had done nothing. In a word, the wasps would devour the honey of the bees.

MRS. B.

Yes, *security* is the grand point; it is security which stimulates industry, and renders labour productive; every step towards security, is a step towards civilization, towards wealth, and towards general happiness.

CAROLINE.

All this is very true; yet an objection to the institution of landed property has just occurred to me which appears of considerable importance. Before land became private property, the earth, you say, was possessed in common by all mankind; every one had an equal claim to it. But the law which institutes landed property takes it from mankind at large to give it to a few individuals; in order therefore to make some men rich, it makes others poor. Now what right has the law to dispossess some in order to enrich others? It should be just, before it is generous.

This objection, however, does not extend to any other than landed property; nothing is more fair than that men should gather the fruits of their labour; that they should possess the houses they have built, the goods they have fabricated; but the land cannot become private property without injury

88   ON PROPERTY.

to others who are thus deprived of their natural
right to it.

MRS. B.

You would then secure to every one the possession of the wealth he may acquire, though you
would refuse him the means of producing it?
You would make him master of his house, but take
away the ground on which it stands; protect his
harvests, but not allow him the property of a field
in which he may raise his crops?

CAROLINE.

I must confess that you have placed my objection
rather in a ridiculous point of view; but that is not
enough, Mrs. B.; you must shew me that it is erroneous before I can consent to relinquish it.

MRS. B.

In countries newly occupied, grants of land are
made to those who are willing to reclaim it from a
state of nature, and the great inequality that we
witness in more modern times is the result of volun-
tary transfers from one individual to another, by
gifts, by bequests, or by sale; it is the necessary
consequence of that freedom and that security of
which we have just seen the origin.

Nature in some instances bestows her gifts with
unbounded and inexhaustible profusion: it is thus
she has given us air and water, which are alike

13

ON PROPERTY. 39

possessed and enjoyed by all. But when she confers her donations with a more sparing hand, as is the case with land, the advantage of all requires that guardians should be appointed to protect and cherish so valuable a gift; and in order that they may have the strongest possible interest in its culture and improvement, they become proprietors, with all the advantages attached to exclusive possession.

The institution of property in land augments the wealth not only of the proprietors, but likewise of all other classes of men.

Land may be considered as the instrument by which alone wealth is created; and we have just seen that the security of its possession gives life and vigour to industry: it is this security which raises the condition of our peasantry so much above that of a savage people who possess the land in common.

CAROLINE.

An institution of such evident and general utility cannot then be considered as unjust.

MRS. B.

Certainly not. It is by the test of general utility that the justice of all laws should be tried; for there are none which do not impose some restraint on the natural liberty of man, and which, in that point of view, might not be deemed objectionable. But with-

40 ON PROPERTY.

out the controul of laws, we have seen that neither the lives, the property, the reputation, nor even the liberty of men are secure; we sacrifice therefore some portion of that liberty to the law; and, in return, it secures to us the remainder, together with every blessing which security can give. Blackstone in his Commentaries says, " Every man, when he " enters into society, gives up a part of his natural " liberty, as the price of so valuable a purchase; " and in consideration of receiving the advantages " of mutual commerce, obliges himself to conform " to those laws which the community has thought " proper to establish. For no man who considers " a moment would wish to retain the absolute and " uncontrouled power of doing whatever he pleases, " the consequence of which is, that every other " man would also have the same power, and there " would be no security to individuals in any of the " enjoyments of life: political, therefore, or civil " liberty, which is that of a member of society, is " no other than natural liberty, so far restrained " by human laws (and no farther) as is necessary " and expedient for the general advantage of the " public.

" That constitution or form of government, that " system of laws, is alone calculated to maintain " civil liberty, which leaves the subject entire " master of his own conduct, except in those points " wherein the public requires some direction or " restraint."

ON PROPERTY.   41

CAROLINE.

You have completely removed all my scruples respecting the institution of landed property, Mrs. B. — let us now therefore return to the progress of wealth and civilization.

MRS. B.

We must not proceed too rapidly; for the progressive steps in the history of civilization are extremely slow, and we must learn to view the developement of human industry in successive and almost insensible degrees.

Civilized nations do not always originate from the settlement of a colony; they frequently arise from a savage state, in which they may remain during a course of centuries. It was in this state we found the Indians on the discovery of America; they were mere hunters; and so long as men behold an unlimited space before them, in which they may wander without obstacle or controul, it is difficult to conceive any circumstances which should lead them to adopt a settled mode of life, and apply themselves to tillage.

In countries abounding with large plains, the pastoral mode of life has prevailed; but for this purpose there must have been established property in cattle, though the land were possessed in common. Such was the case with the ancient Scythians who inhabited the vast plains of Tartary, and with the modern

ON PROPERTY.

Tartars and Arabs, who, to this day, are wandering tribes, and, like the patriarchs of old, live in tents, and travel about with their flocks and herds in search of pasture.

We have observed that men were by nature disposed to idleness, and this disposition is necessarily a great obstacle to the introduction of agriculture; for it requires a considerable degree of foresight and knowledge, and a firm reliance on the security of property, to labour at one season in order to reap the fruits at another. But we may suppose agriculture to be a progressive step from pastoral life; that a tribe of shepherds may have met with enemies in their wandering excursions, and the apprehensions of losing their flocks may have induced them to settle; they would probably chuse a spot defended by nature from attacks of wild beasts, or the incursions of savage neighbours. Thus Cecrops pitched upon the rock on which the citadel of Athens is founded, to build a town. Or they may have been tempted by the attractions of some fruitful spot, under the protection of a neighbouring government able to defend them. Volney in his account of the wandering tribes in Syria, says; " As often as they find peace and security, and a " possibility of procuring sufficient provisions in any " district, they take up their residence in it, and in- " sensibly adopt a settled life and the arts of cultiva- " tion." These arts they must have attained by very

ON PROPERTY. 43

slow degrees — they observed that fruit trees may be multiplied; that nutritious plants may be propagated; that there are seeds which reproduce every year; and that a great variety of animals may be tamed and domesticated. Thus supplied with a new fund of subsistence, their children are better fed, their families increase, and age and infancy are protected and provided for.

But these people are yet acquainted with only the first elements of agriculture; how many fortunate chances must have occurred before they reached the important era of the cultivation of corn ! Wild corn has no where been found, and the Greeks imagined that a divinity descended on earth, to introduce it, and to instruct them in the cultivation of this valuable plant. Athens, Crete, Sicily, and Egypt, all claim the merit of being the original cultivators of corn; but whoever are the people to whom we are indebted for this important discovery, or whatever are the means by which it was accomplished, there is none which has had so great an influence on the welfare of mankind. Feeble as it appears, this plant can resist the summer's heat and the winter's cold. It flourishes in almost every climate, and is adapted not only for the food of man, but for that of a great variety of domestic animals, and it yields by fermentation a pleasant and salubrious beverage. The grain will keep many years, and affords such a durable means

ON PROPERTY.

of subsistence, that danger could no longer be apprehended in trusting to futurity, and plenty was secured during the longest and most unproductive winters.

But the cultivation of this inestimable plant cannot be undertaken without considerable funds, fixed habitations, implements of husbandry *, domestic animals; in a word, establishments which could neither be created nor maintained without the institution of property. Savages have no corn, no cultivation, no domestic animals; they consume and destroy every thing without ever considering re-production; — and how different are the results! We now see millions of men and animals inhabiting an extent of country which would scarcely have sufficed for the maintenance of two or three hundred savages.

CAROLINE.

Let us rest a little, my dear Mrs. B. I am almost bewildered with the number and variety of

---

* These are at first of a very rude and imperfect construction. In some parts of India the plough of a Hindoo, even to this day, is formed of a crooked stick very inartificially sharpened, and not unfrequently drawn by his wife. The use of domestic animals in agriculture is another step towards civilization; but no farming establishment whatever could either be created or maintained without the institution of property.

ON PROPERTY. 45

ideas that you have presented to my mind. I wonder that these things never occurred to me before; but I have been so accustomed to see the world in its present improved state, that my attention was never drawn to the many obstacles and difficulties it must have encountered, and the laborious progressive steps it must have made before society could have attained its present state of perfection.

MRS. B.

Perfection! comparatively speaking I suppose you mean; for it is not long since you were making lamentable complaints of the actual state of society; in which indeed I could not entirely agree with you, though I think that we are still far removed from perfection. But let us continue to trace the progress of wealth and civilization up to their present state, before we begin to find any fault with existing institutions.

CAROLINE.

I think I have now a very clear idea of the important consequences which result from the establishment of property. It puts an end to the wandering life of barbarians, induces men to settle, and inures them to regular labour; it teaches them prudence and foresight; induces them to embellish the face of the earth by cultivation; to multiply the useful tribes of animals and nutritious plants;

46 ON PROPERTY.

and in short, it enables them so prodigiously to augment the stock of subsistence, as to transform a country which contained but a few poor huts and a scanty population into a great and wealthy nation.

CONVERSATION IV.

ON PROPERTY — *continued.*

EFFECTS OF INSECURITY OF PROPERTY.—EXAMPLES FROM VOLNEY'S TRAVELS. — OBJECTIONS RAISED AGAINST CIVILIZATION.—STATE OF BETICA FROM TELEMACHUS.—OBJECTIONS TO COMMUNITY OF GOODS. — ESTABLISHMENT OF JESUITS IN PARAGUAY. — MORAVIANS. — STATE OF SWITZERLAND.—ADVANTAGES RESULTING FROM THE ESTABLISHMENT AND SECURITY OF PROPERTY.

MRS. B.

NOW that we have traced the rise and progress of civilization to the security of property, let us see whether the reverse, that is to say, insecurity of property in a civilized country, will not degrade the state of man, and make him retrace his steps till he again degenerates into barbarism.

CAROLINE.

Are there any examples of a civilized people re-

48   ON PROPERTY.

turning to a savage state? I do not recollect ever
to have heard of such a change.

MRS. B.

No, because when property has once been instituted, the advantages it produces are such, that it
can never be totally abolished; but in countries
where the tyranny of government renders it very
insecure, the people invariably degenerate, the
country falls back into poverty, and a comparative
state of barbarism. We have already noticed the
miserable change in the once wealthy city of Tyre.
Egypt, which was the original seat of the arts and
sciences, is now sunk into the most abject degradation; and if you will read the passages I have
marked for you in Volney's travels, you will find the
truth of this observation very forcibly delineated.

CAROLINE *reads.*

" When the tyranny of a government drives the
" inhabitants of a village to extremity, the peasants
" desert their houses, and withdraw with their fami-
" lies into the mountains, or wander in the plains. It
" often happens that even individuals turn robbers
" in order to withdraw themselves from the tyranny
" of the laws; and unite into little camps, which
" maintain themselves by force of arms; these in-
" creasing become new hordes and new tribes.
" We may say, therefore, that in cultivated coun-

ON PROPERTY. 49

" tries the wandering life originates in the injustice
" or want of policy of the government."

MRS. B.

This, you see, is very much to the point; but
here is another passage equally applicable.

CAROLINE *reads.*

" The silks of Tripoly are every day losing their
" quality from the decay of the mulberry-trees, of
" which scarcely any thing now remains but some
" hollow trunks. Why not plant new ones? That
" is an European observation. Here they never
" plant; because were they either to build or plant,
" the Pacha would say this man has money, and it
" would be extorted from him."

Besides, where there is so little actual security,
what reliance can be placed on futurity? What
reason would the proprietors have to hope that the
mulberry-trees would ever repay them for the trouble
and expense of planting them? Yet I wonder that
the government of the country should not, for its
own sake, encourage the industry of its subjects.

MRS. B.

In the wretched government of the Turks, every
thing is so insecure, from the life and property of
the sovereign, to that of the lowest of his subjects, that
no one looks to futurity, but every man endeavours

50 ON PROPERTY.

to grasp at, and enjoy what is immediately within his reach. The following passage will shew you what sufferers they all are by such a mistaken system of policy.

CAROLINE (reading).

" In consequence of the wretchedness of the go-
" vernment, the greater part of the pachalics are
" impoverished and laid waste. In the ancient
" registers of imports upwards of 3200 villages
" were reckoned in that of Aleppo, but at present
" the collector can scarcely find 4co. Such of our
" merchants as have resided there 20 years, have
" themselves seen the greater part of the environs
" of Aleppo become depopulated. The traveller
" meets with nothing but houses in ruins, cisterns
" rendered useless, and fields abandoned. Those
" who cultivated them are fled into the towns,
" where the population is absorbed, but where at
" least the individual conceals himself among the
" crowd from the rapacious hands of despotism. In
" other countries the cities are in some measure
" the overflow of the population of the country; in
" Syria they are the effect of its desertion. The
" roads in the mountains are extremely bad, as the
" inhabitants are so far from levelling them that they
" endeavour to render them more rugged, in or-
" der, as they say, to cure the Turks of their desire
" to introduce their cavalry.

" The Pacha may applaud himself for penetrat

ON PROPERTY. 51

" ing into the most secret sources of private pro-
" perty, but what are the consequences? The
" people, denied the enjoyment of the fruits of
" their labour, restrain their industry to the supply
" of their necessary wants; the husbandman sows
" only to prevent himself from starving, the arti-
" ficer labours only to maintain his family; if he
" makes any savings he strives to conceal them.
" The people live therefore in poverty and distress,
" but at least they do not enrich their tyrants, and
" the rapacity of despotism is its own punishment."

MRS. B.

The degeneracy of the mighty Persian and Indian monarchies since the conquest of those countries
by the Mahometans, is also clearly deducible from
the insecurity of property, and affords the most
tremendous examples of national decline. Trott, in
his History of Hindostan, informs us that during
the disastrous times of the latter monarchs of
India, the cruelties and oppressions of the agents
of government were such that the farmers burnt
their houses, utensils, and crops, and took refuge
in the woods and mountains, where those who
could neither excite charity nor maintain themselves by the sword, perished through want.

CAROLINE.

What a melancholy picture this is, my dear

D 2

ON PROPERTY.

Mrs. B. ! it is, I think, even more painful to contemplate than the wretchedness of savages; for to their actual misery these people must add the regret of having known better times.

MRS. B.

Dr. Clarke's Travels abound with similar instances of insecurity of property, and legal oppression, which subvert society, and degrade the human species. " In Circassia," he observes, that " the sower scattering seed, or the reaper who gathers the sheaves, are constantly liable to an assault; and the implements of husbandry are not more essential to the harvest than the carbine, the pistol, and the sabre."

Speaking of the Isle of Cyprus, he says: " The soil every where exhibited a white marly " clay, said to be exceedingly rich in its na- " ture, although neglected. The Greeks are so " oppressed by their Turkish masters, that they " dare not cultivate the land; the harvest would " instantly be taken from them if they did. Their " whole aim seems to be, to scrape together barely " sufficient, in the course of the whole year, to " pay their tax to the governor. The omission of " this is punished by torture or by death: and in " case of their inability to supply the impost, the " inhabitants fly from the island. So many emi- " grations of this sort happen during the year that

ON PROPERTY. 53

" the population of Cyprus rarely exceeds 60,000
" persons, a number formerly insufficient to have
" peopled one of its towns."

CAROLINE.

You have made me sensible of the advantages of
civilization; but yet I confess that my mind is not
fully satisfied. Is there no medium between a
savage life and the extreme inequality of condition which we see in the present state of society?
Can we not have conveniencies without luxuries;
plenty without superfluity? I think I have met
with an example of such a people, Mrs. B.; but
I dare not venture to mention my authority, as you
have once before rejected it.

MRS. B.

If you allude to Telemachus, there are many
sound doctrines of political economy in that work;
though it must be acknowledged that it is not free
from error. But let me hear the sentiments of
Fenelon on this subject.

CAROLINE.

Do you remember that delightful picture which
he draws of the inhabitants of Bœtica? There is an
irresistible charm in the description of their happiness; and if fabulous, it is certainly meant at
least to delineate what ought to constitute the hap-

D 3

ON PROPERTY.

piness of nations; equality, community of goods, but few arts and few wants; an ignorance or contempt of luxury, and manners perfectly conformed to the simplicity of nature. I must read you the passage, and you will tell me whether it is not a satire on political economy : —

"They live in common without any partition of "lands, the head of every family is its King. They "have no need of judges, for every man submits "to the jurisdiction of conscience. They possess "all things in common; for the cattle produce "milk, and the fields and orchards fruit and grain "of every kind in such abundance, that a people "so frugal and temperate have no need of pro- "perty. They have no fixed place of abode; but "when they have consumed the fruits, and ex- "hausted the pasturage, of one part of the paradise "which they inhabit, they remove their tents to "another : they have, therefore, no opposition of "interest, but are connected by a fraternal affec- "tion which there is nothing to interrupt. This "peace, this union, this liberty, they preserve by "rejecting superfluous wealth, and deceitful plea- "sure; they are all free, they are all equal.

"Superior wisdom, the result either of long ex- "perience, or uncommon abilities, is the only mark "of distinction among them; the sophistry of fraud, "the cry of violence, the contention of the bar, "and the tumult of battle, are never heard in this

ON PROPERTY. 55

" sacred region, which the Gods have taken under
" their immediate protection; this soil has never
" been distained with human blood, and even that
" of a lamb has rarely been shed upon it. When
" we first traded with these people, we found gold
" and silver used for ploughshares; and, in ge-
" neral, employed promiscuously with iron. As
" they carried on no foreign trade, they had no
" need of money, they were, almost all, either
" shepherds or husbandmen; for as they suffered
" no arts to be exercised among them, but such
" as tended immediately to answer the necessities
" of life, the number of artificers was consequently
" small: besides, a greater part, even of those that
" live by husbandry, or keeping of sheep, are skil-
" ful in the exercise of such arts, as are necessary
" to manners so simple and frugal."

MRS. B.

This, my dear Caroline, is a representation of
what the poets call the Golden age, and requires
only truth to make it perfect. If it were an his-
torical account, all the conclusions you deduce from
it would be just; but it is fiction, which you must
allow makes an essential difference.

Supposing that this earth were a paradise, and
yielded spontaneously all that is now produced by
cultivation; still without the institution of property it
could not be enjoyed; the fruit would be gathered

D 4

56   ON PROPERTY.

before it was ripe, animals killed before they came to maturity; for who would protect what was not their own; or who would economise when all the stores of nature were open to him? There would be a strange mixture of plenty, waste, and famine.

In this country, for instance, where the only common property consists in hedge-nuts and black-berries, how seldom are they allowed to ripen? In some parts of Spain, where the beauty of the climate produces a considerable quantity of good wild fruit, it is customary for the priest to bestow a blessing upon it before any is allowed to be gathered, and this ceremony is not performed till the fruit is considered to be generally ripe; by which means it is prevented from being prematurely gathered. It is with the same view that our game laws prohibit shooting, till the season when the birds have attained their full growth.

CAROLINE.

But though the Bœticans had all their goods in common, they were not without laws for protecting them.

MRS. B.

The earth is not a paradise, and will not spontaneously yield its produce in abundance; and if it were possessed in common, who would set about cultivating this or that spot of ground? Government must allot to every man his daily task, and

ON PROPERTY. 57

say to the one, you must work in this spot; to another, you must work in that. Would these men labour with the same activity and zeal as if they worked on their own account — that is to say, received wages equivalent to their exertions? certainly not. Such a system would transform independent men into slaves, into mere mechanical engines. There would be no inequality of condition, it is true, but the earth would not yield one-tenth part of its actual produce, the population would necessarily be diminished in the same proportion, and if all escaped the distresses of poverty, none would enjoy the acquisition of riches, an enjoyment which, when derived from the exercise of our talents and our industry, is a just and virtuous feeling; it raises men not only in the scale of wealth, but in that of the power of doing good, of enlarging the sphere of human knowledge, with all the inestimable benefits which result from it.

There have, however, really existed establishments founded on a community of goods. That of the Jesuits in Paraguay was of this description. The influence of religion enabled these priests to exercise a despotic sway over the poor Indians whom they had converted to Christianity; it must be allowed that they tempered their power by a patriarchal care of their docile subjects. Such a species of government might perhaps be well adapted to a tribe of ignorant uncivilized Indians, but it

D 5

58   ON PROPERTY.

would never make a free, a happy, an independent, and a wealthy people. I must again repeat it, the industry of man requires the stimulus of exclusive possession and enjoyment; and will always be proportioned to the personal advantage which he derives from it.

There is, indeed, still existing a sect of the same description called Moravians; but it is their religious tenets alone which enable them to keep up such an artificial system of community, and it should be compared rather to a convent of Monks and Nuns, than to a great nation.

CAROLINE.

I find I must give up the point of community of goods; but still I cannot help thinking that the great inequality of conditions which exist in the present state of society, is a serious evil.

In Switzerland, where there is much less inequality of fortune than in this country, I have often admired and almost envied the innocent and simple manners of the people. They seem not to know half our wants, nor to suffer half our cares.

MRS. B.

The Swiss are governed by mild and equitable laws, which render them a virtuous and a happy people; and if they are not a rich and populous nation, it proceeds not from any want of industry,

ON PROPERTY. 59

but from the obstacles opposed both to agriculture and trade by the nature of their country; for they are on the contrary uncommonly active and enterprising. I have often seen men carry on their shoulders baskets of manure up steep ascents inaccessible to beasts of burden, and this for the purpose of cultivating some little insulated spot of ground, which did not appear worth any such labour. The country women wear their knitting fastened round their waists, in order to have it at hand to fill up every little interval that occurs in their domestic employments. If a Swiss woman goes to fetch water from the fountain, or faggots from the wood, her burden is skilfully poised on her head, whilst her fingers busily ply the needles. But industrious as they are, the resources of the country are too limited to enable a father of a family to provide for all his children; some of them are therefore obliged to emigrate, and seek their fortune in a foreign land, which offers greater resources to their industry. Hence the number of Swiss merchants, governesses, shopkeepers, and servants, that are to be met with in almost all countries: would not these people be happier if they found means of exercising their industry and their talents in a country to which they are all so much attached, and which they have so much reason to love. In the energy of youthful vigour men may often quit their own country, and live happily

D 6

60 ON PROPERTY.

in a foreign land; but inquire of the parents who are on the point of separating from their children as soon as they have attained the hopeful age of manhood, whether their country would be less happy for offering them the means of employment and maintenance at home.

The Swiss cannot afford to support a standing army for the defence of their territory; they are therefore under the necessity of engaging their troops in the service of foreign potentates, in order to provide for a part of their population, and to have a resource by calling them home in times of danger. Would not these soldiers be happier in defending their own country, than in shedding their blood as mercenaries in the cause of foreigners? We have a remarkable proof of it, in the effect which their patriotic songs are said to produce on them; when these simple airs recall to their minds their beloved and regretted country, it either drives them to desertion, or renders their lives miserable; and so deep is the impression made by these national airs, that it was found necessary to forbid their being sung by the troops in foreign service.

CAROLINE.

There is no withstanding your attacks, Mrs. B. You drive me from all my strong holds. I expected to have found a safe asylum in the mountains of Switzerland, but I see that I must once

ON PROPERTY. 61

more take refuge in London, where I am sure you
will admit that the contrast between the luxuries of
the rich and the wretchedness of the poor is shock-
ing to every person of common feeling.

MRS. B.

If the wretchedness of the poor were the effect of
the luxuries of the rich, I should certainly agree
with you on that point; but I believe it to be otherwise. However, as the people, whose progress
towards wealth and civilization we have been tracing
in our two last conversations, are yet far from being
sufficiently advanced in their career to be guilty of
any great excess in luxury, we must patiently follow
them in their advancement in knowledge and the
acquisition of wealth before we treat of the subject
of luxury.

CONVERSATION V.

ON THE DIVISION OF LABOUR.

ORIGIN OF BARTER. — DIVISION OF LABOUR. — EXTRACTS FROM SMITH'S WEALTH OF NATIONS ON THE DIVISION OF LABOUR. — ADVANTAGES OF MACHINERY. — EFFECTS OF THE DIVISION OF LABOUR ON THE MORALS AND INTELLECTS OF THE PEOPLE. — RECAPITULATION.

MRS. B.

WE have ascertained that the establishment and security of property were the chief causes of the emancipation of mankind from the shackles of sloth and ignorance; but there are other subordinate causes which tend greatly to promote the progress of industry and civilization. The first of these is the introduction of *exchange* or *barter*.

We observed that when men found they could place a reliance on the security of their possessions,

ON THE DIVISION OF LABOUR. 63

they laboured with redoubled activity, and far from being satisfied with a scanty and temporary maintenance, they provide for the future, they accumulate a little store not only of the necessaries, but of the comforts and conveniencies of life. The one has a stock of arrows for the chace, another of provisions for the winter, a third of clothes or ornaments for his person. They will remain in undisturbed possession of this little property; but those who can no longer obtain it by force or fraud will endeavour to procure it by other means. In the hunting season they will apply to the fabricator of arrows; but they will not go to him with empty hands; they must be provided with something to offer in exchange for the arrows, something which they think will tempt him to part with them; whilst those who have nothing to give in return, must go without the arrows, how much soever they may stand in need of them.

Here then is a new incitement to a spirit of industry. Whoever has accumulated more than he wants of any article, may find means of exchanging the surplus for something that will gratify other desires. As objects of desire increase, the wish to possess and the efforts to obtain them increase also; and the industry of man is exerted either in producing them himself, or in producing something by means of which he may obtain them. Thus the torpid apathy and languid indolence of a savage,

64   ON THE DIVISION OF LABOUR.

yields to the curiosity, the admiration, the desire, the activity, and industry of a civilized being.

The man, for instance, who first cultivates a little spot of ground, may be said to produce in time a general harvest; not only by introducing the art of tillage, but by the powerful impulse which it gives to industry in general. He cannot himself consume the whole produce of his little garden, but he exchanges the surplus for other things of which he stands in need.

CAROLINE.

Besides, he would not have had sufficient time to bestow on the cultivation of his garden, if he had been, at the same time, obliged to provide for all his other wants.

MRS. B.

Very true; those therefore who mean to partake of the fruits of his garden, must contribute towards the supply of those other wants; some will bring him fish from the river, others game from the woods; when his immediate necessities are supplied he will be induced to exchange his vegetables for articles of conveniency, such as baskets to contain his fruit, or some of the rude implements of husbandry; or he may finally be tempted to part with some for mere luxuries, such as rare shells, feathers, and other personal ornaments. His neighbours

ON THE DIVISION OF LABOUR. 65

will therefore be eager to procure and produce articles, which, either from necessity, conveniency, or merely from pleasure, will induce the gardener to part with the produce of his garden ; for this purpose invention will be stimulated, new articles will be produced, skill will be acquired, and a general spirit of industry developed.

CAROLINE.

So far the introduction of barter seems to answer a very useful purpose; but when once industry is roused, why should not every one exert his abilities to supply his own wants, and gratify his desires, without the intervention of barter? If a man happens to be possessed of a superfluous quantity of any commodity, it is no doubt desirable to exchange it for something more wanted : but it seems to me to be an unnatural and circuitous mode of proceeding, to produce something which we do not want, in order afterwards to exchange it for something which we do want.

MRS. B.

Would you then have the baker kill his own meat as well as bake his own bread, brew his own beer, build his own house, make his own clothes, and do a thousand other things, instead of procuring them in exchange through the sale of his bread ?

ON THE DIVISION OF LABOUR.

CAROLINE.

Oh no, it would be impossible to undertake so many occupations; and then he can do one thing better than he can do many: but this separation of trades and employments cannot take place in a savage state.

MRS. B.

No, but it begins to operate as soon as barter is introduced; and it is to this circuitous mode that we owe all our improvements in skill and dexterity; the advantages of which are much more important than you imagine.

When barter became common, it was soon discovered that the more a man confined himself to any one single branch of industry, to the fabrication of bows and arrows for instance, the greater the skill and dexterity he acquired in that particular art; so that he could make bows and arrows not only quicker, but of better workmanship than another man who followed a variety of pursuits.

CAROLINE.

Now I begin to understand the advantage that results from barter, independently of its inspiring a spirit of industry and a taste for a variety of enjoyments. The artist who has acquired a superior degree of excellence in the fabrication of bows and arrows, would gain more, by confining himself entirely to that occupation, and exchanging his

ON THE DIVISION OF LABOUR. 67

merchandize for whatever else he was desirous of obtaining, than by turning his attention to a variety of pursuits.

MRS. B.

No doubt he would, provided he were sure of being able to dispose of all the bows and arrows he could make; for it would be useless to fabricate more than he could sell or exchange; and as no one could become a purchaser, unless he had something to offer in return, a long period of time must elapse before the progress of industry would create a sufficient number of purchasers to enable an individual to earn a livelihood by the fabrication of bows and arrows.

It is therefore only in a more advanced stage of society that the demand for commodities is so great that men find it advantageous to devote themselves wholly to one particular art.

Adam Smith observes, that " in lone houses and " very small villages which are scattered about in " so desert a country as the Highlands of Scotland, " every farmer must be butcher, baker, and brewer " for his own family. In such situations we can " scarcely expect to find even a smith, a carpenter, " or a mason within less than twenty miles of an- " other of the same trade. The scattered families " that live at eight or ten miles distant from the " nearest of them, must learn to perform for them- " selves a great number of little pieces of work, for

ON THE DIVISION OF LABOUR.

" which, in more populous countries, they call in
" the assistance of these workmen."

This separation of employments, which, in political economy, is called the *division of labour*, can take place only in civilized countries. In the flourishing states of Europe we find men not only exclusively engaged in the exercise of one particular art, but that art subdivided into numerous branches, each of which forms a distinct occupation for different workmen.

Here is a beautiful passage in Adam Smith, the merits of which you will now be able to appreciate.

CAROLINE *reads*.

" Observe the accommodation of the most com-
" mon artificer or day-labourer in a civilized and
" thriving country, and you will perceive that the
" number of people of whose industry a part,
" though but a small part, has been employed in
" procuring him this accommodation, exceeds all
" computation. The woollen coat, for example,
" which covers the day-labourer, as coarse and
" rough as it may appear, is the produce of the
" joint labour of a great multitude of workmen.
" The shepherd, the sorter of the wool, the wool-
" comber or carder, the dyer, the scribbler, the
" spinner, the weaver, the fuller, the dresser, with
" many others, must all join their different arts in
" order to complete even this homely production.

ON THE DIVISION OF LABOUR. 69

" How many merchants and carriers, besides, must
" have been employed in transporting the materials
" from some of those workmen to others who often
" live in a very distant part of the country! How
" much commerce and navigation in particular,
" how many ship-builders, sailors, sail-makers, rope-
" makers, must have been employed in order to
" bring together the different drugs made use of by
" the dyer, which often come from the remotest
" corners of the world! What a variety of labour
" too is necessary in order to produce the tools of
" the meanest of those workmen! To say nothing
" of such complicated machines as the ship of the
" sailor, the mill of the fuller, or even the loom of
" the weaver, let us consider only what a variety
" of labour is requisite in order to form that very
" simple machine, the shears with which the
" shepherd clips the wool. The miner, the builder
" of the furnace for heating the ore, the seller of
" the timber, the burner of the charcoal to be made
" use of in the smelting-house, the brickmaker, the
" bricklayer, the workmen who attend the furnace,
" the mill-wright, the forger, the smith, must all of
" them join their different arts in order to produce
" them. Were we to examine, in the same man-
" ner, all the different parts of his dress and house-
" hold furniture, the coarse linen shirt which he
" wears next his skin, the shoes which cover his
" feet, the bed which he lies on, and all the differ-

70 ON THE DIVISION OF LABOUR.

" ent parts which compose it, the kitchen-grate, at
" which he prepares his victuals, the coals which
" he makes use of for that purpose, dug from the
" bowels of the earth, and brought to him by a long
" sea and a long land carriage, all the other uten-
" sils of his kitchen, all the furniture of his table,
" the knives and forks, the earthen or pewter plates
" upon which he serves up and divides his victuals,
" the different hands employed in preparing his
" bread and his beer, the glass window which lets
" in the heat and the light, and keeps out the wind
" and rain, with all the knowledge and art requisite
" for preparing that beautiful and happy invention,
" without which these northern parts of the world
" could scarce have afforded a very comfortable
" habitation, together with the tools of all the dif-
" ferent workmen employed in producing those
" different conveniences; if we examine, I say, all
" these things, and consider what a variety of la-
" bour is employed about each of them, we shall be
" sensible that without the assistance and co-opera-
" tion of many thousands, the very meanest person
" in a civilized country could not be provided, even
" according to what we very falsely imagine the
" easy and simple manner in which he is commonly
" accommodated. Compared, indeed, with the
" more extravagant luxury of the great, his accom-
" modation must no doubt appear extremely simple
" and easy; and yet it may be true, perhaps, that

ON THE DIVISION OF LABOUR. 71

" the accommodation of an European prince does
" not always so much exceed that of an industrious
" and frugal peasant, as the accommodation of the
" latter exceeds that of many an African King, the
" absolute master of the lives and liberties of ten
" thousand naked savages."

It is very true, certainly; and it reminds me of
an observation of Dr. Johnson in the Rambler,
" That not a washerwoman sits down to break-
" fast, without tea from the East Indies, and sugar
" from the West."

I now comprehend your reference to the little
story of the cherry-orchard: it was by dividing
amongst the children the different parts of the process of plaiting straw, that they succeeded so much
better than the boy who was left to perform the
whole of his plait alone.

MRS. B.

I will now point out to you some examples remarked by Adam Smith in illustration of the benefits derived from the division of labour. That of
the pin-manufactory I shall give you in his own
words. He observes, that " A workman not edu-
" cated to this business, nor acquainted with the
" use of the machinery employed in it, could
" scarce, perhaps, with his utmost industry, make
" one pin in a day, and certainly could not make
" twenty. But in the way in which this business

72   ON THE DIVISION OF LABOUR.

" is now carried on, not only the whole work is a
" peculiar trade, but it is divided into a number of
" branches, of which the greater part are likewise
" peculiar trades. One man draws out the wire,
" another straightens it, a third cuts it, a fourth
" points it, a fifth grinds it at the top for receiv-
" ing the head. To make the head requires two or
" three distinct operations; to put it on is a pecu-
" liar business, to whiten the pins is another; it is
" even a trade by itself to put them into the
" paper; and the important business of making a
" pin is, in this manner, divided into about
" eighteen distinct operations, which, in some ma-
" nufactories, are all performed by distinct hands,
" though in others the same man will sometimes
" perform two or three of them. I have seen a
" small manufactory of this kind where ten men
" only were employed, and where some of them
" consequently performed two or three distinct
" operations: but though they were very poor,
" and therefore but indifferently accommodated
" with the necessary machinery, they could, when
" they exerted themselves, make among them
" about twelve pounds of pins in a day. There
" are in a pound upwards of four thousand pins
" of a middling size. Those ten persons, there-
" fore, could make among them upwards of forty-
" eight thousand pins in a day. Each person,
" therefore, making a tenth part of forty-eight

ON THE DIVISION OF LABOUR. 73

" thousand pins, might be considered as making
" four thousand eight hundred pins in a day. But
" if they had all wrought separately and inde-
" pendently, and without any of them having been
" educated to this peculiar business, they certainly
" could not each of them have made twenty,
" perhaps not one pin in a day; that is, certainly,
" not the two hundred and fortieth, perhaps not
" the four thousand eight hundredth part of what
" they are at present capable of performing, in
" consequence of a proper division and combin-
" ation of their different operations."

CAROLINE.

These effects of the division of labour are really
wonderful !

MRS. B.

The instance which Adam Smith quotes in proof
of the dexterity acquired by men, whose labour is reduced to one simple operation, is also very striking.
After observing that a man unaccustomed to a
blacksmith's forge can with difficulty make three
hundred nails in a day, he says that a common blacksmith can forge one thousand, but that he has seen
boys who have been brought up to the art of nall-
making exclusively, acquire such a degree of dexterity as to complete two thousand three hundred
in a day.

E

74 ON THE DIVISION OF LABOUR.

CAROLINE.

The difference is prodigious: but I can conceive it when I observe with what awkwardness a man handles the tools of an art with which he is unacquainted, whilst they are used with ease and dexterity by those who are accustomed to them.

MRS. B.

Then we must consider that when a man's whole attention and talents are turned to one particular object, there is a much greater probability of his discovering means of improving his workmanship, or facilitating and abridging his labour, than if his mind were engaged in a variety of pursuits. It is most frequently to workmen, that we are indebted for improvements in the process and instruments of labour.

Another advantage derived from the division of labour is the regular and uninterrupted manner in which it enables the work to proceed. A labourer who has many diversified occupations not only loses time in going from one to another, but also in settling himself to his different employments; and as soon as his *hand is in*, as the workmen say, he must quit his work to take up another totally different. Thus he must go from his plough to his loom, from his loom to his forge, from his forge to his mill, — but no — there could be neither plough, nor loom, nor forge, nor mill,

ON THE DIVISION OF LABOUR. 75

before a division of labour had taken place; for no man could either find time or acquire skill to construct such machines, unless they could bestow the whole of their labour and attention upon them.

The construction of machines, therefore, we may consider as a refined branch of the division of labour. Their effect in facilitating and abridging labour is almost incredible. How easy, for instance, the operation of grinding corn is rendered by so simple a machine as a windmill! Were this to be done by manual labour, by bruizing it between stones, it would be almost an endless task; whilst in a windmill the natural motion of the air performs nearly the whole of the work.

CAROLINE.

But the cotton-mills we have lately seen are a much more wonderful example of the effect of machinery. In these a steam-engine sets all the wheels and spindles in motion, and performs the work of hundreds of people.

MRS. B.

The great efficacy of machinery in the hands of man, depends upon the art of compelling natural agents, such as wind, steam, and water, to perform the task which he would otherwise be obliged to execute himself; by which means labour is very much abridged, a great deal of human ef-

E 2

76 ON THE DIVISION OF LABOUR.

fort is saved, and the work is often accomplished in a more uniform and accurate manner.

We noticed the skill that could be acquired in the art of forging nails: but the utmost efforts of manual labour fall far short of machinery. A machine has been invented in the United States of America for the purpose of cutting nails out of iron, the operation of which is so rapid that it forms 250 perfect nails in the space of one minute, or 15,000 in an hour.

CAROLINE.

The metals, I suppose, could not have been brought into use, till a considerable progress had been made in the division of labour?

MRS. B.

Certainly not; for it requires the exclusive labour of a great number of men to work a mine. The Mexicans and Peruvians in America, though they had made some progress towards civilization, had never sought for gold in the bowels of the earth, but contented themselves with what they could pick up in the beds of rivers. In Britain, the Cornish mines were worked in very ancient times, and it is even supposed that the Phœnicians had introduced this art among the ancient Britons, with whom they are said to have trafficked for tin and other metals.

ON THE DIVISION OF LABOUR. 77

CAROLINE.

I am perfectly satisfied that the division of labour is a necessary step towards the accumulation of national wealth: but may it not have an injurious effect on the mental faculties of individuals? A man who is confined to one simple mechanical operation, however great the facility and perfection he may acquire in the performance of it, is shut out from all other improvement; his mind will never be roused to exertion by difficulty, interested by variety, or enlightened by comparison. His ideas will be confined within the narrow limits of his monotonous employment, and his rational powers will become so degraded as to render him scarcely superior to the machinery at which he works. Whilst a common husbandman, whose occupations are diversified, and but little aided by machinery, acquires knowledge by experience in his various employments, and, having a much wider range of observation, enjoys a corresponding development of intellect.

MRS. B.

The knowledge of a ploughman is often remarkably distinct in his limited sphere; but yet I have usually found that in conversing upon general topics with a ploughman and with a mechanic, the latter has discovered more intelligence, and that his mind has appeared more active and accustomed to reflection. I conceive this to be owing to the facility

E 3

78 ON THE DIVISION OF LABOUR.

which the arts afford of bringing men together in society. They are carried on in towns, where neighbourhood renders social intercourse much more easy than in scattered hamlets in the country. When they meet together they talk over each other's concerns, read the newspapers, and discuss the politics of the parish, or of the state. This observation is particularly applicable to manufactories, where a number of persons generally work together in the same room, and their employment seldom prevents conversation. Social intercourse, however low the members amongst whom it exists, cannot fail to promote the diffusion of knowledge; they become acquainted with the comforts and conveniences which have been acquired by the more skilful and industrious; they learn to appreciate their value, and are stimulated to acquire the means of obtaining them; a mode of instruction which we have observed to be the most essential step towards dispelling ignorance, and exciting industry.

CAROLINE.

But is there not some danger that the advantages obtained in the improvement of the mind by this state of constant intercourse amongst the lower classes in manufacturing towns, will be more than counterbalanced by the corruption of morals? How much more vice appears to prevail amongst the

ON THE DIVISION OF LABOUR. 79

lower orders in crowded cities, than in the cottages of the peasantry !

MRS. B.

You do not consider the difference of the population; there are often a greater number of people collected together in a manufacturing town than there are scattered over a space of thirty square miles of country: were their morals, therefore, the same, vice would appear much more conspicuous in the town than in the country. Admitting, however, the comparative amount of crimes to be greater in the former, I believe that it is compensated by a more considerable proportion of virtue.

CAROLINE.

But you must allow that we hear much more of the vices than of the virtues of manufacturing towns and great cities.

MRS. B.

Because crimes, from being amenable to the laws, are necessarily made known, whilst virtue seldom receives any public testimony of approbation. Every act of fraud or violence is sounded in our ears, whilst the humanity, the sympathy for sufferings, the sacrifices which the poor make to relieve each other's distresses, are known only to those who enter into their domestic concerns. This has been frequently noticed by medical men who have attended

E 4

80   ON THE DIVISION OF LABOUR.

the lower classes of people in sickness at their own houses.

CAROLINE.

Yet, upon the whole, do you not think that the situation of the poor in the country is better than it is in towns?

MRS. B.

They have each their advantages and disadvantages, and I should imagine that good and evil are pretty equally balanced between them. If the inhabitants of towns are better informed, and can more easily acquire some of the comforts of life, the inhabitants of the country are more vigorous and healthy, more cleanly, and they have the advantage of a more constant and regular demand for the produce of their labour, which is not so liable to be affected by the casualties of war, fashion, and other causes, which often occasion great distress to manufacturers.

But should you still entertain any apprehension that the division of labour may check and repress the intellectual improvement of the lower classes, I should consider this as amply compensated by its prodigious effect in the multiplication of wealth, a circumstance which not only increases the comforts of the poor, but by facilitating the means of acquiring knowledge, ultimately promotes its diffusion among all classes of men. It is to the division of labour that we are indebted for all the

ON THE DIVISION OF LABOUR. 81

improvements in the processes of art, and amongst others for the invention of printing, which has proved the means of so wonderfully extending all kinds of knowledge.

We have now, I think, brought our savages to a considerable degree of advancement in civilization; I would wish you briefly to recapitulate the causes which have produced this happy change, and at our next interview we will continue to trace their progress.

CAROLINE.

Labour seems to be the natural and immediate cause of wealth; but it will produce little more than the necessaries of life until its benefits are extended by the establishment of such a government as can give security to property. The spirit of industry will then be rapidly developed. The surplus produce of one individual will be exchanged for that of another. The facilities thus offered to barter will naturally introduce the division of labour or of employment; and will soon give rise to the invention of machinery, the merits of which we have just discussed.

MRS. B.

Extremely well, Caroline. We shall now take leave of this improved state of society for the present, with a conviction, I hope, that we leave mankind much happier than we found it.

E 5

CONVERSATION VI.

ON CAPITAL.

DISTINCTION OF RICH AND POOR. — ACCUMULATION OF WEALTH. — HOW IT IS DISPOSED OF. — THE POOR LABOUR FOR IT. — CONTRACT BETWEEN THE CAPITALIST AND THE LABOURER.—THE RICH UNDER THE NECESSITY OF EMPLOYING THE POOR. — DEFINITION OF CAPITAL. — HOW CAPITAL YIELDS AN INCOME. — PROFITS MADE BY THE EMPLOYMENT OF LABOURERS. — PRODUCTIVE LABOURERS. — INDEPENDENCE OF MEN OF CAPITAL. — INDUSTRY LIMITED BY EXTENT OF CAPITAL. — INDUSTRY INCREASES IN PROPORTION TO CAPITAL. — CAPITAL AUGMENTED BY THE ADDITION OF SAVINGS FROM INCOME.—HAPPINESS RESULTING RATHER FROM THE GRADUAL ACQUISITION, THAN THE ACTUAL POSSESSION OF WEALTH.

MRS. B.

I N tracing the progress of society towards civilization, we noticed the happy effects resulting from the security of property and the division of

ON CAPITAL. 88

labour. From this period we may also date the distinction of rich and poor.

CAROLINE.

And all the evils that arise from inequality of condition. This, alas! is the dark side of the picture. The weeds spring up with the corn.

MRS. B.

I know not how this distinction can be called an evil. If it does not exist in a savage state, it is because indigence is universal; for no one being able to acquire more than what is necessary for his immediate maintenance, every one is poor. When civilization takes place, the advantages arising from the division of labour enable an industrious skilful man to acquire more wealth than will suffice to gratify his wants or desires. By continued exertion this surplus produce of his industry in the course of time accumulates, and he becomes rich, whilst the less industrious, who acquires merely a daily subsistence, remains poor or possessed of nothing.

CAROLINE.

I see no great advantage in this accumulation of wealth, for it must either be spent or hoarded; if spent, the industrious man is eventually no richer than his idle neighbours; and if hoarded, the accumulation is of no use to any one.

E 6

ON CAPITAL.

MRS. B.

Your dilemma is put with some ingenuity, but you must at least allow that, where more is spent, there is a greater scope for enjoyment; and in regard to hoarding, I hope you are not recurring to your notions about riches and money, and forget that the wealth of which we have been speaking consists of exchangeable commodities, either agricultural or manufactured, many of which are not of a nature to be kept, were men inclined to hoard them. A much better mode of disposing of them has been devised; one which not only secures, but augments them.

CAROLINE.

What can that be?

MRS. B.

This you will hardly understand without some previous explanation.

In civilized society men cannot, as in a state of nature, obtain a subsistence by hunting, or from the spontaneous produce of the earth; because the wilderness has been destroyed by cultivation, and the land has become private property.

CAROLINE.

And when the land is engrossed by the rich, there seems to be no resource left for the poor?

ON CAPITAL.

MRS. B.

What do you suppose the rich do with their wealth?

CAROLINE.

The poor, I am sure, partake very little of it, for the sums the most charitable give away are but trifling compared to what they spend upon themselves.

MRS. B.

I am far from wishing that the poor should be dependant on the charity of the rich for a subsistence. Is there no other mode of partaking of their wealth but as beggars?

CAROLINE.

Not that I know of, unless by stealing. Oh no, I guess now—you mean they may earn it by their labour?

MRS. B.

Certainly. The poor man says to the rich, " You have more than you want, whilst I am destitute. Give me some little share of your wealth for a subsistence; I have nothing to offer in exchange but my labour; but with that I will undertake to procure you more than you part with — if you will maintain me, I will work for you."

CAROLINE.

But is it not usual to pay wages to labourers instead of maintaining them?

86   ON CAPITAL.

MRS. B.

It comes to the same; for the wages purchase
a maintenance; the money merely represents the
things of which the labourer stands in need, and
for which he may exchange it.

CAROLINE.

The labourer may then be supposed to say to
the rich man, " Give me food and clothing, and I
by my labour will produce for you other things
in return."

MRS. B.

Precisely; the rich man exchanges with the
labourer the produce or work that is already done,
for work that is yet to be done. It is thus that he
acquires a command over the labour of the poor,
and increases his wealth by the profits he derives
from it.

CAROLINE.

This is a resource for the poor, I own; but not
enough to satisfy me entirely, for they are left at
the mercy of the rich, and if these did not chuse
to employ them, they would starve.

MRS. B.

True; but what could the rich do without their
assistance?

CAROLINE.

Their wealth would furnish them a plentiful
subsistence.

ON CAPITAL. 87

MRS. B.

At first it might, but in time it would be consumed. Their harvests and their cattle would be eaten, their clothes worn out, and their houses fallen into decay.

CAROLINE.

But you know that the harvests are annually reproduced, new clothes are purchased, and houses repaired or rebuilt: riches easily obtain all these things.

MRS. B.

But who is it that re-produces the harvests? Who manufactures new clothes, and builds new houses, but the poorer classes of men? Without their aid you could spend only what you actually possessed, and when it was gone you would be destitute.

CAROLINE.

True; that is an idea that often perplexed me when I was a child. I thought that in proportion as my father spent his money he must be impoverished; but now I understand that wealth is reproduced by the labour of the poor, and that thence arises an annual income.

MRS. B.

If the value produced by the labourer exceeds what he has consumed, the excess will constitute an income to his employer; and observe, that an

88 ON CAPITAL.

income can be obtained by no other means than by the employment of the poor.

CAROLINE.

Indeed I was perfectly aware that it was necessary to employ labourers for this purpose; but I did not consider that it created reciprocity of benefit, by rendering the poor in a great measure independant of the will of the rich.

MRS. B.

The rich and poor are necessary to each other; it is precisely the fable of the belly and the limbs; without the rich the poor would starve; without the poor the rich would be compelled to labour for their own subsistence.

CAROLINE.

It is very true, Mrs. B.; and this is, I suppose, what you alluded to, when you said that the rich had a means of securing their wealth without hoarding it.

MRS. B.

Yes; the labouring classes consume and re-produce it. Wealth, thus destined for re-production by the employment of labourers, is called *capital.* You have heard of capital before, no doubt?

ON CAPITAL. 89

CAROLINE.

Oh yes; a man of fortune is said to be a man of capital: I always considered these as synonimous terms.

MRS. B.

So they are; and you may have heard also that to spend a capital is very ruinous; that it should be placed in some profitable line, so as to yield an income; that is to say, it must be employed to set labourers to work, and the profit derived from their labour is called revenue or income.

CAROLINE.

If capital is employed in paying the wages of labourers, it is spent and consumed by them, and is lost to the capitalist as much as if he spent it.

MRS. B.

No; capital employed is consumed, but not destroyed: it is at least no more destroyed than the seed sown in the ground, which is re-produced with increase. Thus the capital consumed by labourers is re-produced with increased value in the articles of their workmanship.

CAROLINE.

I know that a capital produces an income; and seem to have a clear idea how this is effected. Yet I have some scruples respecting the mode of obtain-

90   ON CAPITAL.

ing it, which I am not altogether able to remove. I
see that if the labourer re-produces for the
capitalist only as much as he consumes, or, in
other words, commodities equal in value to his
wages, the *income* is only equivalent to the *out-
going;* he restores therefore exactly what the capitalist has advanced him, the latter being neither a
loser nor a gainer by the bargain ; any farther, at
least, than that, by re-production, perishable produce is made to last; and that if more is produced,
it seems but fair that the labourer should have the
whole of his earnings.

MRS. B.

No capitalist would consent to such an agreement. When the poor man applies to the rich one
for a maintenance, offering his labour in return, he
does not say — for the food you give me during the
present year, I will produce an equal quantity of
food next year—because he knows that he would not
be employed on such terms; he must by the prospect of some advantage induce the capitalist to exchange food that is already produced for something
that is yet to be produced.   He therefore says—for
the food you give me now, I will raise you a greater
or more valuable supply next year.

CAROLINE.

It appears to me a hardship, notwithstanding,
that after the rich have engrossed the whole pro-

ON CAPITAL.   91

perty of the land, nothing should be left to the poor beyond their own labour, and that they should not be allowed to reap the whole of the advantages it affords. If I were a legislator, I should be disposed at all events to establish a law compelling the capitalist to allow the labourer the whole of the profit arising from his work. Such a regulation would surely tend to improve the condition of the poor. You smile, Mrs. B., I am afraid you will not allow of my plan?

MRS. B.

I would suggest an addition to it, which is a law to compel the capitalist to employ the labourers; for on your terms none would give them work. The farmer, were he obliged to pay his husband-men the value of the crops they raised, would derive no profit from their sale; he would, therefore, leave his fields uncultivated, the land would lie waste, and the husbandmen starve. Manufacturers for the same reason would discharge their work-men, merchants their clerks; in a word, industry would be paralyzed; and were you to devise a system of certain and inevitable ruin to a country, I do not think you could adopt a more efficacious mode of promoting your design.

CAROLINE.

So much for the wisdom of my laws! I certainly ought to have foreseen these consequences,

92 ON CAPITAL.

since, as you observed before, the inducement for the rich to employ the poor is the advantage the former derive from the latter.

MRS. B.

Undoubtedly. The profits the rich reap from the employment of their capital constitutes their income; without such income the capital, it is true, might, by your compulsatory laws, be re-produced annually; but yielding no income, the capitalist would gradually consume it in the maintenance of his family; and thus his means of employing labourers would annually diminish.

So far from considering the profits which the capitalist derives from his labourers as an evil, I have always thought it one of the most beneficent ordinations of Providence, that the employment of the poor should be a necessary step to the increase of the wealth of the rich.

Thus the rich man has the means of augmenting his capital, not by hoarding, but by distributing it among his labourers, who consume it, and re-produce another and a larger capital—hence have they obtained the name of *productive labourers.*

CAROLINE.

When a man, therefore, becomes possessed of a capital, whether by accumulation of his savings or

ON CAPITAL. 93

by inheritance, it is no longer requisite for him to work for a maintenance, as others will labour for him?

MRS. B.

It depends on the amount of his capital, and the extent of his desires. If it will yield an income sufficient to maintain him and his family with the degree of comfort or affluence which satisfies his ambition, he may live in idleness; if not, he will work himself; or at least superintend his labourers. This is the case with the farmer, the merchant, the master manufacturer, each of whom superintend their respective concerns.

Do you understand now, that no productive enterprize can be undertaken without capital. Capital is necessary to pay labourers, to purchase materials to work upon, instruments to work with; in short to defray the whole expense attached to the employment of labourers.

CAROLINE.

But a man may undertake a productive enterprize without employing labourers: for instance, if he gather mushrooms on a common, he requires no capital for that purpose; no tools are used, the earth produces mushrooms spontaneously, and every one has a right to gather them. The same may be said of nuts and wild strawberries.

94   ON CAPITAL.

MRS. B.

These are small remnants of the resources of a
savage state, in which subsistence is derived from
the spontaneous produce of the earth: but the employments which require no capital, are very inconsiderable, and occur only during a short season of
the year.

CAROLINE.

There is one, which appears to me of great importance — fishing. Fishermen are in no want of
capital; the fish costs them merely the trouble of
catching. Oh no! I am mistaken; I forgot the
nets and the boats that are necessary for fishing;
besides, the men must have something to subsist
on, when the weather will not allow them to venture
on the water.

But there is another case, Mrs. B.; I have
known persons who were worth nothing, and yet
who set up in business on credit.

MRS. B.

That is no exception; for credit is the employment of the capital belonging to another.

CAROLINE.

Well, it is a melancholy reflection that one must
always possess something in order to gain more.
He then who has nothing to begin with, has no
means of escaping from poverty.

ON CAPITAL. 95

MRS. B.

Poverty is a word of vague signification. If you mean to express by it a state of positive indigence, the labourer who earns a subsistence from day to day, cannot come under that description. But if you use the word poverty in opposition to wealth, that is to say, to the possession of capital, labourers, though usually in that state, are not necessarily condemned to it. A healthy and hard-working man may, if he be economical, almost always lay aside something as the beginning of a little capital, which by additional savings accumulates.

CAROLINE.

That is true. Thomas, our under gardener, who is a very intelligent, industrious man, was saying the other day to one of his fellow-labourers, that as soon as he had laid by a little money to begin the world with, he intended to marry. But it seems to me that if my father would give him a cottage, and an acre or two of ground, he might raise vegetables for market, and by these means support himself and his family.

MRS. B.

In that case your father would supply the capital. The cottage and the land is a capital, but they will not do alone. Thomas would besides require garden tools to work with, and an assistant,

96   ON CAPITAL.

if not several, to prepare the ground. Then he must not only subsist himself, but maintain his family till the produce of his garden can be brought to market. In the course of three or four years, from the earnings of his daily labour he may have amassed a little capital sufficient to enable him to undertake this; he will then no longer be a labourer for hire, but will work on his own account. It is thus every thing has a beginning; the largest fortunes have often had no greater origin.

Now, supposing Thomas to be able to rent an acre of land when he is worth 100*l.*, he may rent ten acres when he is worth 1000*l.*, but he cannot rent more; he cannot increase his farm, beyond his means of paying for it; his industry, therefore, is limited by the extent of his capital.

CAROLINE.

I do not quite understand that.

MRS. B.

Let us imagine a tradesman, a shoe-maker for instance, to be master of a capital which will enable him to maintain ten workmen, and that the following year he finds that he has gained 100*l.* by the profits derived from their labour. This 100*l.* constitutes his income; if he spend it, his capital remains what it was before: but if he adds it to his capital it will enable him to maintain and

ON CAPITAL. 97

provide work for a greater number of journeymen. Let us say that he can now employ twelve instead of ten men; these will make him a greater quantity of shoes, and the additional profits arising from their sale will, if added to his capital, still farther increase his means of employing workmen. Thus the demand for labour, or, in other words, employment for the poor, will ever increase with the increase of capital, and be limited only by its deficiency.

CAROLINE.

But we must not forget that the master shoemaker and his family are to be maintained out of these profits; the whole of them cannot, therefore, be added to his capital.

MRS. B.

Certainly not. The expenses of his family consume, in general, by far the greater part of a man's income; but if he is prudent, he will lay aside as much as can be spared, and these savings will enable him to enlarge and improve his business, of whatever description it may be.

CAROLINE.

Thus a farmer would be able to extend and improve the cultivation of his farm by increasing the number of his labourers — and a merchant proportionally to extend his commercial dealings — so that

F

98   ON CAPITAL.

the richer a man becomes, the more it will be in his
power to increase his wealth?

MRS. B.

Yes; the second thousand pounds is often acquired with less difficulty than the first hundred.

CAROLINE.

That is hard upon those who have nothing. The
rich landed proprietors buy up all the little farms;
rich merchants engross all the great commercial
speculations; in a word, the great fish devour the
small ones.

MRS. B.

There is no truth in that comparison. He who
accumulates a large fortune by his industry injures
no one; on the contrary, he confers a benefit on
the community. You will understand this better
by and by. In the mean time I must observe to
you, that happiness, so far as it is dependant on
wealth, consists less in the possession of riches than
in the pleasure of acquiring them. Every degree
of increasing prosperity is attended with its enjoyment. Your gardener, who saves his earnings
with the prospect of settling at the end of two or
three years, has probably more satisfaction in the
prospect of his future wealth than he will have in
the possession of it; as long as he continues making
annual additions to his capital, the same source of

ON CAPITAL. 99

enjoyment will be preserved, but will never excite so strong an interest as at first. Merchants will tell you that their first gains gave them greater pleasure than all their subsequent accumulations. Nature has wisely attached happiness to the gradual acquisition, rather than to the actual possession of wealth, thus rendering it an incitement to industry; and we shall hereafter see that this progressive state of prosperity is most conducive also to the happiness of nations.

CONVERSATION VII.

ON CAPITAL — *continued.*

OF FIXED CAPITAL. — DISTINCTION BETWEEN FIXED
AND CIRCULATING CAPITAL. — EXAMPLES OF THE
DIFFERENT KINDS OF CAPITAL. — OF SLAVES. —
FIXED CAPITAL AND CIRCULATING CAPITAL EQUAL-
LY BENEFICIAL TO THE LABOURING CLASS. —
MACHINERY ADVANTAGEOUS TO THE LABOURING
CLASSES. — QUOTATION FROM MACPHERSON ON
THE ADVANTAGES OF MACHINERY. — QUOTATION
FROM MR. SAY'S TREATISE ON POLITICAL ECO-
NOMY.

MRS. B.

I HAVE some further remarks to make to you
on the nature of capital.

A land owner, when he increases his capital by
savings from his income, may probably, instead of
employing the whole of his additional capital on
husbandmen, find it more advantageous to lay out
some part of it on workmen to build barns and
outhouses, to store his crops and shelter his cattle;

ON CAPITAL. 101

he may plant trees to produce timber, build cottages, and bring into cultivation some of the waste land on his farm.

A manufacturer also, in proportion as he increases the number of his workmen, must enlarge his machinery or implements of industry.

CAROLINE.

But the capital laid out in buildings, tools, and machinery will not yield a profit, like that which is employed in the payment of workmen, the produce of whose labour is brought to market?

MRS. B.

The farmer and manufacturer would not lay out their capital in this way, did they not expect to reap a profit from it. If a farmer has no barn or granary for his corn, he will be compelled to sell his crops immediately after the harvest, although he might probably dispose of them to greater advantage by keeping them some time longer. So a manufacturer, by improving or enlarging his machinery, can, with less labour, perform a greater quantity of work, and his profits will be proportionate.

Thus, for instance, when a manufacturer can afford to establish a steam-engine, and employ a stream of vapour as a substitute for the labour of men and horses, he saves the expense of more than half the number of hands he before employed.

F 3

102 ON CAPITAL.

The capital laid out in this manner is called *fixed capital;* because it becomes fixed, either in land, in buildings, in machinery or implements of art; it is by keeping this capital in possession, and using it, that it produces an income. Whilst the capital employed in the maintenance of productive labourers, whose work is sold and affords an immediate profit, is distinguished by the name of *circulating capital.*

The produce of a farm, or the goods of a manufacturer, afford no profit until they are brought to market, and sold or exchanged for other things. This description of capital is, therefore, constantly circulating. It is transferred first from the master to the labourer, in the form of wages and raw materials, then from the labourer it is returned to the master, in the form of produce or workmanship of increased value; but the latter does not realize his profits until this produce is sold to the public, who turn it to their use, and are therefore called the consumers of it.

CAROLINE.

I think I understand the difference between fixed and circulating capital perfectly. A farmer derives profit from his implements of husbandry by their use, while kept in his possession; and from his crops by parting with them. But to which kind of capital should the farming cattle be referred?

ON CAPITAL. 103

MRS. B.

It depends upon the nature of the cattle. The value of the labouring cattle is fixed capital, like the implements of agriculture; thus the horses which draw the plough, as well as the plough itself, are fixed capital. But sheep and oxen intended for market are circulating capital.

CAROLINE.

But should the plough be drawn by oxen, Mrs. B., how would you settle the point then? for whilst they labour for the farmer they are fixed capital; but when they are sold to the butcher they become circulating capital.

MRS. B.

They alternately belong to each of these descriptions of capital; because the farmer makes his profit, first by keeping, and afterwards by selling them.

CAROLINE.

I do not understand why you should call the maintenance of labouring *men* circulating capital, whilst you consider that of labouring *cattle* as fixed capital: they appear to me to be exactly similar.

MRS. B.

And so they are. The maintenance of cattle as well as that of labourers is circulating capital; that maintenance is in both cases consumed and re-

F 4

104 ON CAPITAL.

produced with advantage; it is therefore by parting with it that profits are derived. But the value of the cattle themselves is fixed capital, and if labourers, like cattle, were purchased, instead of being hired, thus becoming the property of their employers, they also would be fixed capital.

CAROLINE.

And this, I suppose, is the case with the poor Africans in the West Indies?

MRS. B.

Yes, and with slaves of every description. Even the peasantry of Russia and Poland are in general considered as fixed capital, because their state of vassalage is such as to amount to slavery, the proprietors of the land having a right to their labour without remuneration : and the value of an estate in Russia is not estimated by the number of acres, but the number of slaves upon it; in the same manner as a West Indian plantation. A similar state of vassalage prevailed throughout most parts of Europe some centuries ago; but in later times the progress of civilization has been such, that I believe every country, excepting Russia and Poland, has emancipated the labouring classes, experience having proved that the more free and independent men are, the more industrious they become, and the better the land is cultivated.

ON CAPITAL.

CAROLINE.

I wish that the West-Indian planters could be induced to adopt this opinion.

MRS. B.

The time will no doubt arrive when slavery will be abolished in every civilized country. But important changes ought not to be introduced without extreme caution. The minds of men should be freed from the degrading fetters of ignorance, before they can reap advantage from personal emancipation. An ingenious author observes, " that liberty is an instrument with which men may either make their fortune or destroy themselves; that they should therefore be taught the use of it before it is intrusted to their hands." In all cases we shall find that gradual and progressive improvement is invariably conducive to the happiness of mankind, whilst sudden and violent revolutions are always attended with danger. But we are deviating from our subject.

CAROLINE.

Well then, to return to it. I thought at first that I understood the difference of fixed and circulating capital perfectly; but I find upon reflection, that I am at a loss to determine to which kind of capital several articles of property belong. For instance, is the money laid out in the improvement of land, fixed or circulating capital?

F 5

106 ON CAPITAL.

MRS. B.

The money laid out on waste land to bring it into a state fit for cultivation, such as inclosing, draining, ditching, preparing the soil, &c. is fixed capital; and so is that which is employed in the improvement of land already cultivated. If it is the proprietor who lays out capital on land which he lets, he receives in remuneration an increase of rent: if the farmer, he makes greater profits. But the money laid out in the regular course of cultivation, such as ploughing, sowing, reaping, &c., consists, as we have before observed, partly in fixed and partly in circulating capital.

CAROLINE.

I must say that I prefer the employment of wealth in the form of circulating, rather than in that of fixed capital. Granaries, barns, machinery, &c. may be advantageous to the proprietors, but they must be injurious to the labouring classes; for the more a man lays out as fixed capital, the less remains to be employed as circulating capital, and therefore the fewer labourers he can maintain.

MRS. B.

You must always remember that the greatest good you can do the labouring classes, is to increase the consumable produce of the country. Whilst plenty of the necessaries of life is raised, it signifies

ON CAPITAL. 107

little to whom it belongs; for whoever may be the proprietors of this wealth, they can derive no advantage from it but by employing it; that is to say, by maintaining with it productive labourers. The more abundant, therefore, this wealth is, the more people will be employed.

Now it is evident that whatever tends to improve or facilitate labour, increases the productions of the country; and if fixed capital should eventually occasion the raising a greater produce than circulating capital, it must be more beneficial to the labourers as well as to the capitalist.

CAROLINE.

So it appears; and yet I cannot understand how this operates with regard to machinery. We cannot substitute the powers of nature for human industry without throwing people out of work. How then can the poor derive any benefit from inventions and improvements which prevent their being employed?

MRS. B.

It may appear paradoxical, but it is nevertheless true, that whatever abridges and facilitates labour will *eventually* increase the demand for labourers.

CAROLINE.

Or, in other words, to turn people out of work is the most certain means of procuring them em-

F 6

108   ON CAPITAL.

ployment! — This is precisely the objection I was making to the introduction of new machinery.

MRS. B.

The invention of machinery, I allow, is at first attended with some partial and temporary inconvenience and hardship; but on the other hand, the advantages resulting from it are almost incalculable both in extent and duration. When any new machine or process whatever which abridges or facilitates labour is adopted, the commodity produced by it falls in price, the low price enables a greater number of persons to become purchasers, the demand for it increases, and the supply augments in proportion; so that eventually more hands are employed in its fabrication than there were previous to the adoption of the new process. When, for instance, the machine for weaving stockings was first invented, it was considered as a severe hardship on those who had earned a maintenance by knitting them; but the superior facility with which stockings were made in the loom, rendered them so much cheaper, that those, who before were unable to purchase them, could now indulge in the comfort of wearing them, and the prodigious increase of demand for stockings enabled all the knitters to gain a livelihood, by spinning the materials that were to be woven into stockings.

ON CAPITAL. 109

CAROLINE.

That was a resource in former times, but household spinning is scarcely ever seen since Arkwright's invention of spinning jennies. Where are the spinners now to find employment? The improvements in machinery drive these poor workmen from one expedient to another, till I fear at last every resource will be exhausted.

MRS. B.

No; that cannot be the case. Where there is capital the poor will always find employment. In countries possessed of great wealth we see prodigious works undertaken. Roads cut through hills, canals uniting distant rivers, magnificent bridges, splendid edifices, and a variety of other enterprises which give work to thousands, independently of the usual employment of capital in agriculture, manufactures, and trade. What is the reason of all this? It is in order that the rich may employ their capital; for in a secure and free government no man will suffer any part of it to lie idle; the demand for labour is therefore proportioned to the extent of capital. Industry, we have already observed, knows no other limits. The capitalist who employs a new machine is no doubt the immediate gainer by it; but it is the public who derive from it the greatest and most lasting advantage. It is they who profit by the diminution of the price of the goods fabri-

110   ON CAPITAL.

cated by the machine; and, singular as it may appear, no class of the public receives greater benefit from the introduction of those processes which abridge manual labour, than the working classes, as it is they who are most interested in the cheapness of the goods.

CAROLINE.

Well, Mrs. B., I must confess myself vanquished, and beg pardon of Mr. Watts for having ventured to doubt the beneficial effects of his steam-engine; and of Sir Richard Arkwright for having found fault with his spinning jennies.

MRS. B.

I will read you a passage in Macpherson's History of Commerce which will shew you the degree of estimation in which the inventions of Arkwright were held by that writer.

" If Mr. Arkwright made a great fortune, he " certainly deserved it; for the advantages he con- " ferred upon the nation were infinitely greater " than those he acquired for himself; and far more " solid and durable than a hundred conquests. " Instead of depriving the working poor of employ- " ment by his vast abridgment of labour, that very " abridgment has created a vast deal of work for " more hands than were formerly employed; and " it was computed that in 1785, about 25 years " after the invention of his spinning jennies, that

15

ON CAPITAL. 111

" half a million of people were employed in the
" cotton manufactures of Lancashire, Cheshire,
" Derby, Nottingham, and Leicester. And it is
" but justice to the memory of Sir Richard Ark-
" wright to say that he was unquestionably one of
" the greatest friends to the manufacturing and
" commercial interests of this country, and to the
" interest of the cotton planters in almost all parts
" of the world, and that his name ought to be
" transmitted to future ages, along with those of the
" most distinguished benefactors of mankind."

CAROLINE.

This is indeed a magnificent eulogium of Sir
Richard Arkwright, but not more so, it appears,
than he really deserves.

MRS. B.

I shall conclude my observations on the benefits
arising from machinery by reading to you some
remarks on the invention of printing, extracted
from Mr. Say's excellent treatise on Political
Economy.

" Au moment ou elle fut employée une foule de
" copistes durent rester inoccupés, car on peut
" estimer qu'un seul ouvrier imprimeur fait autant
" de besogne que 200 copistes. Il faut donc
" croire que 199 ouvriers sur 200 resterent sans
" ouvrage. Hé bien, la facilité de lire les ouvrages

112 ON CAPITAL.

" imprimés, plus grande que pour les ouvrages
" manuscrits, le bas prix auquel les livres tombe-
" rent, l'encouragement que cette invention donna
" aux auteurs pour en composer un bien plus grand
" nombre, soit d'instruction, soit d'amusement,
" toutes ces causes firent, qu'au bout de très peu de
" temps, il y eut plus d'ouvriers imprimeurs em-
" ployés, qu'il n'y avoit auparavant de copistes. Et
" si à présent on pouvoit calculer exactement non
" seulement le nombre des ouvriers imprimeurs,
" mais encore des industrieux que l'imprimerie
" fait travailler, comme graveurs de poinçons,
" fondeurs de caractères, relieurs, libraires, on
" trouveroit peut-être que le nombre des personnes
" occupées par la fabrication des livres est cent
" fois plus grand que celui qu'elle occupoit avant
" l'invention de l'imprimerie."

CAROLINE.

And the number of readers must have increased
in a still greater proportion. You may recollect
observing, in our conversation on the division of
labour, that the invention of printing was a circumstance most favourable to the diffusion of
knowledge.

MRS. B.

Thus you see that capital, whether fixed or circulating, invariably promotes the increase of the

ON CAPITAL. 113

produce of the country; we may, therefore, I think,
define capital to be any accumulated produce which
tends to facilitate future productions. And the
capital of a country is composed of the aggregate
property of all its inhabitants.

CONVERSATION VIII.

ON WAGES AND POPULATION.

EXTREME LIMITS OF WAGES. — WAGES REGULATED BY THE PROPORTION WHICH CAPITAL BEARS TO POPULATION. — SMALL CAPITAL CREATES SMALL DEMAND FOR LABOUR, LOW WAGES, AND GREAT PROFIT TO THE CAPITALIST. — INCREASE OF CAPITAL CREATES GREATER DEMAND FOR LABOUR, HIGHER WAGES, AND LESS PROFIT TO THE CAPITALIST. — NECESSITY OF RAISING SUBSISTENCE BEFORE OTHER WORKS ARE UNDERTAKEN. — HOW WAGES ARE LOWERED BY THE INCREASE OF POPULATION WITHOUT AN INCREASE OF CAPITAL. — EFFECT OF SCARCITY OF PROVISIONS ON WAGES. — EFFECT OF RAISING WAGES DURING A SCARCITY. — OF A MAXIMUM PRICE OF PROVISIONS. — EFFECT OF DIMINUTION OF POPULATION BY SICKNESS ON THE RATE OF WAGES. — IT IS NOT WORK BUT FUNDS THAT CREATES A DEMAND FOR LABOUR. — WAGES IN IRELAND. — WAGES IN TOWN AND COUNTRY.

MRS. B.

IN our last conversation I think we came to this conclusion, that capital is almost as beneficial to

ON WAGES AND POPULATION. 115

the poor as to the rich; for though the property of the one, it is by its nature destined for the maintenance of the other.

CAROLINE.

It comes to the labourer in the form of wages, but as we must allow the capitalist a profit on his work, I should like very much to know what proportion that profit bears to the wages of the labourer.

MRS. B.

It varies extremely, but the wages of the labourer can never be permanently less than will afford him the means of living, otherwise he could not labour.

CAROLINE.

On the other hand, they can never be equal to the whole value of the work he produces, for if his master made no profit by him he would not employ him.

MRS. B.

Such then are the two extremes of the wages of labour, but they admit of many intermediate degrees of variation. If besides furnishing subsistence for himself, the wages of the labourer would not enable him to maintain a wife and bring up a family, the class of labourers would gradually diminish, and the scarcity of hands would then raise their wages, which would enable them to live with more comfort

116   ON WAGES AND POPULATION.

and rear a family; but as the capitalist will always keep wages as low as he can, the labourer and his family can seldom command more than the necessaries of life.

CAROLINE.

By the necessaries of life do you mean such things only as are indispensably necessary for its support?

MRS. B.

No; I mean such food, clothing, and general accommodation as the climate and custom of the country have rendered essential to the preservation of the life, health, and decent appearance of the lowest classes of the people. Fuel, for instance, and warm clothing are necessary articles in this country; but they are not so in Africa. Civilization and the progress of wealth and manufactures have greatly extended the scale of necessaries; the use of linen is now considered as necessary by all classes of people, and shoes and stockings in England, at least, almost equally so. Houses with glazed windows and a chimney are become necessaries; for if our poor were deprived of such accommodation it would very materially increase mortality amongst them. In Ireland the peasantry bring up their children in a mud cabin, the door of which answers also the purposes of window and chimney.

ON WAGES AND POPULATION. 117

CAROLINE.

Then would it not be better that the labouring classes here should, like the Irish, accustom themselves to hardships and inconveniencies, rather than indulge in a degree of comfortable accommodation, the privation of which in a season of distress is attended with so much misery?

MRS. B.

No; I would on the contrary wish rather to extend than contract the scale of the necessaries of life. There is more health, more cleanliness, more intellect, and more happiness developed in an English cottage than in an Irish cabin. There is more strength, vigour, and industry in an English peasant, who feeds on meat, bread, and vegetables, than in an Irish one, who subsists on potatoes alone.

CAROLINE.

No doubt I would wish the lower classes every comfort which they can afford, but their wages will not always allow them such gratifications. What is it that determines the rate of wages?

MRS. B.

It depends upon the proportion which capital bears to the labouring part of the population of the country.

118 ON WAGES AND POPULATION.

CAROLINE.

Or, in other words, to the proportion which subsistence bears to the number of people to be maintained by it?

MRS. B.

Yes, it is this alone which regulates the rate of wages, when they are left to pursue their natural course. It is this alone which creates or destroys the demand for labour. In order to render it more clear to you, let us simplify the question by examining it on a small scale — let us suppose for instance that we have founded a colony in a desert island; that the settlers have divided the land amongst them, and cultivated it for their own subsistence, and that being both proprietors and labourers, they reap the whole reward of their industry. Thus situated, should a ship be wrecked on the coast, and some of the crew effect their escape to shore, what would ensue? They would furnish a supply of labourers, who would be dependent on the original settlers for maintenance and employment.

CAROLINE.

But if those settlers have not raised a greater quantity of subsistence than is necessary for their own use, how can they maintain the new-comers? Without capital, you know, they cannot employ labourers.

ON WAGES AND POPULATION. 119

MRS. B.

You are perfectly right. But it is probable that the most industrious of them will have raised somewhat more subsistence than is absolutely necessary for their own consumption. They will possess some little stock in reserve, which will enable them to maintain and employ at least a few of the shipwrecked crew. Yet as these poor destitute men will all be anxious to share in this little surplus, each will offer his labour in exchange for the smallest pittance that will support life. Thus the capital of the island being inadequate to the maintenance of its population, the competition amongst the labourers to get employment will render wages extremely low, and the capitalist will derive a high profit from the industry of his labourers. A small capital, therefore, creates but a small demand for labour.

CAROLINE.

By demand for labour do you mean the demand of the poor for work, or of the capitalist for workmen?

MRS. B.

Certainly the latter. The demand for labour means the demand for labourers, by those who have the means of paying them for their work, whether it be in the form of wages, maintenance, or any other kind of remuneration.

But what will happen in our colony, when the

120   ON WAGES AND POPULATION.

labourers shall have richly repaid their employers by the fruits of their industry?

CAROLINE.

By raising a more plentiful harvest they would of course have a more plentiful subsistence.

MRS. B.

The harvest, you must observe, belongs, not to the men who produced it, but to their masters; how therefore does it follow of course, that the labourers obtain a larger share of it?

CAROLINE.

I suppose that their masters having more capital, are willing to bestow a larger proportion of it on their labourers.

MRS. B.

I believe that the capitalist will always make as high a profit as he can upon the work of his labourers; and that when his capital increases, he will chuse rather to increase the number of his workmen than the rate of their wages. But the power of employing more labourers increases the demand for labour; and this, as I shall explain to you, eventually raises the wages or reward of labour.

The capital of the settlers will probably be so much augmented by the industry of the labourers, that the difficulty will no longer consist in maintaining the new comers, but in finding employment

ON WAGES AND POPULATION. 121

for the new capital. The possessors of this surplus capital will be eager to procure the services of the labourers; one perhaps to build a hut, another to fence a field, a third to construct a boat, and so on. For the surplus, unless employed, will yield no profit; the competition therefore will no longer be amongst the labourers to obtain work, but amongst the masters to obtain workmen; and this will necessarily raise the price of wages, and consequently diminish the profits of the capitalist.

CAROLINE.

Oh, that is very clear. If John offers a man a shilling a day to work at his house, and Thomas gives eighteen-pence to those who will build his boat, while James pays two shillings for fencing his field; wages must rise to two shillings a day: for if John and Thomas did not give as much as James, the latter would monopolize all the labourers.

MRS. B.

You see therefore that it is the additional capital produced by the labour of these men, which by increasing the demand for labour raises their wages. Thus whenever capital for the maintenance of labourers abounds, the capitalist must content himself with smaller profits, and allow his workmen a more liberal remuneration. Hence as national opulence

G

122 ON WAGES AND POPULATION.

increases, the labouring poor are more munificently rewarded, and the profits of capital diminish.

CAROLINE.

Oh, that is charming! that is exactly what I wish. But, Mrs. B., if during the second year our colonists employ their labourers in building houses and fencing fields, instead of cultivating them, subsistence will again fall short, and the labourers will be reduced to their former necessitous condition; unless having once experienced such distress, they guard against it in future.

MRS. B.

That does not depend on the choice of the labourers who must do the work they are hired to perform, of whatever nature it may be. But their employers will be careful to provide for their maintenance, for they know that those who should neglect to make such a provision for their future services would be deprived of them. They cannot work without subsistence, nor will they work without an ample subsistence whilst any of the colony has it to offer them. If John therefore does not raise so great a harvest as James, he will not be able, the following year, to employ so many workmen. Each landed proprietor therefore will take care to direct the labour of his workmen towards raising

ON WAGES AND POPULATION. 123

the requisite subsistence, before he employs them in any other description of labour.

Now let us suppose that the shipwrecked crew had brought wives with them, and reared families: would that have affected the rate of wages?

CAROLINE.

Their wages would remain the same; but as they would have to maintain their wives and children as well as themselves, they would not fare so well.

MRS. B.

And if there was not food enough for them all, the most weakly of the children would die, not precisely of hunger, but of some of those diseases which want of sufficient and proper food engenders. It is evident, therefore, that a labourer ought not to marry unless his wages are adequate to the maintenance of a family; or unless he has, like your gardener, some little provision in store to make up the deficiency.

Suppose now after several years of prosperity, that a hurricane makes such devastation amongst the crops of our colonists as to reduce the harvest to one half what it was the preceding year. What effect would this have on the wages of labour?

CAROLINE.

It would of course reduce them, for the subsist-

G 2

124   ON WAGES AND POPULATION.

ence would be diminished. But in what manner the reduction would take effect I do not exactly see.

MRS. B.

In order to trace its consequences step by step, we may suppose that John, finding his capital will not maintain more than one half of the number of labourers he before employed, reluctantly discharges the other half. These poor men wander about the colony seeking for work, but instead of finding any, they meet only with companions in distress who have lost their employment for similar reasons; thus without resource they return to their masters, and intreat to be employed on lower terms. John, who had discharged these men not for want of work to give them, but for want of funds to pay them, is happy in his reduced circumstances to employ labourers at lower wages. He therefore makes a new agreement with them, and determines to discharge those whom he had originally retained in his service unless they will consent to work for him on the same terms. These men, aware of the difficulty of finding employment elsewhere, are compelled by necessity to accept the conditions, and thus wages are reduced to one half their former rate throughout the colony.

CAROLINE.

It appears as evident as possible. I have only one objection to make, which is, that though this

ON WAGES AND POPULATION. 125

may be the case in our colony, it certainly is not so in other places. Wages, so far from being reduced, are, I believe, frequently raised during a scarcity; at least there are great complaints amongst the poor if that is not done.

MRS. B.

In countries where money is used, the reduction of wages does not take place in the manner I have described. In such countries it is unnecessary to make any change in the rate of wages, because the high price of provisions during a scarcity produces a similar effect. If you continue to pay your labourer the same wages when the articles of provision on which he subsists have doubled in price, his wages are really diminished one half, because he can procure with them only one half of what he did before the scarcity.

CAROLINE.

But this is a kind of imposition upon the poor labourers, who, I suppose, are at least as ignorant as I am of political economy, and do not know that a shilling is worth more at one time than it is at another, and therefore during a scarcity continue to work at the usual rate of wages for want of knowing better.

MRS. B.

Knowledge in this instance would only teach

G 3

126 ON WAGES AND POPULATION.

them that they must bear with patience an unavoidable evil. The alternative, for the capitalist, when his capital is diminished, is to reduce, either the number of his labourers, or the rate of their wages — or rather, I should say, the remuneration of their labour; for the wages remain nominally the same. Now is it not more equitable to divide the maintenance amongst the whole of the labouring class, than to feed some of them amply, whilst the remainder starve?

CAROLINE.

No doubt it is; but would it not, in this instance, be allowable for the legislature to interfere, and oblige the capitalist to raise the rate of wages in proportion to the rise of price of provisions, so as to afford the labourers their usual quantity of subsistence? I think the rate of wages ought to be regulated by the price of bread, as that is the principal subsistence of the poor; so as to enable them to purchase the same quantity of bread whatever its price may be.

MRS. B.

Or, in other words, that every man may eat his usual quantity of bread, however deficient the harvest is in its produce; for unless you could find means to increase the quantity of subsistence, it will avail nothing to raise the rate of wages.

ON WAGES AND POPULATION. 127

CAROLINE.

Very true; yet two shillings will purchase twice the quantity of bread that one will; is not that true also, Mrs. B.? and yet these truths appear incompatible.

MRS. B.

One of them must therefore be an error; two shillings would not purchase twice the quantity of bread that one did if wages were doubled, because provisions would continue to rise in price in proportion to the advance on wages.

CAROLINE.

But I would prohibit the farmer from raising the price of his corn and his cattle, and then there would be no necessity for the butcher and the baker raising the price of meat and bread. It is not just that the farmer, when he has a bad crop, should throw his misfortune on the public, and be the only person who does not suffer from it; which is the case if he raises the price of his produce in proportion to its scarcity.

MRS. B.

The farmer consumes, as well as produces provisions; and as a consumer he partakes of the evil of the advance of price. If he sell his corn for twice the usual price, what he consumes at home stands

G 4

128   ON WAGES AND POPULATION.

him in the same value, for such is the price it would fetch at market.

But supposing it possible to prevent the rise in price during a scarcity, what consequences would ensue? Keep in mind the important point, that the harvest has yielded but half its usual product; that whilst the wages of labour and the price of provisions undergo no alteration, the labourers purchase and consume the usual quantity of food, and at the end of six months . . . .

CAROLINE.

You need not finish the sentence, Mrs. B.; at the end of six months the whole stock of provisions would be consumed, and the people who excited my commiseration would be starved.

MRS. B.

This would infallibly be the case, were such a measure persevered in; but though it has often been attempted by sovereigns more benevolent than wise, to set limits to the price of provisions, the consequences soon became so formidable as to compel the legislature to put a stop to a remedy which was as ineffectual as it was pernicious. * " In the year 1315 England was afflicted by a " famine, grievous beyond all that ever were known " before, which raised the price of provisions far

---

* Macpherson's Annals of Commerce

ON WAGES AND POPULATION. 129

" above the reach of the people of middling classes.
" The parliament, in compassion to the general
" distress, ordered that all articles of food should
" be sold at moderate prices, which they took
" upon themselves to prescribe. The consequence
" was that all things, instead of being sold at or
" under the maximum price fixed by them, be-
" came dearer than before, or were entirely with-
" held from the market. Poultry were rarely to
" be seen. Butchers' meat was not to be found at
" all. The sheep were dying of a pestilence, and
" all kinds of grain were selling at most enormous
" prices. Early the next year the parliament,
" finding their mistake, left provisions to find their
" own price."

Thus you see that the rise in the price of provisions is the natural remedy to the evil of scarcity.
It is the means of husbanding the short stock of
provisions, and making it last out to the ensuing
harvest. Government should never interfere, either
with the price of provisions or the rate of wages;
they will each find their respective level if left
uncontrolled.

But to return to our colony. What effect would
it produce on wages, were some contagious malady
to carry off one half of the labourers?

CAROLINE.

It would increase the demand for the labour of

G 5

130 ON WAGES AND POPULATION.

those which remained, and consequently raise their wages.

MRS. B.

We may generally state, therefore, that when the number of labourers remains the same, the rate of wages will increase with the increase of capital, and lower with the diminution of it; and that if the amount of capital remain the same, the rate of wages will fall as the number of labourers increase, and rise as the number of labourers diminish; or, as mathematicians would express it, the rate of wages varies directly as the quantity of capital, and inversely as the number of labourers.

Macpherson mentions that " a dreadful pesti-
" lence, which originated in the eastern regions,
" began its ravages in England in the year 1348,
" and is said to have carried off the greater part
" of the people, especially in the lower ranks of
" life. The surviving labourers took advantage of
" the demand for labour and the scarcity of hands
" to raise their prices. The king, Edward I.,
" thereupon enacted the statute of labourers, which
" ordained that all men and women under 60 years
" of age, whether of free or servile condition, hav-
" ing no occupation or property, should serve any
" person of whom they should be required, and
" should receive only the wages which were usual
" before the year 1346, or in the five or six pre-
" ceding years, on pain of imprisonment, the em-

ON WAGES AND POPULATION. 131

" ployers being also punishable for giving greater
" wages. Artificers were also prohibited from de-
" manding more than the old wages; and butchers,
" bakers, brewers, &c. were ordered to sell their
" provisions at reasonable prices. The ' ser-
" vants having no regard to the said ordinance,
" but to their ease and singular covetise,' refused
" to serve unless for higher wages than the law
" allowed them. Therefore the parliament, by
" another statute, fixed the yearly and daily wages
" of agricultural servants, artificers, and labourers,
" the payment of threshing corn by the quarter,
" and even the price of shoes. They also forbad
" any person to leave the town in summer wherein
" he had dwelt in the winter, or to remove from
" one shire to another.

" Thus were the lower classes debarred by laws,
" which in their own nature must be inefficient,
" from making any effort to improve their situation
" in life."

CAROLINE.

I had always imagined that a great demand for
labour was occasioned by some great work that was
to be executed, such as digging a canal, making
new roads, cutting through hills, &c.; but it seems
that the demand for labour depends, not so much
on the quantity of work to be done as on the quantity of subsistence provided for the workmen.

G 6

132 ON WAGES AND POPULATION.

MRS. B.

Work to be performed is the immediate cause of the demand for labour; but however great or important is the work which a man may wish to undertake, the execution of it must always be limited by the extent of his capital; that is to say, by the funds he possesses for the maintenance or payment of his labourers. The same observation applies to the capital of a country, which is only an aggregate of the capital of individuals; it cannot employ more people than it has the means of maintaining. All the waste land capable of cultivation in the country might be called work to be done, but there can be no demand for labourers to do that work, until a sufficient quantity of subsistence has been raised to support such an additional number of labourers as would be required for that purpose. In our conversation on capital we observed, that in countries of large capital great works were undertaken, such as public buildings, bridges, iron rail-ways, canals, &c. All these things are a sign of redundance of wealth.

CAROLINE.

In Ireland I understand that the wages of common labourers are much lower than in England: is it on account of the capital of that country being less adequate to the maintenance of its population?

ON WAGES AND POPULATION. 133

MRS. B.

That is, no doubt, one of the principal causes of the low price of labour in that country; but there are many other causes which affect the price of labour, arising from the imperfection of its government. The Irish are far less industrious than the English. Arthur Young, in his travels through Ireland, observes, that " husbandry labour is " very *low priced*, but not *cheap*. Two shillings " a-day in Suffolk is cheaper than sixpence a-day in " Cork. If a Huron would dig for two-pence " a-day, I have little doubt but that it might be " dearer than the Irishman's sixpence."

CAROLINE.

But, Mrs. B., the price of labour does not only vary in different countries, but very considerably in different parts of the same country. In purchasing some cutlery a few days ago, I was shewn country and town made knives and forks, apparently the same, yet the difference in price was considerable. Upon inquiring the cause, I was informed that it was owing to wages being so much higher in London than in the country.

MRS. B.

And if you had inquired the cause of the high rate of wages of London workmen, you would have heard that it was on account of their being better

ON WAGES AND POPULATION.

workmen; the ablest artificers generally resort to London, as the place where their skill will be most duly appreciated, and where their employers can best afford to reward it.

It is but just to remunerate labourers according to their ability. Your head gardener does less work than any of the men under him; yet he has the highest wages, on account of the skill and experience he has acquired. A working silversmith has on this account higher wages than a taylor or a carpenter.

But where skill is not requisite, the hardest and most disagreeable kinds of labour are best paid: this is the case with blacksmiths, iron founders, coal heavers, &c.

A consideration is also had for arts of an unwholesome, unpleasant, or dangerous nature, such as painters, miners, gunpowder makers, and a variety of other analogous employments.

CONVERSATION IX.

ON WAGES AND POPULATION.
Continued.

HIGH WAGES NOT INVARIABLY ACCOMPANYING GREAT CAPITAL. — GREAT CAPITAL AND LOW WAGES IN CHINA. — SMALL CAPITAL AND HIGH WAGES IN AMERICA. — ADVANTAGES OF NEW SETTLED COUNTRIES. — POVERTY THE NATURAL CHECK TO POPULATION. — GREAT POPULATION ADVANTAGFOUS ONLY WHEN RESULTING FROM PLENTY. — INCREASING WEALTH PREFERABLE TO ANY STATIONARY CAPITAL. — MISTAKE IN ENCOURAGING POPULATION. — POPULATION OF MANUFACTURING TOWNS. — INDUSTRY PIECE WORK.

CAROLINE.

I HAVE been reflecting a great deal on our last conversation, Mrs. B., and the conclusions I have drawn from it are, that the greater the capital a country possesses, the greater number of people it can maintain, and the higher the wages of labour will be.

MRS. B.

The greater the stock of subsistence, the more people may be maintained by it, no doubt; but your second inference is not at all a necessary conclusion. China is a very rich country, and yet wages are I believe no where so low. The accounts which travellers give of the miserable state of the inferior classes, are painful to hear; and their poverty is not the result of idleness, for they run about the streets with tools in their hands, begging for work.

CAROLINE.

That is owing to the immense population of China; so that, though the capital of the country may be very considerable, still it is insufficient for the maintenance of all its inhabitants.

MRS. B.

You should therefore always remember that the rate of wages does not depend upon the absolute quantity of capital, but upon its quantity relative to the number of people to be maintained by it. This is a truth which, however simple, is continually lost sight of, and hence arise errors without number in political economy. If China had ten times the wealth it actually possesses, and its population were at the same time tenfold as numerous, the people would not be better fed.

America, on the other hand, is a country of very

ON WAGES AND POPULATION. 137

small capital, and yet wages are remarkably high there.

CAROLINE.

How do you account for that? for the demand for labour, you know, can be only in proportion to the extent of capital.

MRS. B.

The capital of America, though small when compared with those of the countries of Europe, is very considerable in proportion to the number of people to be maintained by it. In America, and in all newly settled countries as yet thinly inhabited, the wages of labour are high, because capital increases with prodigious rapidity. Where land is plentiful and productive, and the labourers to cultivate it scarce, the competition amongst the landholders to obtain labourers is so great as to enable this class to raise their demands, and the higher the wages the labourer receives, the sooner he has it in his power to purchase a piece of land and become landholder himself. Thus the class of labourers is continually passing into the class of proprietors, and making room for a fresh influx of labourers, both from the rising generation and from emigrations from foreign countries.

CAROLINE.

America has then the double advantage, of high wages and low price of land; no wonder that it is so thriving a country.

138 ON WAGES AND POPULATION.

MRS. B.

The progress of wealth and improvement is no where so rapid, as in the settlement of a civilized people in a new country; provided they establish laws for the security of their property, they require no other incitement to industry. In the new settlements of America, where the experienced farmer with his European implements of husbandry is continually encroaching on the barren wilderness, want is almost unknown, and a state of universal prosperity prevails. We may form some judgment of the rapid increase of their capital by that of their population. The facility with which the Americans acquire a maintenance sufficient to bring up a family encourages early marriages, and gives rise to numerous families; the children are well fed, thriving, and healthy; you may imagine how small are the proportion that die in comparison to the number born, when I inform you that their population doubles itself in about 23 years!

CAROLINE.

But does not such an immense increase of population reduce the rate of wages?

MRS. B.

No, because their capital increases in a still greater proportion; and as long as that is the case, wages, you know, will rise rather than fall. But

ON WAGES AND POPULATION. 139

what I have said relative to America refers only to the United States of that country; which have the advantage of a free government protecting the property of all classes of men. In the Spanish settlements, where the government is of a very different description, the condition of the people is far less flourishing. The population of Mexico, one of the finest provinces of Spanish America, does not double itself in less than 48 years.

CAROLINE.

Yet I do not well understand why the poor should be worse off in England where there is a large capital, than in America where there is a small one.

MRS. B.

Because you are again forgetting the fundamental rule which I have laid down for you, that capital must always be considered with reference to the number of people to be employed and maintained by it.

In England, and all the old established countries of Europe, the population has gradually increased till it has equalled the means of subsistence; and as Europe no longer affords the same facility for the growth of capital as a newly settled country, if the population goes on augmenting, it may exceed the means of subsistence, and in that case the wages of labour will fall instead of rising, and the condition of the poor become very miserable.

140 ON WAGES AND POPULATION.

CAROLINE.

But how is it possible for population to increase beyond the means of subsistence? Men cannot live without eating.

MRS. B.

No; but they may live upon a smaller portion of food than is necessary to maintain them in health and vigour; children may be born without their parents having the means of providing for them. Increase of population therefore under such circumstances cannot be permanent; its progress will be checked by distress and disease, and this I apprehend to be one of the causes of the reduced state of the poor in this country.

CAROLINE.

I declare I always thought that it was very desirable to have a great population. All rich thriving countries are populous: great cities are populous; wealth, which you esteem so advantageous to a country, encourages population; and population in its turn promotes wealth, for labourers produce more than they consume. You recollect how rich our colony became by the acquisition of the labour of the ship-wrecked crew; their first arrival was attended with some inconvenience, it is true; but I should say as you do with respect to machinery, the inconvenience is small and temporary, the advantage both durable and extensive.

ON WAGES AND POPULATION. 141

MRS. B.

You are quite mistaken if you imagine that I do not consider a great population as highly advantageous to a country, where there is a capital which will afford wages sufficient for a labourer to bring up his children; for population is not usually increased by the acquisition of a number of able labourers, (as was the case in our colony,) but by the birth of helpless infants who depend entirely upon their parents for subsistence. If this subsistence is not provided, the children are born merely to languish a few years in poverty, and to fall early victims to disease brought on by want and wretchedness. They can neither increase the strength, the wealth, nor the happiness of the country. On the contrary, they weaken, impoverish, and render it more miserable. They consume without reproducing, they suffer without enjoying, and they give pain and sorrow to their parents without ever reaching that age when they might reward their paternal cares. Yet such is the fate of thousands of children wherever population exceeds the means of subsistence.

CAROLINE.

What a dreadful reflection this is! But you do not suppose that there are any children actually starved to death?

142　　ON WAGES AND POPULATION.

MRS. B.

I hope not; but the fate of those poor infants is scarcely less deplorable who perish by slow degrees for want of proper care and a sufficiency of wholesome food. A large family of young children would require the whole of a mother's care and attention; but that mother is frequently obliged to leave them to obtain by hard labour their scanty meal. Want of good nursing, of cleanliness, of fresh air, and of wholesome nourishment, engenders a great variety of diseases which either carry them off, or leave them in such a state of weakness that they fall a sacrifice to the first contagious malady which attacks them. It is to this state of debility, as well as to the want of medical advice and judicious treatment, that must be attributed the mortality occasioned by the small pox and measles amongst the lower classes of children, so much greater than in those of the upper ranks of society.

Nor are the fatal effects of an excess of population confined to children. A sick man, who might be restored to health by medical assistance and a proper diet, perishes because he can afford to obtain neither. A delicate or an infirm woman requires repose and indulgence which she cannot command. The necessaries of life vary not only with the climate and customs of a country, but with the age, sex, and infirmities of the individuals who

ON WAGES AND POPULATION. 143

inhabit it; and wherever these necessaries are deficient, mortality prevails.

Do you understand now why the rate of wages and the condition of the poor is better in countries which, like America, are growing rich; than in those which, like England, have long accumulated large capitals, but whose wealth is either stationary or making but slower progress?

CAROLINE.

Yes; it is because when capital augments very rapidly, plenty precedes the increase of population, and labour is in great demand and well rewarded. But when wealth, however great, has long been stationary, population has risen up to the means of subsistence, or perhaps gone beyond it, so that wages fall and distress comes on.

MRS. B.

This is what I formerly alluded to when I told you that you would find that the acquisition of wealth was more advantageous to a country, as well as to an individual, than the actual possession of it.

I must read you a passage of Paley on this subject, in which he expresses himself with remarkable perspicuity.

" The ease of subsistence and the encourage-
" ment of industry depend neither upon the price

144   ON WAGES AND POPULATION.

" of labour, nor upon the price of provisions; but
" upon the proportion which the one bears to the
" other. Now the influx of wealth into a country
" naturally tends to advance this proportion; that
" is, every fresh accession of wealth raises the
" price of labour, before it raises the price of
" provisions.

" It is not therefore the quantity of wealth col-
" lected into a country, but the continual increase
" of that quantity, from which the advantage arises
" to employment and population. It is only the
" accession of wealth which produces the effect;
" and it is only by wealth constantly flowing into,
" or springing up in a country, that the effect can
" be constant."

You must not, however, imagine that the capital
of this country remains stationary; on the contrary, we are making rapid advances in wealth,
though we cannot pretend to equal the progress of
a newly settled country. In confirmation of this,
Arthur Young observes, that wages had risen about
one-third, both in England and Ireland, within the
last 20 years; which proves that capital has been
increasing in a greater ratio than population. But
it must be observed, that it is about 30 years since
he gave this account; and the severe checks which
industry has received since that period throughout
the greater part of Europe, from a constant state
of the most expensive warfare, has, I fear, greatly

ON WAGES AND POPULATION. 145

retarded the progress of capital, without equally affecting that of population; but if the increase of the latter has occasionally outstripped the means of subsistence, it is no less owing to the ill-judged conduct of the upper classes than to the imprudence of the lower orders of people.

CAROLINE.

You allude, I suppose, to the encouragement of early marriages amongst the poor?

MRS. B.

Yes; we observed that when a great population springs from ample means of subsistence, it is the highest blessing a country can enjoy; the children brought up in plenty, attain a healthy and vigorous manhood, with strength to defend, and industry to enrich their country. Those who have not reflected on the subject, have frequently confounded cause and effect, and have, with you, considered a great population under all circumstances as the cause of prosperity. Hence the most strenuous efforts have been made, not only by individuals, but even by the legislature, to encourage early marriages and large families, conceiving that by so doing they were promoting the happiness and prosperity of their country.

H

146   ON WAGES AND POPULATION.

CAROLINE.

This is a most unfortunate error. But when population is again reduced, the evil corrects itself; for capital being thus rendered more adequate to the maintenance of this diminished population, the wages of labour will again rise.

MRS. B.

Certainly. But it often happens that as soon as the labouring classes find their condition improved, whether by a diminution of numbers, or an augmentation of capital, which may spring up from some new source of industry, marriages again increase, a greater number of children are reared, and population once more outstrips the means of subsistence; so that the condition of the poor, after a temporary improvement, is again reduced to its former wretchedness.

CAROLINE.

That is precisely what has occurred in the village near which we live. It was formerly, I have heard, but a small hamlet, the inhabitants of which gained a livelihood as farmers' labourers. Many years ago a cotton manufacture was set up in the neighbourhood, which afforded ample employment for the poor; and even the children, who were before idle, could now earn something towards their maintenance. This, during some years, had an admirable effect in raising the condition of the labouring classes. I have heard my grandfather

ON WAGES AND POPULATION.   147

say that it was wonderful to see how rapidly the village improved, how many new cottages were built, and what numerous families they contained. But this prosperous state was not of long duration: in the course of time the village became over-stocked with labourers, and it is now sunk into a state of poverty and distress worse than that from which it had so recently emerged.

MRS. B.

You see, therefore, that this manufacture, which at first proved a blessing to the village, and might always have continued such, was, by the improvidence of the labourers, converted into an evil. If the population had not increased beyond the demand for labour, the manufacture might still have afforded them the advantages it at first produced.

CAROLINE.

This then must be the cause of the misery which generally prevails amongst the poor in manufacturing towns, where it would be so natural to expect that the facility of finding work would produce comfort and plenty.

MRS. B.

And it proves that no amelioration of the condition of the poor can be permanent, unless to industry they add prudence and foresight. Were

H 2

148 ON WAGES AND POPULATION.

all men as considerate as your gardener, Thomas, and did they not marry till they had secured a provision for a family, or could earn a sufficiency to maintain it; in short, were children not brought into the world until there was bread to feed them, the distress which you have just been describing would be unknown, excepting in cases of unforeseen misfortunes, or unless produced by idleness or vice.

CAROLINE.

And is it not to these latter causes that a great part of the misery in manufacturing towns should be ascribed? I have heard it observed that skilful workmen, who could earn a livelihood by three or four days' labour in the week, would frequently spend the remainder of it in idleness and profligacy.

MRS. B.

I believe that it is much more common for great gains to act as a stimulus to industry. Like every other human quality, industry improves in proportion to the encouragement it receives, and it can have no greater encouragement and reward than high wages. It sometimes happens, it is true, that workmen act in the way you mention, but such conduct is far from being common; the greater part, when their wages are liberal, keep steadily to their work, and if they are paid by the piece, are even apt to overwork themselves.

ON WAGES AND POPULATION. 149

CAROLINE.

That I have observed. My father lately agreed to pay a certain sum for digging a sunk fence in our pleasure-grounds; and two of the under-gardeners engaged to do it after the day's work was over. I thought they would repent of their undertaking, when they came to such hard labour, after having performed their usual task; but I was astonished at their alacrity and perseverance: in the course of a week they completed the job, and received the price in addition to their usual wages. I wonder that work is not always paid by the piece, it is such an encouragement to industry.

MRS. B.

All kinds of work are not susceptible of being so paid; for instance, the care of a garden could not be divided into jobs, and the gardener be paid so much for planting trees, so much for cleaning borders, so much for mowing grass, &c. Besides I doubt whether it would be desirable that this mode of payment should be generally adopted, on account of the temptation it affords to labourers to overwork themselves; for notwithstanding all the advantages of industry, one would never wish it to be pushed to that extreme which would exhaust the strength of the labouring classes, and bring on disease and infirmity. The benefits resulting from

H 3

150 ON WAGES AND POPULATION.

industry are an increase of the comforts and conveniencies of life; but it would be paying too dear for these to purchase them by a sickly and premature old age.

In order to be of permanent service to the labouring classes we must not rest satisfied with encouraging industry; but we should endeavour by instruction to awaken their minds to a sense of remote consequences, as well as of immediate good, so that when they have succeeded in rendering their condition more comfortable, they may not rashly and inconsiderately increase their numbers beyond the means of subsistence.

CAROLINE.

But if population be constantly kept within the limits of subsistence, would it not always remain stationary?

MRS. B.

Certainly not; if the people are industrious capital will increase; and the increase of population will follow of course, and with advantage.

CAROLINE.

I now see evidently, that population should never be encouraged but where there is great plenty of subsistence and employment.

MRS. B.

And *then* it requires no encouragement. If men so often marry without having made any pro-

ON WAGES AND POPULATION. 151

vision for a family, there is no danger of their not marrying when a subsistence is easily obtained; and their children will be healthy and long-lived in proportion as they are well fed, clothed, and taken care of.

CONVERSATION X.

ON THE CONDITION OF THE POOR.

OF THE CULTIVATION OF COMMONS AND WASTE LANDS. — OF EMIGRATION. — EDUCATION OF THE LOWER CLASSES. — BENEFIT CLUBS. — SAVING BANKS. — PAROCHIAL RELIEF. — ALMS AND PRIVATE CHARITIES. — REWARDS.

CAROLINE.

IN our last conversation, Mrs. B., you pointed out the evils arising from an excess of population; they have left a very melancholy impression on my mind. I have been reflecting ever since whether there might be any means of averting them, and of raising subsistence to the level of population, rather than suffering population to sink to the level of subsistence. Though we have not the same resource in land as America; yet we have large tracts of waste land, which by being brought into cultivation would produce an additional stock of subsistence.

ON THE CONDITION OF THE POOR. 153

MRS. B.

You forget that industry is limited by the extent of capital, and that no more labourers can be employed than we have the means of maintaining; they work for their daily bread, and without obtaining it, they neither could nor would work. All the labourers which the capital of the country can maintain being disposed of, the only question is, whether it be better to employ them on land already in a state of cultivation, or in breaking up and bringing into culture new lands; and this point may safely be trusted to the decision of the landed proprietors, as it is no less their interest than that of the labouring classes that the greatest possible quantity of produce should be raised. To a certain extent it has been found more advantageous to lay out capital in improving the culture of old land, rather than to employ it in bringing new land into tillage; because the soil of the waste land is extremely poor and ungrateful, and requires a great deal to be laid out on it before it brings in a return. But there is often capital sufficient for both these purposes, and of late years we have seen not only prodigious improvements in the processes of agriculture throughout the country, but a great number of commons inclosed and cultivated.

H 5

154 ON THE CONDITION OF THE POOR.

CAROLINE.

I fear you will think me inconsistent, but I cannot help regretting the inclosure of commons; they are the only resource of the cottagers for the maintenance of a few lean cattle. Let me once more quote my favourite Goldsmith:

> " Where then, ah where shall poverty reside,
> " To 'scape the pressure of contiguous pride?
> " If to some common's fenceless limits stray'd,
> " He drives his flock to pick the scanty blade,
> " Those fenceless fields the sons of wealth deride,
> " And e'en the bare worn common is deny'd."

MRS. B.

You should recollect that we do not admit poets to be very good authority in political economy. If, instead of feeding a few lean cattle, a common can, by being inclosed, fatten a much greater number of fine cattle, you must allow that the quantity of subsistence will be increased, and the poor, though in a less direct manner, will fare the better for it. Labourers are required to inclose and cultivate those commons, the neighbouring cottagers are employed for that purpose, and this additional demand for labour turns to their immediate advantage. They not only receive an indemnity for their loss of right of common, but they find purchasers for the cattle they can no

ON THE CONDITION OF THE POOR.   155

longer maintain, in the proprietors of the new in-
closures.

When Finchley Common was inclosed, it was
divided amongst the inhabitants of that parish;
and the cottagers and little shopkeepers sold the
small slips of land which fell to their share to men
of greater property, who thus became possessed of
a sufficient quantity to make it answer to them to
inclose and cultivate it; and the poorer classes
were amply remunerated for their loss of com-
monage by the sale of their respective lots.

CAROLINE.

But if we have it not in our power to provide
for a redundant population by the cultivation of
our waste lands, what objection is there to sending
those who cannot find employment at home, to
seek a maintenance in countries where it is more
easily obtained, where there is a greater demand
for labour? Or why should they not found new
colonies in the yet unsettled parts of America?

MRS. B.

Emigration is undoubtedly a resource for an
overstocked population; but one that is adopted in
general with great reluctance by individuals; and is
commonly discouraged by governments, from an
apprehension of its diminishing the strength of the
country.

H 6

156 ON THE CONDITION OF THE POOR.

CAROLINE.

It might be wrong to encourage emigration to a very great extent; I meant only to provide abroad for those whom we cannot maintain at home.

MRS. B.

Under an equitable government there is little danger of emigration ever exceeding that point. The attachment to our native land is naturally so strong, and there are so many ties of kindred and association to break through before we can quit it, that no slight motive will induce a man to expatriate himself. An author deeply versed in the knowledge of the human mind says, "La seule bonne loi contre les emigrations, est celle que la nature a a gravé dans nos cœurs." On this subject I am very willing to quote the Deserted Village:

> " Good heaven! what sorrows gloom'd that parting day
> " That call'd them from their native walks away."

Besides, the difficulties with which a colony of emigrants have to struggle before they can effect a settlement; and the hardships they must undergo, until they have raised food for their subsistence, are so discouraging, that no motive less strong than that of necessity is likely to induce them to settle in an uncultivated land.

Some capital too is required for this as well as for all undertakings; the colonists must be provided

ON THE CONDITION OF THE POOR. 157

with implements of husbandry and of art; and supplied with food and clothing until they shall have succeeded in producing such necessaries for themselves.

Were emigration therefore allowed, instead of being checked, scarcely any would abandon their country but those who could not find a maintenance in it. But should emigration ever become so great as to leave the means of subsistence easy and plentiful to those who remain, it would naturally cease, and the facility of rearing children, and maintaining families, would soon fill the vacancy in population.

There are some emigrations which are extremely detrimental to the wealth and prosperity of a country; these however are not occasioned by poverty, but result from the severity and hardships imposed by arbitrary governments on particular classes of men. Want of toleration in religion has caused the most considerable and numerous emigrations of this description. Such was that of the Huguenots from France at the revocation of the edict of Nantz. They were a skilful and industrious people, who carried their arts and manufactures into Germany, Prussia, Holland, and England, and deprived France of some of her most valuable subjects. Spain has never recovered the blow which her industry received by the expulsion of the Moors, under Ferdinand and Isabella; not all the wealth of America has repaid her for this loss.

158 ON THE CONDITION OF THE POOR.

But to return to the population of England; the more we find ourselves unable to provide for an overgrown population, the more desirous we should be to avail ourselves of those means which tend to prevent the evil; — such, for instance, as a general diffusion of knowledge, which would excite greater attention in the lower classes to their future interests.

CAROLINE.

Surely you would not teach political economy to the labouring classes, Mrs. B. ?

MRS. B.

No; but I would endeavour to give the rising generation such an education as would render them not only moral and religious, but industrious, frugal, and provident. In proportion as the mind is informed, we are able to calculate the consequences of our actions: it is the infant and the savage who live only for the present moment; those whom instruction has taught to think, reflect upon the past and look forward to the future. Education gives rise to prudence, not only by enlarging our understandings, but by softening our feelings, by humanizing the heart, and promoting amiable affections. The rude and inconsiderate peasant marries without either foreseeing or caring for the miseries he may entail on his wife and children; but he who has been taught to value the comforts and decencies

ON THE CONDITION OF THE POOR. 159

of life, will not heedlessly involve himself and all
that is dear to him in poverty, and its long train
of miseries.

CAROLINE.

I am very happy to hear that you think instruction may produce this desirable end, since the zeal
for the education of the poor that has been
displayed of late years gives every prospect of
success; and in a few years more, it may perhaps
be impossible to meet with a child who cannot read
and write.

MRS. B.

The highest advantages, both religious, moral,
and political, may be expected to result from this
general ardour for the instruction of the poor. No
great or decided improvement can be effected in
the manners of the people but by the education of
the rising generation. It is difficult, if not impossible, to change the habits of men whose characters
are formed, and settled; the prejudices of ignorance
that have grown up with us, will not yield to
new impressions; whilst youth and innocence may
be moulded into any form you chuse to give them.
But independently of schools and the various
institutions for the education of youth, there is an
establishment among the lower classes which is peculiarly calculated to inculcate lessons of prudence
and economy. I mean the Benefit Clubs, or Friendly
Societies; the members of which, by contributing a

160　ON THE CONDITION OF THE POOR.

small stipend monthly, accumulate a fund which furnishes them relief and aid in times of sickness or distress. These associations have spread throughout the country, and their good effects are rendered evident by comparing the condition of such of the labouring classes as belong to them with those of the same district who have no resource in times of distress, but parochial relief or private charity. The former are comparatively cleanly, industrious, sober, frugal, respecting themselves, and respected by others; depending in times of casual sickness or accident on funds created by their own industry, they maintain an honourable pride and independance of character: whilst the latter, in a season of distress, become a prey to dirt and wretchedness; and being dissatisfied with the scantiness of parish relief, they are often driven to the commission of crimes. It is above a century since these clubs were first instituted; they have received encouragement both from government and individuals, and have spread throughout the country. I dare say that your prudent gardener Thomas is a member of one of them.

CAROLINE.

Yes; and he belongs to one which can boast of peculiar advantages, as most of the gentlemen in the neighbourhood subscribe to it; in order by increasing the fund, and consequently the amount of

ON THE CONDITION OF THE POOR.   161

the relief which the distressed members can receive,
to encourage the poor to belong to it.

MRS. B.

That is an excellent mode of bestowing charity,
for you are not only sure that you relieve the necessitous, but also the industrious poor.   A similar
plan has been adopted, within these few years, in a
village in the neighbourhood of London, and has
been attended with the greatest success.   Various
schemes had been devised by the charitable inhabitants of this village to relieve the necessities of their
poor, and so much was done for them by the opulent, that they found little need to exert their own
industry; whilst the poor in the neighbouring pa-
rishes, attracted by the munificence of the charitable
donations, flocked to the place; so that notwithstanding all their bounty, the rich still found themselves surrounded by objects of penury and distress.
Convinced at length that they created as much
poverty as they relieved, they came to a resolution
of completely changing their system.   They established benefit clubs, and the sums which they
before gave away in alms, were now subscribed to
these societies, so as to afford very ample relief to
its members in cases of distress.   The consequence
was, that the idle poor abandoned the place, and
the industrious poor were so well provided for, that
the village has assumed quite a new aspect, and

162 ON THE CONDITION OF THE POOR.

penury and want are scarcely any more to be seen.

An institution has within a short time been established in Scotland, and is, I understand, now rapidly spreading in England, which is likely to prove still more advantageous to the lower classes than the benefit clubs. " The object of this institution," says the Edinburgh Review, No. 49., " is to open " to the lower orders a place of deposit for their " small savings, with the allowance of a reasonable " monthly interest, and with full liberty of with- " drawing their money, at any time, either in " whole or in part, — an accommodation which it " is impracticable for the ordinary banks to fur- " nish. Such an establishment has been called " *a Saving Bank.*"

These institutions give the greatest encouragement to industry, by securing the property of the labouring poor. How frequently it happens that an industrious man, after having toiled to accumulate a small sum, is tempted to lay it out in a lottery ticket, is inveigled by sharpers to a gambling table, or induced by adventurers to engage in some ill-judged and hazardous speculation; to lend it to a distressed or a treacherous friend, — not to mention the risk of its being lost or stolen. If we succeed in establishing banks in different districts in England, where the poor may without difficulty or trouble deposit the trifle they can spare from their

ON THE CONDITION OF THE POOR. 163

earnings, and where, as an additional inducement, some interest is allowed them for their money, all this mischief will be avoided, and we may hope that the influence of prudential habits will gradually raise the poor above the degrading resource of parochial assistance; and enable us in the course of time to abolish the poor rates; a tax which falls so heavily on the middling classes of people, and which is said to give rise to still more poverty than it relieves.

CAROLINE.

I cannot understand that.

MRS. B.

The certainty that the parish is bound to succour their wants, renders the poor less apprehensive of indigence than if they were convinced that they must suffer all the wretchedness it entails. When a young man marries without having the means of supporting his family by his labour, and without having saved some little provision against accidents or sickness, he depends upon the parish as a never-failing resource. A profligate man knows that if he spend his wages at the public-house instead of providing for his family, his wife and children can at worst but go to the poor-house. Parish relief thus becomes the very cause of the mischief which it professes to remedy.

164   ON THE CONDITION OF THE POOR.

CAROLINE.

It appears to me to encourage the worst species of poverty, that arising from idleness and ill-conduct.

MRS. B.

The greatest evil that results from this provision for the poor is, that it lowers the price of labour; the sum which the capitalist is obliged to pay as poor rates necessarily reduces the wages of his labourers, for if the tax did not exist, his capital being so much more considerable, the demand for labour, and consequently its remuneration, would be greater. But the poor rates bestow in the form of alms, but too frequently on the idle and profligate, that wealth which should be the reward of active industry; if the amount of the poor rates were added to the circulating capital of the country, the independent labourer might earn a better livelihood for himself and his family than he can now do; and, without the degrading resource of parish relief, might lay by a portion to provide for sickness and old age.

When it was once proposed to establish a poor's rate in France, the committee of mendicity, in rejecting it, thus expressed themselves on that of England:

" Cet exemple est une grande et importante leçon
" pour nous, car independamment des vices qu'elle
" nous présente et d'une dépense monstreuse, et

ON THE CONDITION OF THE POOR. 165

" d'un encouragement necessaire à la fainéantise,
" elle nous découvre la plaie politique de l'Angle-
" terre la plus dévorante, qu'il est également dan-
" gereux pour sa tranquillité, et son bonheur, de
" détruire ou de laisser subsister."

CAROLINE.

But what is to be done, the poor cannot be allowed to starve, even when idle and vicious?

MRS. B.

Certainly not; and besides the wife and children of a profligate man are often the innocent
victims of his misconduct. Then there are frequently cases of casual distress, which no prudence
could foresee nor guard against; under these circumstances the poor rates could not be abolished
without occasioning the most cruel distress. I
know therefore of no other remedy to this evil
than the slow and gradual effect of education; by
enlightening the minds of the lower classes their
moral habits are improved, and they rise above
that state of degradation in which all feelings of
dignity and independance are extinguished.

CAROLINE.

But, alas! how many years will elapse before
these happy results can take place. I am impatient that benefits should be immediately and uni-

166 ON THE CONDITION OF THE POOR.

versally diffused; their progress is in general so slow and partial, that there is but a small chance of our living to see their effects.

MRS. B.

There is some gratification in looking forward to an improved state of society, even if we should not live to witness it.

CAROLINE.

Since it is so little in our power to accelerate its progress, we must endeavour to be contented: but I confess that I cannot help regretting the want of sovereign power to forward measures so conducive to the happiness of mankind.

MRS. B.

You might possibly fail in your projects by attempting too much. The Emperor Joseph II. endeavoured at once to transform a bad government into a good one, and by adopting arbitrary and violent measures to accomplish his purpose, without paying any regard to the habits and manners, the prejudices and ignorance of his subjects, created ill-will and opposition, instead of co-operation; and ended by leaving them but little more advanced than he found them. I cannot too often repeat to you that gradual improvement is always

ON THE CONDITION OF THE POOR. 167

preferable, and more likely to be permanent than that which is effected by sudden revolution.

But of all modes of bestowing charity, that of indiscriminate alms is the most injudicious. It encourages both idleness and imposition, and gives the bread which should feed the industrious poor, to the indolent and profligate. By affording certain support for beggars, it trains up people to those wretched means of subsistence as regularly as men are brought up to any respectable branch of industry. This is more especially notorious in Catholic countries, where alms-giving is universally considered as a religious duty; and particularly in those towns in which richly endowed convents and religious establishments dispense large and indiscriminate donations.

Townsend, in his travels in Spain, tells us, that " The Archbishop of Grenada once had the cu-" riosity to count the number of beggars to whom " he daily distributes bread at his doors. He " found the men 2000, the women 3024, but at " another time the women were 4000.

" Leon, destitute of commerce, is supported by " the church. Beggars abound in every street, all " fed by the convents and at the bishop's palace. " Here they get their breakfast, there they dine. " Beside food at St. Marca's, they receive every " other day, the men a farthing, the women and " children half as much. On this provision they

168   ON THE CONDITION OF THE POOR.

" live, they marry, and they perpetuate a miserable
" race. Were it possible to banish poverty and
" wretchedness by any other means than by in-
" dustry and unremitted application, benevolence
" might safely be permitted to stretch forth the
" hand, and without distinction to clothe the naked,
" feed the hungry, give drink to the thirsty, and
" furnish habitations to the desolate. But the
" misfortune is, that undistinguished benevolence
" offers a premium to indolence, prodigality, and
" vice."

CAROLINE.

All this is very true: but you must allow that it
is extremely painful to pass, so frequently as we do,
objects of distress in the streets, without affording
them some trifling assistance.

MRS. B.

I cannot blame any one for indulging feelings
of humanity; to pity and relieve the sufferings of
our fellow creatures is one of the first lessons
which nature teaches us: but our actions should
be regulated by good sense, not blindly directed
by undistinguishing compassion. We should certainly consider it as a duty to ascertain whether the
object whom we relieve is in real want, and we
should proportion our charity not only to his distress, but also to his merits. We ought to do much
more for an industrious family, whom unforeseen

ON THE CONDITION OF THE POOR. 169

or unavoidable accidents have reduced to poverty, than for one who has brought on distress through want of a well-regulated conduct. When we relieve objects of this latter description, it would be well at the same time to bestow a trifling reward on some individual among the labouring classes of the neighbourhood distinguished for his industry and good conduct. This would counteract the pernicious effect which cannot fail to be produced by assisting the indolent, whilst we suffer the industrious to remain without reward.

CAROLINE.

But the advantages and comforts derived from industry constitute its natural recompence, and it seems to require no other reward.

MRS. B.

Nor would it, if a similar result could not be obtained without effort; but when a hard-working labourer observes that the family of his idle neighbour is as well provided for as his own — that the hand of charity supplies them with what he earns by the sweat of his brow — such reflections are apt to produce discontent, and tend to check his industry. While, therefore, we tacitly encourage idleness by relieving the distress it produces, we at the same time discourage that laborious industry which passes unnoticed. The value of pecuniary

I

170 ON THE CONDITION OF THE POOR.

rewards is increased by their being bestowed as a mark of approbation; so far from exciting a sense of humiliating dependance, they produce a feeling of a very opposite nature, which raises and improves the character — a consciousness of merit seen and approved by those to whom the poor look up. Such sentiments soften whilst they invigorate the labours of the industrious. Thus if help for the distressed, and rewards for the meritorious poor were to go hand in hand, the one would do as much towards the prevention of poverty as the other towards relieving it.

CAROLINE.

I had an opportunity last summer of witnessing a mode of improving the condition of the labouring poor, in which the system of rewards was introduced with the happiest effect. An extensive piece of ground was laid out in gardens by a great landed proprietor in Hertfordshire, for such of his labourers as had none attached to their cottages. He let the ground to them at the low rate of sixpence a-year each. These gardens were sufficiently large to provide an ample supply of common vegetables for the labourer's family, and to employ his leisure hours in its cultivation; but not so extensive as to tempt him to withdraw his attention from his daily labour, and render the produce an article of sale. As a further means of exciting

ON THE CONDITION OF THE POOR. 171

industry, the proprietor annually distributes three prizes as rewards to those whose gardens are found to be in the highest state of cultivation. This judicious mode of rewarding industry has been beneficial also in producing a spirit of emulation amongst the rival gardeners, whose grounds being separated only by paths, the comparative state of each is easily determined.

MRS. B.

This is indeed an excellent plan; the leisure hours which the labourers might probably have passed at the alehouse are occupied in raising an additional stock of wholesome food, and the money which would have been spent in drinking is saved for a better purpose — it may form perhaps the beginning of a capital, and in process of time secure a little independence for himself and his family.

CONVERSATION XI.

ON REVENUE.

MODES OF EMPLOYING CAPITAL TO PRODUCE REVE-
NUE. — WHICH OF THESE IS MOST ADVANTAGEOUS.
— VARIES ACCORDING TO THE STATE OF THE
COUNTRY. — GARNIER'S OBSERVATIONS ON THE
EMPLOYMENT OF CAPITAL. — EQUALITY OF
PROFITS AFFORDS A CRITERION OF THE DUE DIS-
TRIBUTION OF CAPITAL. — NATURAL ARRANGE-
MENT OF THE DISTRIBUTION OF CAPITAL.—
EQUALITY OF PROFITS IN AGRICULTURE, MANU-
FACTURES, AND TRADE. — WHY THOSE PROFITS
APPEAR UNEQUAL.

MRS. B.

IN our last conversation we have in some measure digressed from our subject; but I trust that
you have not forgotten all we have said upon the
accumulation of capital. Let us now proceed to
examine more specifically the various modes in
which it may be employed in order to produce a
revenue or income. Capital may be invested:

ON REVENUE. 173

In Agriculture,
Mines,
Fisheries,
Manufactures, and
Trade.

CAROLINE.

Of all these ways of employing capital, agriculture, no doubt, must be the most advantageous to the country, as it produces the first necessaries of life.

MRS. B.

In these northern climates it is almost as essential to our existence to be clothed and lodged as to be fed; and manufactures are, you know, requisite for these purposes.

CAROLINE.

True; but then agriculture has also the advantage of furnishing the raw materials for manufactures; it is the earth which supplies the produce with which our clothes are made and our houses built.

MRS. B.

Yet without manufactures these materials would not be produced; it is the demand of the manufacturer for such articles which causes them to be raised by the farmer; agriculture and manufactures thus re-act on each other to their mutual advantage.

I 3

174 ON REVENUE.

CAROLINE.

It may be so; but still it does not appear to me that they can be equally beneficial to the country. Manufactures do not, like agriculture, actually increase the produce of the earth; they create nothing new, but merely put together under another form the materials with which they are supplied by agriculture.

MRS. B.

True: but by such operations they frequently increase the value of these materials an hundred fold. And you are mistaken if you suppose that agriculture can do more than arrange and combine the particles of bodies under a new form. In this respect it differs from manufactures merely from the circumstance of the process being performed by nature in the bosom of the earth, and in a manner which eludes our observation. But agriculture is no more capable than manufactures of creating a single new particle of matter; it is merely by a chemical change of combination that it alters their form and nature, and increases their value.

CAROLINE.

But in agriculture nature facilitates the labours of man; she seems to work together with the husbandman; and provided that he but ploughs the field and sows the seed, she performs all the remainder of the task. It is nature that unfolds the

ON REVENUE. 175

germ, and raises up the plant out of the ground; she nourishes it with genial showers, she ripens it with sun-beams, and leaves the farmer little more to do than to gather in the fruits of her labours.

How different is the case in manufactures! *There* man must perform the whole of the work himself; and notwithstanding the aid he derives from his mechanical inventions, it is all the result of his own toil; whether it be the labour of the head or the hands, it is all art.

MRS. B.

We are accustomed to speak of art in opposition to nature, without considering that art itself is natural to man. He is endowed with the faculties of invention and contrivance, which give him a considerable degree of command over the powers of nature, and render them in a great measure subservient to his use. He studies the peculiar properties of bodies in order to turn them to his advantage; he observes that light bodies float on the surface of the water, and he builds himself a boat; he feels the strength of the wind, and he raises sails; he discovers the powers of the magnet, and he directs his course by it to the most distant shores: but the water which supports the vessel, the wind which wafts it on, and the magnet which guides it, are all natural agents compelled by the art of man to serve his purposes. We cannot,

I 4

176   ON REVENUE.

therefore, say that it is in agriculture alone that nature lends us her assistance. The miller is as
much indebted to nature for grinding his corn as
the farmer is for raising it. In manufactures her
share of the labour is sometimes even more considerable than in agriculture. You may recollect
our observing that the effect of machinery in
facilitating labour, consisted chiefly in availing
ourselves of the powers of nature to perform the
principal part of the work; and there are some
processes of art for which we seem almost wholly
indebted to nature. In bleaching, it is the air and
light which perform the entire process; in the preparation of fermented liquors, we are ignorant even
of the means which nature employs to accomplish
this wonderful operation. In short, it would be
difficult to point out any species of labour in which
nature did not perform a share of the task.

CAROLINE.

That is very true; and it requires only a little
reflection to discover how much we owe to her
assistance in every work of art. We could not
make a watch without the property of elasticity
natural to steel, which enables us to construct a
spring; nor could the spring be fabricated without
the natural agency of fire, rendered subservient
to art.

But, Mrs. B., in agriculture we avail ourselves of

ON REVENUE. 177

machinery as well as of those secret operations of nature which produce vegetation?

MRS. B.

Undoubtedly we do; for every tool which facilitates manual labour is a machine — the spade and hoe, which save us the trouble of scratching up the earth with our hands — the plough and harrow, which still more facilitate the process — the flail, which prevents the necessity of rubbing out the corn — and the threshing machine, which again diminishes the labour. Machinery is, however, not susceptible of being applied to rural occupations with the same degree of perfection as to the arts, because the processes of agriculture are extremely diversified, carried on over an extensive space, and dependant to a very considerable degree on the vicissitudes of the seasons over which we have no control.

Agriculture, manufactures, and commerce, are all essential to the well being of a country; and the question is not whether an exclusive preference should be given to any one of these branches of industry, but what are the proportions which they should bear to each other in order to conduce most to the prosperity of the community.

CAROLINE.

That is all I ask. I never imagined that every

I 5

178   ON REVENUE.

other interest should be sacrificed to that of agriculture; but I feel persuaded that in this country at least, trade and manufactures meet with greater encouragement than agriculture.

MRS. B.

That is a point on which I cannot pretend to decide; and when you are a little better acquainted with the subject, you will be more aware of its difficulty.

CAROLINE.

But surely political economists ought to know in what proportions the capital of a country should be distributed among these different branches of industry?

MRS. B.

It is not easily ascertained, because these proportions vary exceedingly in different countries according to their local situation or peculiar circumstances. In America, for instance, or any new country in which land is cheap, population but thinly scattered, and capital scarce, the prevailing branch of industry will be agriculture. For in such countries, when a labourer accumulates a little money, which (where wages are so high) he is soon enabled to do, he is immediately tempted by the cheapness of land, to lay it out in a farm; and though the wealth of the Americans is so rapidly inereasing, they have hitherto found it more advan-

ON REVENUE. 179

tageous to import the greater part of their manufactured goods, than to establish manufactures at home, a circumstance not so much to be ascribed to a deficiency of capital, as to their having a more profitable use for it.

CAROLINE.

And in England, where the population is abundant and land comparatively scarce, we must find it advantageous to take their corn in exchange for our manufactures.

MRS. B.

No doubt; if old countries were not to purchase elsewhere some part of the agricultural produce they consume, new countries would not raise more than they required for their own consumption, for want of a foreign market to dispose of it.

In this country where land is dear, if a labourer makes a little money, he never thinks of purchasing land; he cannot even afford to rent a farm; but he may set up a shop, or invest his capital in the manufacturing line.

There are other circumstances which affect the destination of capital; such as the local situation of a country; if it abound with rivers and sea-ports, so great a facility for the disposal of its manufactures in foreign parts, will render that branch peculiarly advantageous.

I 6

180   ON REVENUE.

CAROLINE.

So then if agriculture suits one country best, manufactures are more profitable to another, and thus they mutually accommodate each other?

MRS. B.

Exactly. If in England the proportion of capital employed in manufactures be more than is requisite for our own use, it is because we find our advantage in supplying other countries with manufactured produce; were that not the case, we should be at a loss for employment for so large a capital as the country possesses. In proportion therefore as the channel of agriculture fills, capital overflows, into those of manufactures and trade. Agriculture thus leads to manufactures and trade as youth leads to manhood; the progress of the former is the most rapid, the latter adds the vigour and stability of mature growth. Garnier, in his introduction to his French edition of Adam Smith's Essay, remarks on this subject, that,

" It is almost in every instance an idle refine-
" ment to distinguish between the labour of those
" employed in agriculture, and those employed
" in manufactures and commerce; for wealth is
" necessarily the result of both descriptions of la-
" bour, and consumption can no more take place
" independantly of the one than of the other. It
" is by their simultaneous concurrence that any

ON REVENUE. 181

" thing becomes consumable, and of course that
" it comes to constitute wealth. The materials of
" all wealth originate in the bosom of the earth,
" but it is only by the aid of labour that they can
" ever truly constitute wealth; it is industry and
" labour which modify, divide, and combine the
" various productions of the soil, so as to render
" them fit for consumption."

CAROLINE.

But, Mrs. B., though political economists cannot
specify the proportion of capital which should be
employed in these several branches of industry,
have they no means of judging whether they are
actually employed in that proportion which is most
conducive to the welfare of a country? Men follow
their own taste and inclination in the employment
of their capital, and I fear the public benefit has
very little weight in the scale.

MRS. B.

Fortunately there is a better guide than mere
inclination to regulate our choice in the employment of capital, and *that* is *interest.* Men are induced to invest their capital in those branches of
industry which yield the greatest profits; and the
greatest profits are afforded by those employments
of which the country is the most in need.

182   ON REVENUE.

CAROLINE.

I do not exactly understand why there should be such a perfect coincidence between the wants of the public and the interest of the capitalist?

MRS. B.

The public are willing to give the highest price for things of which they stand in greatest need. Let us suppose there is a deficiency of clothing for the people, the competition to obtain a portion of it raises the price of clothing, and increases the profits of the manufacturer of clothes. What will follow? Men who are making smaller profits by the cultivation of land will transfer some of their capital to the more advantageous employment of manufacturing clothes; in consequence of this more clothes will be made, the deficiency will no longer exist, the eager competition to purchase them will subside, they will fall in price, and reduce the profits of the manufacturer to those of agriculture — or should these profits fall still lower, the farmer will take back the capital he had placed in manufactures to restore it to agriculture.

CAROLINE.

Then the profits of agriculture and manufactures will always be, or at least tend to be, upon a footing of equality.

ON REVENUE. 183

MRS. B.

Yes; *tend to be;* that is a very proper qualification, for these changes are not produced on a sudden. The tendency to equalization of profits takes place not only in agriculture and manufactures, but in every other branch of industry. In a country where capital is allowed to follow its natural course, it will always flow into that channel which affords the highest profits, till all employments of capital are nearly upon the same level.

CAROLINE.

You say nearly, why not exactly the same?

MRS. B.

Because, generally speaking, agricultural pursuits are more congenial to the tastes of the majority of mankind than manufactures or commerce: and hence in countries where fertile land is to be obtained at an easy rate, a man no sooner acquires a little capital than he is desirous of purchasing land, and retiring even to remote and almost unpeopled districts, where he can live as the lord of his little domain; as is the case in America at present. Yet this preference will not lead beyond a certain limit, therefore it may be stated that the profits of different employments of capital are nearly upon a level.

184 ON REVENUE.

CAROLINE.

How admirably nature makes all her arrangements! The more I learn of political economy, the more it appears to me, that the institution of laws which control her operations are generally productive of greater evil than good.

MRS. B.

That may frequently be the case, but *generally* is too comprehensive a term. Every law that is enacted infringes more or less upon the natural order of things; and yet I should not hesitate to say that the worst system of laws is preferable to no government at all. Art, we have observed, is natural to man; it is the result of reason, and leads him onwards in the progressive path of improvement. Instead of being chained down like the brute creation by instinct, he is free to follow where inclination leads. But as soon as he enters into a state of society he feels the necessity of a control which nature has not imposed, and his reason enables him to devise one. He enacts laws, which are more or less conducive to his good in proportion as his rational faculties are developed and cultivated. Many of these laws, no doubt, are inimical to his welfare; yet the balance upon the whole is in their favour; the advantages resulting from the single law of the institution of property has conferred a greater benefit on mankind than

ON REVENUE. 185

all the evils which spring from the worst system of government.

CAROLINE.

But this level — this equality of profit to which you say every branch of industry naturally tends, cannot yet have taken place in England, since manufactures and trade are here allowed to yield greater profits than agriculture.

MRS. B.

You are mistaken in that opinion. It is true that it is more common to see merchants and manufacturers accumulate large and rapid fortunes than farmers. They are a class who generally employ capital upon a much larger scale, hence their riches make a greater shew. Yet, upon the whole, trade and manufactures do not yield greater profits than agriculture.

CAROLINE.

I cannot understand why the merchant and manufacturer should grow richer than the farmer unless they make larger profits.

MRS. B.

You must observe that though a farmer does not so frequently and rapidly amass wealth as a merchant, neither is he so often ruined. The risks a man encounters in trade are much greater than in farming. The merchant is liable to severe

ON REVENUE.

losses arising from contingencies in trade, such as war, changes of fashion, bad debts, which scarcely affect the farmer; he must therefore have a chance of making proportionally greater profits.

CAROLINE.

That is to say, that the chances of gain must balance the chances of loss?

MRS. B.

Yes; the merchant plays for a larger stake. If therefore he be so skilful or so fortunate as to make more than his average share of gains, he will accumulate wealth with greater rapidity than a farmer; but should either a deficiency of talents or of fortunate circumstances occasion an uncommon share of losses, he may become a bankrupt.

CAROLINE.

But, Mrs. B., you should, on the other hand, consider that the farmer is exposed to the risk attending the uncertainty of the seasons, a cause which is continually operating, and over which we have no control.

MRS. B.

Yet, in these climates, the loss occasioned by such causes are seldom attended with ruinous consequences; for seasons which prove unfavourable to one kind of produce are often advantageous to an-

ON REVENUE. 187

other. And besides, the produce of agriculture consisting chiefly of the necessaries of life, the demand for it cannot well be diminished; the price, therefore, will rise in proportion to the scarcity. Farmers, you know, are sometimes accused of making the greatest gains in a bad harvest; though I do not believe that to be the case.

We may then conclude that though agriculture, manufactures, and trade, do upon the whole afford similar profits, these profits are, amongst farmers, more equally shared than amongst merchants and manufacturers, some of whom amass immense wealth, whilst others become bankrupts.

The rate of profit, therefore, upon any employment of capital is proportioned to the risks with which it is attended; but if calculated during a sufficient period of time, and upon a sufficient number of instances to afford an average, all these different modes of employing capital will be found to yield similar profits.

It is thus that the distribution of capital to the several branches of agriculture, manufactures, and trade, preserve a due equilibrium, which, though it may be accidentally disturbed, cannot, whilst allowed to pursue its natural course, be permanently deranged. If you are well convinced of this you will never wish to interfere with the natural distribution of capital.

You must not, however, consider this general

188 ON REVENUE.

equality of profits as being fixed and invariable, even in countries where government does not interfere with the direction of capital. A variety of circumstances occasion a temporary derangement of it. The invention of any new branch of industry, or the improvement of an old one, will raise the profits of capital invested in it; but no sooner is this discovered, than others, who have capital that can be diverted to the new employment, engage in this advantageous concern, and competition reduces the profits to their due proportion. A remarkably abundant harvest may occasionally raise the rate of agricultural profits, or a very bad season reduce them below their level. The opening of a trade with a new country, or the breaking out of a war which impedes foreign commerce, will affect the profits of the merchant: but these accidents disturb the equal rate of profits, as the winds disturb the sea; and when they cease, it returns to its natural level.

CONVERSATION XII.

ON REVENUE DERIVED FROM PRO-PERTY IN LAND.

ON RENT.—HIGH PRICE OF AGRICULTURAL PRO-DUCE THE EFFEST, NOT THE CAUSD OF RENT.—CAUSES OF RENT; I.THE FIRTILITY OF THE EARTH; 2. DIVERSITY OF SOIL AND SITUATION REQUIRING DIFFERENT DEGREES OF EXPENCE TO RAISE SIMILAR PRODUCE —ORIGIN OF RENT. — RENT INCREASES POSITIVELY IN A PROGRESSIVE COUN-TRY, AND DIMINISHES RELATIVELY.—HIGH PRICE OF RAW PRODUCE NECESSARY TO PROPORTION THE DEMAND TO THE SUPPLY. — MONOPOLY OF LAND. — MONOPOLY DEFINED.

CAROLINE.

I HAVE been reflecting much upon the subject of revenue, Mrs. B.; but I cannot comprehend how farmers can afford to pay their rent if they do not make more than the usual profits of capital. I had imagined that they began by raising greater produce from the same capital than merchants or

190 REVENUE FROM LANDED PROPERTY.

manufacturers, but that the deduction of their rent eventually reduced their profits below those of other branches of industry.

MRS. B.

You were right in the first part of your conjecture, but how did you account for the folly of farmers in chusing a mode of employing their capital which after payment of their rent yielded them less than the usual rate of profit?

CAROLINE.

I believe that I did not consider that point. I had some vague idea of the superior security of landed property; and then I thought they might be influenced by the pleasures of a country life.

MRS. B.

Vague ideas will not enable us to trace inferences with accuracy, and to guard against them we should avoid the use of vague and indeterminate expressions. For instance — when you speak of the security of landed property being advantageous to a farmer, you do not consider that in the capacity of farmer a man possesses no landed property; he *rents* his farm; if he *purchases* it, he is a landed proprietor as well as a farmer. It is not therefore the security of landed property which is beneficial to a

REVENUE FROM LANDED PROPERTY. 191

farmer, but the security or small risk in the raising and disposing of his crops.

A farmer when he reckons his profits, takes his rent into consideration; he calculates upon making so much by the produce of his farm as will enable him to pay his rent besides the usual profits of his capital; he must expect therefore to sell his crops so as to afford that profit, otherwise he would not engage in the concern. Farmers then really produce more by the cultivation of land than the usual rate of profit; but they are not greater gainers by it, because the surplus is paid to the landlord in the form of rent.

CAROLINE.

So then they are obliged to sell their produce at a higher price than they would otherwise do, in order to pay their rent: and every poor labourer who eats bread contributes towards the maintenance of an idle landlord?

MRS. B.

You may spare your censure, for rent does not increase the price of the produce of land. It is because agricultural produce sells for more than it cost to produce, that the farmer pays a rent. Rent is therefore the *effect* and not the *cause* of the high price of agricultural produce.

192 REVENUE FROM LANDED PROPERTY.

CAROLINE.

That is very extraordinary! If landed proprie-tors exact a rent for their farms, how can farmers afford to pay it, unless they sell their crops at a higher price for that purpose?

MRS. B.

A landlord cannot exact what a tenant is not willing to give; the contract between them is volun-tary on both sides. If the produce of the farm can be sold for such a price as will repay the farmer the usual rate of profit on the capital employed, and yet leave a surplus, farmers will be found who will willingly pay that surplus to the landlord for the use of his land.

CAROLINE.

But if the profits of agriculture are not the effect of rent, why are they not reduced by competition, and brought down to the usual rate of profit? Why does not additional capital flow into that channel, and by increasing the supply of agricultu-ral produce reduce its price?

MRS. B.

In the first place, agriculture is not susceptible of an unlimited augmentation of supply, like manu-factures. If hats and shoes are scarce, and sell at extraordinarily high prices, a greater number of men will set up in the hat and shoemaking busi-

REVENUE FROM LANDED PROPERTY. 193

ness, and by increasing the quantity of those commodities reduce their price. But land being limited in extent, farmers cannot with equal facility increase the quantity of corn and cattle. It might however be done to a very considerable extent by improvements in husbandry, and bringing new lands into cultivation. But, in the second place, to whatever extent this were accomplished, it would not have the effect of permanently diminishing the price of those commodities which constitute the necessaries of life, because population would increase in the same proportion, and the additional quantity of subsistence would therefore be required to maintain the additional number of people; so that there would remain (after allowing a short period for the increase of population) the same relative proportion between the supply and the demand of the necessaries of life, and, consequently, no permanent reduction of price would take place. The necessaries of life therefore differ in this respect from all other commodities; if hats or shoes increase in plenty they fall in price, but the necessaries of life have the peculiar property of creating a demand in proportion to the augmentation of the supply.

CAROLINE.

But what is it that makes agricultural produce sell at so high a price as to afford a rent? If it is

K

194 REVENUE FROM LANDED PROPERTY.

not rent that occasions the high price, there must be some other cause for it.

MRS. B.

There are several circumstances which concur to raise and maintain the price of agricultural produce above its cost of production, and enable the farmer to pay rent. Its first source is what upon a superficial view would seem to have the effect of diminishing price; it is that invaluable quality with which Providence has blessed the earth, of bringing forth food in abundance; an abundance more than sufficient to maintain the people who cultivate it. For if those who occupy the land and raise the crops, consumed the whole of them, there would be no surplus to sell at any price to others; and under such circumstances it would be impossible that the cultivator of the soil should pay rent. But the natural fertility of the earth is such as to render almost all soils capable of yielding some surplus produce which remains after the farmer has paid all the expences of cultivation, including the profits of his capital. It is from this fund that he pays his rent. The quantity of this surplus produce varies extremely, according to the degree of fertility of the soil, and enables a farmer to pay a higher or a lower rent.

CAROLINE.

But, Mrs. B., in countries newly settled, where

REVENUE FROM LANDED PROPERTY. 195

the greatest choice of fertile land is to be had, and where we are told that the harvests are so productive, as in many parts of America, no rent is paid?

MRS. B.

Wherever land is so plentiful that it may be cultivated by any one who takes possession of it, of course no man will pay a rent. But the cultivator nevertheless makes such a surplus produce as would enable him to pay rent. The only difference is, that instead of transferring it to a landlord, he keeps the whole himself. This is the reason that such rapid fortunes are made by new settlers, in a fine climate and a fertile soil.

It is the fertility of the soil then which *enables* the cultivator to pay a rent; but we must look for another cause which *induces* him to do so.

CAROLINE.

You speak as if it were left to his option, Mrs. B.; and if that were the case, I do not think that rent would ever be paid.

MRS. B.

We shall see presently how far you are right. — When a newly settled country increases in capital and in population, fresh land is taken into cultivation, and after all the most fertile districts are occupied, soil of an inferior quality, or less advan-

K 2

196 REVENUE FROM LANDED PROPERTY.

tageously situated, will be brought under tillage. Now, corn, or any agricultural produce, raised upon less fertile soils, will stand the farmer in a greater expense, more labour, more manure; and more attention will be required to raise a less abundant crop, and the cost of its production will, upon the whole, be greater.

CAROLINE.

The original settlers who had the first choice of the land have then an advantage over the others; they will make the greatest profits, and accumulate fortunes soonest. For the several crops, when brought to market, if of the same quality, will sell for the same price, whatever difference there may have been in the cost of their production. Nay, it is even likely that the crops which cost the least in their production, may fetch the highest price; for the most fertile soil will, in all probability, yield the finest produce.

MRS. B.

The first settlers have also another advantage; they will have selected the most favourable situations as well as the most fruitful soil; their fields will flourish on the borders of a navigable river, or surround the town which they have built; affording them a resource both for a home and a foreign market. Whilst those who cultivate land in more

REVENUE FROM LANDED PROPERTY. 197

remote parts must add all the charges of conveyance to the market where the produce is sold, or the port from whence it is exported. Let us suppose that the first settlers make 30 per cent., whilst the latter make only 20 per cent. of their capital. With the double advantage of the most fertile soil, and free from rent, it is no wonder if the first settlers should rapidly amass large capitals, and it is not improbable that towards the decline of life they may be desirous of retiring from the fatigues of an active life, yet without wishing to sell their property. Under these circumstances, do you not think that they would readily find new settlers, who, rather than undertake to cultivate remote districts, of perhaps a still inferior soil, would pay an annual sum for the use of their land, and become their tenants?

CAROLINE.

That is very true: it would answer to the new comers to give the 10 per cent. which the first settlers make above the others, in consequence of having the most eligible land.

MRS. B.

This, then, is the origin of *Rent.* If the tenant pay 10 per cent., which is equal to one-third of what the proprietor made by cultivation, his profits will be reduced to 20 per cent., and will consequently be upon a level with those of the second

K 3

REVENUE FROM LANDED PROPERTY.

settlers, who remain both proprietors and farmers; and thus the profits of the farmer are reduced from 30 to 20 per cent.

CAROLINE.

And those of other branches of industry will, I suppose, be reduced to the same rate, in order to maintain the level of equality of profits?

MRS. B.

Of course. But when the profits of agriculture are 20 per cent., accumulation will still proceed with rapidity; and as the country grows rich and populous, the demand for corn will increase, and fresh land will be required to be brought into cultivation. The new land being either more remote, or of an inferior quality, will be cultivated under still greater disadvantages, and will not yield, let us suppose, above 10 per cent. profits. As soon as this happens, the second settlers will be able to obtain a rent for *their* land. For it will be as advantageous to a farmer to pay 10 per cent. whilst he makes 20, as to give nothing for the use of the land when he makes only 10 per cent. of his capital.

The general profits of capital are thus again reduced, from 20 to 10 per cent.

CAROLINE.

But do not those who first rented land continue making 20 per cent. by cultivating it?

MRS. B.

Only as long as their leases last; for as soon as their landlords find that the profits of capital are reduced to 10 per cent. they will not allow their tenants to make more, but require all the surplus profits above that sum to be paid them in the form of rent. Thus every fresh portion of land that is taken into cultivation, either of inferior quality or less favourably situated, produces the double effect of raising rents and reducing the profits of capital.

CAROLINE.

But if profits continue to decrease with every fresh portion of land that is ploughed up, they will, in the course of time, be reduced to nothing; and then the progress both of cultivation and of population must stop, else there will be a scarcity of food.

MRS. B.

As soon as that scarcity is felt, corn will rise in price, and this by increasing the profits of the farmer will induce him again to take new land into cultivation. This occurs more or less at every progressive step made in agriculture, and prevents the profits from being reduced to nothing. Every time that new land is brought into culture, the price of raw produce, and consequently the profits of farming, must have previously risen. No new land *can* be cultivated

200 REVENUE FROM LANDED PROPERTY.

till capital has accumulated to maintain and employ a greater number of labourers. And no new land *will* be cultivated till population has so far increased as to raise the price of corn, and make it answer to the agriculturist to break up new land for tillage.

CAROLINE.

And when the crops from the new land come to market, I suppose corn will again be reduced in price?

MRS. B.

Yes; or what comes to the same, wages will rise: but the fall from this cause will only be temporary; for when higher wages enable a labourer to rear a greater number of children, population will, in the course of time, again outstrip the progress of capital, and the same consequences will again recur. Thus agricultural produce and population alternately take the lead. But independently of the temporary rise and fall in the price of corn which they occasion, every fresh portion of land that is taken into cultivation diminishes the profits of capital, and raises the rent of land, and the price of raw produce; for in proportion as recourse must be had to land of an inferior quality to provide food for the increasing population, the expense of producing it is increased. For every quartern of corn, and loaf of bread, whether raised on the finest soils at the least cost of production,

REVENUE FROM LANDED PROPERTY. 201

or yielded by land the most unfavourably circumstanced, will fetch the same price in the market.

CAROLINE.

It is curious enough to think that of two similar loaves of bread brought on table, the cost of production of one of them may perhaps have been nearly twice as much as that of the other; and that one may have paid three-pence, whilst the other has only paid a halfpenny towards the rent.

The price of raw produce in general is then regulated by the expense of producing it on soils of the worst quality, or the most disadvantageously situated?

MRS. B.

Yes; provided you include in the cost of production the profits of the farmer, for though the worst soils may not afford a rent, they must bring the cultivator a profit; and if the produce of such land ceased to afford him profits it would be thrown out of cultivation.

CAROLINE.

The high price of agricultural produce is then owing to the necessity of raising part of it at an additional expense on inferior soils?

MRS. B.

Yes; for this has at the same time the effect of

K 5

202 REVENUE FROM LANDED PROPERTY.

raising the rents of the land of superior quality. We may, therefore, define *rent* to be that part of the surplus produce of the land which remains after all the expenses of cultivation are deducted.

CAROLINE.

Under such disadvantages I only wonder that the price of corn, and of raw produce, should not be higher than it is.

MRS. B.

The natural rise in the price of raw produce, owing to the cultivation of inferior soils, is in a great measure counterbalanced by other circumstances. Every year improvements are made in agriculture, which increase the produce without proportionally increasing the expenses of cultivation, and enable corn to be brought cheaper to market. Besides, though land of an inferior quality is at first cultivated at an additional expense, it improves by tillage, so that the cost of production gradually diminishes, and by draining, manuring, and other ameliorating processes of agriculture, an ungrateful soil is in the course of time not unfrequently rendered fertile. Disadvantages of situation are also remedied with the progress of society, the neighbourhood increases in population, new towns are built and new markets opened; if therefore it were not indispensably necessary to

15

REVENUE FROM LANDED PROPERTY. 203

continue bringing fresh land into cultivation to provide for an ever growing population, corn would be produced at less expense, and would fall instead of rising in price.

CAROLINE.

But if all the surplus produce which remains, after the expenses of production are deducted, go to the landlord in the form of rent, improvements in agriculture will not lower the price of raw produce, but will increase the rent.

MRS. B.

I beg your pardon; you have just observed that the price of raw produce in general is regulated by the expense of producing it on soils of the worst quality, and the most disadvantageously situated; therefore, the more we diminish the expense of raising it on such soils, and the more we can remedy the disadvantages of situation, the lower we shall fix the standard price of raw produce. The cost of production of a loaf of bread raised on land of the lowest description is now one shilling; if by improvements in agricultural labour we could reduce it to ten-pence, bread in general would sell at that price.

CAROLINE.

All this is perfectly clear; but I am not at all pleased to learn that as a country advances in the

K 6

204 REVENUE FROM LANDED PROPERTY.

accumulation of wealth, *rent*, the portion of the idle landlord, augments, while *profits*, the portion of the industrious farmer, diminishes.

MRS. B.

These idle landlords, of whom you complain, neither lower the profits of capital nor raise the price of agricultural produce. If you understand what I have said on rents, you must be aware that the reduction of profits is occasioned by the diversity of soils successively brought into cultivation, and that the natural high price of agricultural produce is owing to the surplus which remains after all the expenses of cultivation are defrayed. Were rents, therefore, to be abolished, the only effect produced would be to enable farmers to live like gentlemen, as they would be enriched by that share of the produce of their farms which before fell to the lot of the landlord.

CAROLINE.

And would not that be a very desirable change? Is it not better that those who labour should grow rich, rather than those who live upon the fruits of the labour of others?

MRS. B.

The yeomanry are a classs of farmers who cultivate their own property; and if you wish to eu-

REVENUE FROM LANDED PROPERTY. 205

courage their industry you must allow them to reap the full reward of their labours, — to accumulate wealth, and when wealthy to indulge in ease and repose, and to *let* their land to others, if they prefer this plan to that of cultivating it themselves. Were landed proprietors prohibited from letting their land when rich, they would nevertheless become idle, and would neglect the farming business, which being left to the care of servants, the cultivation would suffer, and the country, as well as the proprietor, be injured by the diminution of produce. In civilized countries, landed property has been obtained by industry, or by wealth, the fruits of industry, and should be secured in its full value, not only to the individual who has earned it, but to his heirs for ever.

Besides, though it is true that rents rise as a country advances in prosperity, this rise is not in proportion to the increasing produce of the soil. Rent formerly used to bring in to the landlord one-third of the produce of his land; it has since fallen to one-fourth, and has lately been estimated as low as one-fifth; so that the landlord, whilst he receives a higher rent, has a smaller share of the whole produce.

CAROLINE.

That is some consolation. But could no means be devised to abolish rents, and compel farmers to reduce in consequence the price of their produce,

206 REVENUE FROM LANDED PROPERTY.

so that neither the landlord nor the farmer, but the public, should enjoy the benefit of the surplus produce, which constitutes rent? Surely this would reduce the price of provisions, and of all agricultural produce.

MRS. B.

Admitting that it did so, what advantages do you expect would result from the reduction of prices? When a measure of compulsion, especially one so complicated, is proposed, I am always suspicious of its consequences.

CAROLINE.

But the good that would result is so evident; if food were cheaper, people would be able to consume more, and the poor would have plenty.

MRS. B.

How so? would the land be more productive in consequence of the abolition of rent? and if more should not be produced, how could the people consume more? An increased consumption without an increased supply will, as we have remarked on a former occasion, lead to a famine. The price of a quartern loaf is now one shilling; I conclude, therefore, that at that price the consumption of bread will be so proportioned to the quantity wanted, that the stock of wheat will last till the next harvest. The adoption of your com-

REVENUE FROM LANDED PROPERTY. 207

pulsory measures might reduce the price of a quartern loaf to nine-pence, and every poor family being thus enabled to increase their consumption of bread, the stock of wheat would not last out till the ensuing harvest. Then the following year, instead of raising more corn to make up the deficiency, the poorest land, which yields no rent, and but just affords the profits of capital at the present price of raw produce, would, by such a diminution of price, be thrown out of cultivation; and the produce of the country would thus be considerably diminished.

CAROLINE.

Very true. I did not foresee that consequence. And a scarcity would perhaps raise the price of bread higher than it was before.

MRS. B.

How much would it be necessary for bread to rise in price in order to make the corn last till the next crops came in?

CAROLINE.

To the price at which it now sells, one shilling.

MRS. B.

We return then to the rent-price, though no rent is paid: you see, therefore, the fallacy of your

208 REVENUE FROM LANDED PROPERTY.

measures. The high price, of which you so bitterly complain, is the price necessary to proportion the consumption to the supply, so as to make it last till the ensuing harvest.

CAROLINE.

So far from being mortified, Mrs. B., I am delighted with my disappointment, as it has been the means of convincing me that if the poor are obliged to pay a high price for the necessaries of life, it is for their own benefit, as well as that of the mighty lords of the land; since it ensures them a uniform supply throughout the year. And I the more willingly acquit rent of the accusation of high prices, since I find there are two other sources from whence that evil may spring.

MRS. B.

I think you may add, that as these high prices are necessary to regulate the consumption and prevent scarcity, or even famine, you no longer consider them as an evil. An inquiry into the effects of human laws and institutions often discovers error; but whatever flows in the course of nature springs from a pure source, and the more accurately we examine it, the more admiration we shall feel for its Author.

Thus though rent cannot in itself be considered as an evil, since we have traced it to the natural

REVENUE FROM LANDED PROPERTY. 209

fertility of the earth, and its diversity of soil; yet every artificial measure which tends to raise the price of agricultural produce, so as to enable the farmer to pay a higher rent, is certainly injurious. Therefore restrictions on the free importation of corn, or any other species of raw produce, which raises the price of those articles at home, is taking an additional sum out of the pockets of the consumer to put into that of the landlord. For rent may be considered as a necessary tax which the consumer pays to the landlord; the farmer is merely the vehicle of conveyance from the one to the other.

CAROLINE.

And has such a measure immediately the effect of raising rents?

MRS. B.

Not until the leases are expired; during their existence the farmer enjoys all the adventitious gains or suffers all the losses that may occur; but when his lease is renewed it must correspond with the rate of profit, and rise or fall in proportion to the gains which the farmer expects to make, so as to give the whole of the surplus produce to the landlord, and leave only the usual profits of capital to the farmer. It may happen, indeed, either from ignorance or carelessness, and sometimes from motives of humanity, that the landlord does not exact all that the farmer can afford to pay; but

210 REVENUE FROM LANDED PROPERTY.

these are accidental circumstances, and the whole of the surplus produce is considered as the fair and usual rent. The contract between the farmer and the landlord is naturally in favour of the latter, for this reason: every man possessed of a little capital is capable of engaging in a farm, and as the land to be let is limited in extent, there are always more men desirous of renting farms than there are farms to be let. The landholders may, therefore, be considered as exercising a species of monopoly towards farmers, being possessed of a commodity the demand for which exceeds the supply; competition to obtain it, therefore, enables the landholder to exact the highest rent which the farmer can afford to pay; that is, to relinquish the whole of the surplus produce of agriculture to the landlord.

CAROLINE.

I do not exactly know the meaning of the term *monopoly;* but I had always understood it to be a very unjust and improper thing.

MRS. B.

Monopoly is the exclusive privilege of any person, or set of persons, to possess or sell any particular commodity. When sanctioned by government it is generally prejudicial, because it prevents the free competition of other sellers, which would tend to the reduction of the price of the commodity in

REVENUE FROM LANDED PROPERTY. 211

question. Thus if any set of men were exclusively privileged to deal in tea or coffee, there being no rival traders to enter into competition with and undersell them, they can raise the price of those articles higher than will afford the usual profits, and the extra profit is unfairly taken from the consumers of tea and sugar. Granting a monopoly is therefore a very improper measure of government, excepting in cases in which it can be proved that the restrictions imposed are of general benefit to the community.

CAROLINE.

I cannot conceive any case in which general good can result from giving one set of men such an advantage over the rest of the community.

MRS. B.

To grant a patent for a useful discovery or invention is authorising a temporary monopoly, which is decidedly advantageous, from the encouragement it affords to ingenuity, investigation, and perseverance; qualities which are highly beneficial to the progress of industry. But I wonder that you should hesitate respecting the advantages derived from the monopoly of land; for this monopoly simply means, that the land shall not belong in common to all mankind, as nature designed it, but that it shall be exclusively possessed, sold, or dis-

212 REVENUE FROM LANDED PROPERTY.

posed of by a particular set of men; — in short, it is nothing more than the institution of property in land, the advantages of which are so unquestionable. It is perhaps the only monopoly of a permanent nature which the law ought to sanction. If the monopoly extended to the produce of the earth, it would then indeed partake of the evil effects of monopolies in general — excess of price, owing to deficiency of competition.

CAROLINE.

But can land be a monopoly, without the price of its produce being affected by it?

MRS. B.

Yes; because the produce of the land depends not so much upon the quantity of land as upon the quantity of capital employed on it, and this is comparatively unlimited and perfectly free from monopoly. Property in land is therefore a monopoly of a very peculiar nature, confined entirely to one of the instruments of production; and so far is it from raising the price of the fruits of the earth, that it is absolutely necessary both to their production and to their preservation.

CONVERSATION XIII.

ON REVENUE DERIVED FROM THE CULTIVATION OF LAND.

TWO CAPITALS EMPLOYED ON LAND. — TWO REVE-
NUES DERIVED FROM IT. — OF THE CAPITAL AND
PROFITS OF THE FARMER. — OF THE DURATION
AND TERMS OF LEASES. — OF TYTHES. — EX-
TRACT FROM PALEY.—OF PROPRIETORS FARMING
THEIR OWN ESTATES. — EXTRACT FROM TOWNS-
END'S TRAVELS. — FARMS HELD IN ADMINISTRA-
TION. — ADVANTAGE OF AN OPULENT TENANTRY.
— METAYER SYSTEM OF FARMING. — SMALL
LANDED PROPERTIES. — EXTRACT FROM ARTHUR
YOUNG'S TRAVELS. — DAIRY ESTABLISHMENTS IN
SWITZERLAND.— SMALL FARMS.— SIZE OF FARMS
IN BELGIUM AND TUSCANY. — OF. MINES. — OF
FISHERIES.

CAROLINE.

FROM what you said in our last conversation I
perceive that agriculture yields two distinct
incomes; one to the proprietor, the other to the
cultivator of the land.

214 REVENUE FROM CULTIVATION OF LAND.

MRS. B.

And it employs also two capitals to produce those incomes; the one to purchase, the other to cultivate the land. A man who lays out money in the purchase of land becomes a landed proprietor, and obtains a revenue in the form of rent. He who lays out capital in the cultivation of land, becomes a farmer, and obtains a revenue in the form of produce.

CAROLINE.

What do you mean by the capital of the farmer, Mrs. B.? I thought that the land was the capital from which he derived his profits.

MRS. B.

You mistake; the land is the capital of its proprietor, and as such yields him a revenue; whatever the farmer obtains from it, is derived from cultivation; that is to say, from the labour and expense he bestows on the soil. The land is the machine with which he fabricates agricultural produce, and the income he derives from it is the revenue of the capital employed in working this machine. A farmer requires capital to pay his labourers, and to purchase his farming-stock, such as cattle, waggons, ploughs, &c. It is the bare land and the farming buildings which he rents. The crops which are upon the ground when the agreement is made are paid for independantly, and

REVENUE FROM CULTIVATION OF LAND. 215

become the property of the farmer. Unless therefore he has a capital to defray these expenses, he cannot take the lease of a farm.

CAROLINE.

I always supposed that the produce of a farm was sufficient to defray its expenses; nor can I understand how profits are to be derived from a farm, if the cultivation and rent cost more than its produce will repay.

MRS. B.

It is not so. The capital of the farmer is employed as the means of cultivating his farm; and when at the end of the year, after paying his rent, his labourers, and keeping his stock in repair, he finds himself in possession not only of his original capital, but also of a surplus or profit, it is a proof that the farm produces more than the cost of its rent and cultivation. The case is similar in all employment of capital. The manufacturer who lays it out in the purchase of raw materials, and in paying the labour which is afterwards expended on them; or the merchant whose capital is employed in the purchase of goods for sale, could not carry on their respective occupations without first laying out their capital: but it is returned to them, together with the profits that have accrued by its employment. Each of these occupations bring in

216 REVENUE FROM CULTIVATION OF LAND.

more than is laid out, but none of them could be carried on without a capital.

CAROLINE.

Oh yes; I recollect the labourer produces for his employer more than he receives from him as wages, and this surplus is the source of his master's profit; but if the farmer had not wherewithal to pay his labourers' wages, he could not set them to work.

It is then upon the capital which a farmer employs on his land, that he calculates his profits?

MRS. B.

Yes. Let us suppose that a farmer employs a capital of the value of 3000*l.* on his farm : he may, possibly, after deducting the rent and the expenses of cultivation, make ten per cent., or 300*l.* profit.

CAROLINE.

That is to say, that at the end of the year he would find himself 300*l.* richer than he was before?

MRS. B.

Provided that he had spent none of his gains during the course of the year. But as his family are commonly maintained by the produce of the farm, he will at the end of the year be actually richer or poorer according to the proportion which his domestic expenses have borne to his gains. But

REVENUE FROM CULTIVATION OF LAND. 217

these cannot be considered as a deduction from his profits, as the expense of the maintenance of his family must fall upon his revenue in whatever way it is obtained.

CAROLINE.

And what is the usual rent paid for such a farm?

MRS. B.

It depends in a great measure upon the extent and condition of the land. A considerable farm, in a good state of cultivation, and possessing the advantage of a fertile soil, may not require a capital of more than 3000*l.* to carry it on; whilst a farm of only half that extent, if in a bad condition, and with an ungrateful soil, may require as large a capital to be laid out on it. But a very different rent would be paid for these two farms.

CAROLINE.

Of course the large productive farm must pay a higher rent than the smaller ill-conditioned one?

MRS. B.

And the difference of rent will equalize the profits which a farmer would derive from employing the same quantity of capital on each of these farms. Taking an average of the state of culture, a farm which requires 4000*l.* capital may pay a rent of about 200*l.*, the share of the farmer being nearly half as much again as that of the landlord.

L

218 REVENUE FROM CULTIVATION OF LAND.

CAROLINE.

You said in our last conversation, that the rent of land had lately been estimated as low as $\frac{1}{5}$th of the produce. A farm, such as you have described, would therefore yield produce worth 1000*l.*, in which case the profits of the farmer would be above three times as great as those of the landlord?

MRS. B.

You forget that from the total produce must be deducted not only the rent, but also the expenses of cultivation; these are generally estimated at one half of the produce, after deducting the rent; there will remain therefore 400*l.*, which is 10 per cent. profit on the 4000*l.* capital employed on the farm. If from this sum the farmer saves 50*l.*, he may lay it out in the improvement of his land, which will render the produce more plentiful the following year; an advantage of which he will derive the full benefit, as his rent will remain the same to the end of the lease.

CAROLINE.

But on granting a new lease, the proprietor, I suppose, would expect a higher rent for a farm that had been thus improved?

MRS. B.

No doubt; it is therefore desirable that land should not be let on short leases, because farmers

REVENUE FROM CULTIVATION OF LAND. 219

would have no inducement to improve the condition of their land without the prospect of reaping the benefit of it for some years to come.

CAROLINE.

But towards the end of the lease, this objection would remain in force?

MRS. B.

True: but to prevent this farmers generally obtain a renewal of their leases some time before they are elapsed. Besides it would be contrary to the interest of the landlord to deal hardly with his tenants on such occasions, as it would discourage them from improving their farms; an advantage in which the landlord must eventually partake.

In Staffordshire, Nottinghamshire, and some other parts of the country, it is not customary to grant leases; the tenants hold their farms at the will of the landlord. There is, however, a sort of conventional agreement between the parties, that except in cases of misconduct, the farmer shall not be removed, nor have his rent raised during a certain period. Some people are of opinion that this mode of letting land is preferable to granting a lease; because they say the industry of the farmer is stimulated both by hope and fear; the hope of profit from his labours, and the fear of being

L 2

220 REVENUE FROM CULTIVATION OF LAND.

turned out should he neglect the improvement of his farm: but in arguing thus they do not consider that this fear must operate in two ways, for in proportion to the improvement which the farmer makes, so is the temptation to the landlord, if he be needy or illiberal, to turn him out, or to exact an increase of rent. In short, there can be no greater check to industry than the insecurity of the profits it produces; and how can a farmer feel his interests secure whilst he is dependant on the will of his landlord?

CAROLINE.

Besides, though a farmer may repose great confidence in the character of the individual whose land he holds, the uncertainty of life renders him dependant also upon his heir, and this may perhaps be some wild extravagant youth, who, without regard to his ultimate interest, will exact the highest rents from his tenants.

MRS. B.

Security is, no doubt, the most important point for the encouragement of industry; and the greatest, indeed the only encouragement which government can give to agriculture, is to secure to the farmer all the power over the soil that is necessary for its perfect cultivation, and to ensure him the profits of every improvement he may make. I will read you a passage from Paley on this subject:

REVENUE FROM CULTIVATION OF LAND. 221

" The principal expedient by which laws can
" promote the encouragement of agriculture, is to
" adjust the laws of property as nearly as possible
" by the following rules; 1st, To give to the oc-
" cupier all the power over the soil which is neces-
" sary for its perfect cultivation. 2dly, To assign
" the whole profit of every improvement to the
" persons by whom it is carried on. Now it is in-
" different to the public in whose hand this power
" of the land resides, if it be rightly used; it mat-
" ters not to whom the land belongs if it be well
" cultivated.

" Agriculture is discouraged by every constitu-
" tion of landed property which lets in those who
" have no concern in the improvement to a parti-
" cipation of the profit. This objection is appli-
" cable to all such customs of manors as subject
" the proprietor, upon the death of the lord or te-
" nant, or the alienation of the estate, to a fine
" apportioned to the improved value of the land.
" But of all institutions which are in this way ad-
" verse to cultivation and improvement, none is so
" noxious as that of tythes. When years perhaps
" of care and toil have matured an improvement,
" when the husbandman sees his new crops ripen-
" ing to his industry, the moment he is ready to
" put his sickle to the grain, he finds himself com-
" pelled to divide his harvest with a stranger.
" Tythes are a tax not only upon industry, which

L 3

222 REVENUE FROM CULTIVATION OF LAND.

" feeds mankind, but upon that species of exertion
" which it is the aim of all wise laws to cherish
" and promote."

CAROLINE.

It is indeed much to be regretted that a provision for the clergy should not be raised in some other manner.

MRS. B.

Since all right of property is derived from legal institutions, the clergy have an equal right to their tythes as the landed proprietors to their estates; yet so severely does this law fall upon the cultivators of land, that I believe few of the clergy venture to levy tythes to the extent of their rights; they cannot do it without incurring the ill will and opposition of their parishioners. How defective then must that institution be, which dispossesses one man of the fruits of his industry, whilst it will not allow another to take, without exciting vexation and disturbance, that which the law has assigned him as his property.

Tythes are a portion of the surplus produce of agriculture, destined for the maintenance of the clergy. They should be considered, therefore, as a portion of rent, for if the farmer did not pay tythes to the rector of his parish, his rent would be raised proportionally; and indeed lands tythe free always yield a higher rent.

REVENUE FROM CULTIVATION OF LAND. 223

Would it not be better, then, that tythes should be paid by the farmer to his landlord in the form of rent, and that they should be through him transmitted to the clergyman; the tythes would then bear a proportion to the rent, and not to the annual produce of the land? By such a regulation the clergy would know on what income to depend, and the farmer would not have the vexation of seeing any part of the fruits of his labour gathered by another. It would destroy that source of ill will and contention between the clergy and their parishioners, and that opposition of interests which are so prejudicial both to religion and morals; and it would remove that constant check on industry, which is so severely felt in the present mode of levying tythes.

CAROLINE.

Such an alteration would certainly be advantageous to all parties.

Since it is so desirable for the cultivator to have unlimited power over the soil, I should have thought that it would have been particularly advantageous for landed proprietors to cultivate their own estates, instead of letting them to farmers; and yet it is a common observation that gentlemen make the least profits by agriculture. This is the more unaccountable, because, being both landlord and farmer, the proprietor must receive

L 4

224 REVENUE FROM CULTIVATION OF LAND,

the two incomes comprised in the produce of the land, rent and profit.

MRS. B.

But recollect that he also employs two capitals, in order to make the two incomes; the one to purchase the land, the other to cultivate it. The reason why gentlemen who cultivate their own estates do not usually make profits equal to those of a common farmer, is either because they do not understand the business so well, or that they do not bestow the same care and attention upon it. The common farmer usually devotes the whole of his time to his farm, either in the capacity of bailiff, or that of labourer; while the gentleman farmer never earns the wages of labour, and generally leaves the important office of bailiff to be performed by a substitute; therefore were the gentleman to raise as plentiful crops as the farmer, they would be produced at a more considerable expense, and his gains would be proportionally diminished. As to the value of the rent, it must be reckoned independantly, as he receives it in his quality of landlord.

CAROLINE.

It would then probably increase the agricultural produce of the country, if gentlemen were always to let their land instead of farming it themselves.

REVENUE FROM CULTIVATION OF LAND. 225

MRS. B.

On the contrary, I believe it to be very desirable that some few gentlemen, in different parts of the country, should cultivate their own estates. Being generally men of greater information than common farmers, they are more willing to make experiments, and adopt any new mode in the various agricultural processes which may appear eligible. Besides, the land is frequently better improved in the hands of the proprietor than in those of a labouring farmer; as the proprietor has usually the advantage of a larger capital to lay out on his land, and then he is not restrained by the apprehension that his rent will be ultimately raised in proportion to the additional value which he gives to the land.

Townsend, in his Travels in Spain, has made some very judicious observations on English gentlemen farmers.

" By residing," he says, " on their own estates, " they not only spend money among their tenants, " which by its circulation sets every thing in mo- " tion, and becomes productive of new wealth, but " their amusement is to make improvements. By " planting, draining, and breaking up lands which " would have remained unprofitable, they try new " experiments, which their tenants could not af- " ford, and which, if successful, are soon adopted " by their neighbours. They introduce the best

L 5

226 REVENUE FROM CULTIVATION OF LAND.

" breed of cattle, the best implements of hus-
" bandry, and the best mode of agriculture; they
" excite emulation, they promote the mending of
" the roads, and secure good police in the villages
" around them. Being present, they prevent their
" tenants from being plundered by their stewards.
" They encourage those who are sober, diligent,
" and skilful; and they get rid of those who would
" impoverish their estates. Their farmers, too,
" finding a ready market for the produce of the
" soil, become rich, increase their stock, and by
" their growing wealth make the land more pro-
" ductive than it was before."

CAROLINE.

You have enumerated so many advantages on
the opposite side of the question, that I begin to
think that it would be more beneficial to the country that all landed proprietors should cultivate their
own estates; for though they might not be great
gainers by it themselves, yet the country would
derive all the advantage from the improvement of
the soil, and the introduction of scientific agriculture.

MRS. B.

A few gentlemen farmers in each county will be
sufficient for the latter purpose. Were it common
for proprietors to farm their own estates, I am convinced that it would be extremely injurious to

REVENUE FROM CULTIVATION OF LAND. 227

agricultural produce ; for no command of capital, no scientific knowledge, can, in a general point of view, compensate for the keen and vigilant eye of the industrious farmer, who sees that every thing is turned to the best account.

CAROLINE.

I should suggest as a medium between these two modes, that a landed proprietor should neither farm his estate, nor let it, but employ an agent to cultivate it for him, whose salary should be proportioned to the produce which he raises on the land.

MRS. B.

Such I believe was the species of tenure by which farms were held by the vassals of the nobles when they were first emancipated from slavery, and that military services were no longer, as in feudal times, considered as a sufficient remuneration for the occupancy of land. To give the cultivator any interest in the produce he raises acts certainly as a spur to his industry; but it is one much less powerful than the security and independance of the leasehold farmer, who after paying a stipulated rent enjoys the whole advantage of the efforts of his industry.

Townsend informs us, that most of the great estates in Spain are held in administration, that is, cultivated by agents or stewards for the account of

L 6

228 REVENUE FROM CULTIVATION OF LAND.

the proprietor; and it is principally to this cause that he attributes the low state of agriculture " No country," he observes, " can suffer more than " Spain for want of a rich tenantry, and perhaps none " in this respect can rival England. We find univer- " sally that wealth produces wealth, but then to pro- " duce it from the earth, a due proportion of it much " be in the pocket of the farmer. Many gentlemen " among us, either for amusement, or with a view " to gain, have given attention to agriculture, and " have occupied much land; they have produced " luxuriant crops, and have introduced good hus- " bandry; but I apprehend few can boast of having " made much profit; and most are ready to confess " that they have suffered some loss. If, then, re- " siding on their own estates, with all their atten- " tion they are losers, how great would be the " loss if in distant provinces they employed only " stewards to plough, to sow, to sell, and to eat up " the produce of their lands."

There are, however, in warmer climates, some species of produce, which from their peculiar nature farmers would not venture to undertake to cultivate on their own account, and proprietors would be un- willing to trust entirely to their management. Such is the culture of the vine and the olive, plants which require the utmost care and attention during a num- ber of years before they begin to yield any fruit, and farmers are seldom sufficiently opulent to engage in

REVENUE FROM CULTIVATION OF LAND. 229

a species of husbandry, the profits of which are so
long protracted. On the other hand, as these plants
may be very materially injured by being allowed to
bear fruit either prematurely or too luxuriantly; and
as the interest of the farmer looks rather to immediate than remote profits, it is not considered safe to
trust such plantations entirely to his care. Vineyards and olive-grounds are therefore, I am informed, cultivated by the farmer in half account
with the proprietor, who shares with him equally
the expenses and the profits. This is called the
Métayer system of cultivation: it was formerly very
common on the continent for all kinds of produce,
and still prevails in Italy, where the land is so extremely subdivided, that the métayer farmers, frequently subsisting upon half the produce of not more
than three or four acres of land, are scarcely superior in condition to our peasantry. In France and
Switzerland this system of farming is confined
almost exclusively to the culture of the vine and the
olive. But how requisite soever the system may be
for particular plantations, the usual mode in this
country of granting leases, I conceive to be, not only
most advantageous to the farmer, but ultimately so
to the landed proprietor, who can procure the
highest rent for the land best cultivated; and it
is also most beneficial to the country by yielding
the greatest produce. But in Spain this mode
could not be adopted for want of an affluent te-

230 REVENUE FROM CULTIVATION OF LAND.

nantry. The wealth of the country is chiefly en-grossed by the nobles and clergy; there is a total deficiency of yeomen, or farmers who cultivate their own land; and the middling classes are few in number, and so destitute of capital, that they are incapable of taking a lease of land.

CAROLINE.

I often wish that the property of land was more subdivided in this country. How delightful it would be to see every cottage surrounded by a few acres belonging to the cottager, which would enable him to keep a cow, a few pigs, and partly at least to support his family on the produce of his little farm. Do you recollect Goldsmith's lines?

> " A time there was, e'er England's griefs began,
> " When every rood of ground maintain'd its man :
>   " But now alas ! . . . .
> " Along the lawn where scatter'd hamlets rose,
> " Unwieldy wealth and cumb'rous pomp repose,
> " And every want to luxury allied."

MRS. B.

I shall point out to you a passage in Arthur Young's Travels in France, in which this question appears to be ably discussed.

CAROLINE *reads.*

" I saw nothing respectable in small properties " except most unremitting industry. Indeed it is

REVENUE FROM CULTIVATION OF LAND. 231

" necessary to impress on the reader's mind that
" though the husbandry I met with in a great
" variety of instances was as bad as can well be
" conceived, yet the industry of the possessors was
" so conspicuous and meritorious that no com-
" mendations would be too great for it. It was
" sufficient to prove that property in land is the
" most active instigator to severe and incessant
" labour. And this truth is of such force and
" extent that I know no way so sure of carrying
" tillage to a mountain-top as by permitting the
" adjoining villagers to acquire it in property; in
" fact we see that in the mountains of Languedoc
" they have conveyed earth in baskets on their
" backs to form a soil where nature has denied it."

MRS. B.

Land that is too poor to afford a rent may still
yield sufficiently to pay the proprietor for its cultivation; it is therefore the property of such soils
alone which will ensure their being cultivated.—
But go on.

CAROLINE *reads.*

" But great inconveniency arises in small pro-
" perties from the universal division which takes
" place after the death of the proprietor. Thus I
" have seen some farms which originally consisted
" of 40 or 50 acres reduced to half an acre, with a
" family as much attached to it as if it were an

282 REVENUE FROM CULTIVATION OF LAND.

" hundred acres. The population flowing from
" this extreme division is often but the multiplica-
" tion of wretchedness. Men increase beyond the
" demand of towns and manufactures, and the
" consequence is distress and numbers dying of
" diseases arising from insufficient nourishment.
" Hence small properties much divided form the
" greatest source of misery that can be conceived.

" In England small properties are exceedingly rare;
" our labouring poor are justly emulous of being
" the proprietors of their cottages, and that scrap
" of land which forms the garden ; but they seldom
" think of buying land enough to employ them-
" selves. A man that has two or three hundred
" pounds with us, does not buy a field but stocks a
" farm. In every part of England in which I have
" been, there is no comparison between the case of
" a day-labourer and of a very little farmer : we
" have no people that fare so hard and work so ill
" as the latter. No labour is so wretchedly per-
" formed and so dear as that of hired hands accus-
" tomed to work for themselves ; there is a disgust
" and listlessness that cannot escape an intelligent
" observer, and nothing but real distress will drive
" such little proprietors to work at all for others.
" Can any thing be apparently so absurd as a
" strong, heavy man walking some miles and
" losing a day's work in order to sell a dozen of
" eggs or a chicken, the value of which would not

REVENUE FROM CULTIVATION OF LAND. 233

" be equal to the labour of conveying it, were the
" people usefully employed?"

CAROLINE.

This reminds me of a poor woman in Savoy,
who kept a few cows among the mountains two or
three leagues distant from Geneva. Having no other
market for her milk, she carried it regularly every
day to that town for sale; thus the greater part of
her time was spent upon the road, whilst it might
certainly have been much more profitably employed had she been dairy-maid to some considerable farmer, who, having milk enough to turn
it to butter and cheese, could in that state send it
wholesale to market.

MRS. B.

The inconvenience you allude to has of late
years been obviated in many of the villages of
Switzerland, especially in the neighbourhood of
Geneva, by the introduction of a peculiar species
of public dairy establishments, which, I understand, originated in the plains of Lombardy. To
these dairies, called *Fruitières*, the farmers in the
vicinity bring their daily stock of milk, which is
converted into butter and cheese, and returned to
them in that form, the establishment retaining
only such a portion as is necessary to defray its
expences.

There are also considerable dairy establishments

234 REVENUE FROM CULTIVATION OF LAND.

in the Swiss mountains, but these are commonly private property; the proprietor of the mountain pasture usually hiring cows of the neighbouring farmers, who are commonly repaid in the manufactured produce of the dairy.

Small landed properties are extremely common in Switzerland. The canton De Vaud consists chiefly of such, and they do not seem to be attended with the mischievous consequences which Arthur Young describes; for the country is well cultivated, and landed property is not reduced to that minute division which entails wretchedness.

CAROLINE.

I heard a gentleman who is recently returned from France say, that three servants, whom he had hired at Marseilles, had all been men of landed property; but that the portion of inheritance to each had been so small that they had disposed of it to other members of their families, in order to hire themselves as servants.

MRS. B.

When this or any other cause prevents the extreme partition of landed property, the principal objections to small properties are removed; and the disadvantage arising from deficiency of capital may be in a great measure compensated by the stimulus given to the industry of a man who cultivates his own land. This system is perhaps best

REVENUE FROM CULTIVATION OF LAND. 235

calculated for mountainous countries, where the strongest motives to industry are required, to induce men to climb the steep rock in order to cultivate a small patch of earth favourably situated on its acclivity.

CAROLINE.

I have heard that the condition of the lower agricultural classes in France has been very much improved by the sale of the national domains, at the commencement of the Revolution in that country; that it has enabled the small farmers and many of the peasantry to become landed proprietors, and thus to cultivate their own land; and that this subdivision of property has proved so beneficial that, notwithstanding all the evils they have since had to contend with, they are yet in a very thriving condition. This does not seem to agree with Arthur Young's statements?

MRS. B.

By the sale of the national domains, very small proprietors, whose land was scarcely equal to the maintenance of their families, were enabled to enlarge their farms. The ill consequences arising from an extreme subdivision of land would thus be remedied. But we must recollect that at the commencement of the French Revolution, the restrictive and oppressive laws which checked the progress of every branch of industry were abolished; this gave

236 REVENUE FROM CULTIVATION OF LAND.

vigour to agricultural pursuits. Then the sale of confiscated lands, at a period when its tenure was considered as extremely insecure, rendered them so cheap, that it was almost as easy to purchase an estate in France as in America, with the additional advantage of its being already in a state of cultivation. These circumstances all concurred to improve the condition of the small landed proprietors. With a view of amassing little capitals to lay out upon their new domains, they have acquired habits of industry and economy, and such habits are of themselves a treasure to a country. These small capitals which are now growing up in France, will no doubt prove a source of prosperity; but as the French law divides the landed property of a man dying without a will among all his children equally, it may probably in time lead to that extreme division of landed property which is attended with such injurious effects.

CAROLINE.

And are there the same objections to small leasehold farms as to small landed properties?

MRS. B.

In a great measure. It is poverty alone which induces a man to take a very small farm; and a poor farmer cannot make those exertions which are requisite for good husbandry. The profits of a considerable farmer enable him to improve his land;

REVENUE FROM CULTIVATION OF LAND. 237

those of a small one are entirely consumed in the maintenance of his family; his land is therefore badly cultivated, and he has little or no surplus produce to send to market.

I met with a remarkable instance of the disadvantage of extremely small farms during a visit to a considerable landed proprietor in Hampshire. He made me observe a field in which a number of labourers were employed ploughing and sowing turnips, and pointed out a man whose appearance was far less creditable than that of the other labourers.

That man,' said he, ' rents this single field, and resides in the wretched cottage you see at the end of it: the common labourers are better fed and clothed than himself, because he cannot earn so good a livelihood by his farm as they can by their daily work. Unable to afford the expense of hiring a team of horses to plough his field, and not knowing where to procure sheep to eat off the turnips which should be the crop next in rotation, his intention was to have let the field lie fallow; when I proposed to him to undertake to plough and sow it, on condition that my sheep should eat off the turnips on the ground, by which means they would manure it, and his field would be returned to him in a much better state than if suffered to be fallow. To this proposal he assented, and thus we shall both be gainers.'

252 REVENUE FROM CULTIVATION OF LAND.

CAROLINE.

And the country will profit by both their gains, for the sheep will be fattened by turnips, which, without such an agreement, would not have been grown; and the farmer's ensuing crop will be more productive from the land having been manured by the sheep.

But what sized farms do you suppose to be most beneficial to a country?

MRS. B.

That must vary extremely, according to the local situation, the nature of the climate and soil, and the capital of the farmer. In Belgium, which is esteemed one of the best cultivated countries in Europe, I am informed that the farms are upon an average about 40 acres; and in Tuscany, another spot remarkable for the excellence of its agriculture, the farms seldom exceed 10 or 15 acres, all cultivated upon the metayer system; but in this favoured climate the fields yield such abundant crops that the produce approaches more nearly to that of a Belgic farm, than you would imagine from the difference of their extent.

In this country there is, I think, a strong predilection in favour of considerable farms. Were I to give an opinion, I should say that a farm should never be so large that the farmer cannot superintend the whole of the cultivation himself; nor so small

REVENUE FROM CULTIVATION OF LAND. 239

as not to enable him to keep up that farming stock establishment necessary for the most perfect husbandry. But this is a point which may be safely left to regulate itself. I do not apprehend that this country can suffer by the different size of farms; for there are very few small landed properties; and as it is the interest of the landlord to draw the greatest possible income from his estate, he will let his farms of such dimensions as he conceives his tenant will be able to turn to the best account. To a very opulent farmer he may be induced to grant a lease of a large farm; whilst he will refuse that of a single field to a cottager who would exhaust instead of improving the soil.

The advantages of considerable farms have been so ably delineated in one of the last numbers of the Edinburgh Review, that I shall read you the passage:

" It is quite evident that some of the most valu-
" able mechanical inventions could never have
" come into general use if there had been no farms
" of more than 100 or 150 acres; that no great
" improvement could have been made in our live
" stock; that there would have been still less room
" than there is at present for the division of labour,
" and for its accumulation for the purpose of dis-
" patch at particular seasons; that there would not
" have been that systematic arrangement by which
" every different quality of soil is made to produce

240 REVENUE FROM CULTIVATION OF LAND.

" those crops, and to feed those sorts of animals for
" which it is best calculated; that it would have
" been almost impracticable to practise convertible
" husbandry at all, which by combining tillage and
" pasturage on the same farm, contributes so power-
" fully to sustain and augment the fertility of the
" soil; that the surplus produce for the supply of
" towns would have been inconsiderable at all
" times, and from the general poverty of small
" tenants brought to market in too great abundance
" in the early part of the season, instead of appor-
" tioning it over the whole year; and in bad seasons
" there would have been no surplus at all :—and that
" in short, as no person of capital or enterprize
" would ever have entered into the profession, our
" extensive moors and morasses, and indeed all our
" inferior soils, must have remained in their natural
" state, or been partially and most unprofitably
" improved under the delegated management of
" great proprietors."

It is now, I think, high time to conclude the subject of agriculture; and it is necessary to say only
a few words on Mining, a branch of industry which
I have placed next to agriculture, on account of its.
analogy to it, in affording a rent.

Mines, like land, generally yield a rent to the
proprietor as well as profits to the undertaker
whose capital is employed in working them. The
coal-mines, notwithstanding the great assistance

REVENUE FROM CULTIVATION OF LAND. 241

derived from machinery, give work to several hundred thousand labourers who earn their maintenance, besides the profits of their employer and the rent of the proprietor; and this rent is in general more considerable than that of agricultural land, as the produce of coal mines is more valuable than that of the soil.

CAROLINE.

The mines that contain metals are, I suppose, of still greater value?

MRS. B.

Yes, and their rent proportionally higher; but the profits of the capitalist who rents them, and of the labourers who work them, is not greater. As the value of a mine, however, depends upon the quantity, as well as on the quality of the metal it affords, it frequently happens that a lead mine will fetch a higher rent than a silver mine. The expense of working coal mines is less than that of metallic mines. The coal requires nothing more than to be extracted from the earth: but with the metals the labour is much more complicated; they must be separated from the ore in the furnace, and undergo variety of processes before they are fit for the purposes of art.

The risk and uncertainty attending mining is greater than that of any other employment of capital; and accordingly we find both larger for-

M

242 REVENUE FROM CULTIVATION OF LAND.

tunes made, and more people ruined in that than in any other branch of industry.

CAROLINE.

The chance of gain then compensates for the risk of loss; but upon the whole I suppose the profits are similar to those derived from other modes of employing capital?

MRS. B.

I am inclined to believe the profits of mining to be rather lower than the common standard. In all hazardous enterprises men are prone to trust to their good fortune, and generally consider the chances more in their favour than an accurate calculation would warrant. This is evinced by the readiness with which men venture to stake their money in the lottery, though it is well known that the chances of gain are decidedly against them. A mine is a more advantageous lottery no doubt than that of government, but it contains a prodigious number of blanks, and only a few great prizes. Sanguine hopes and expectations in some measure supply the place of actual gains; yet if the average profits of mining should at any time fall so low as to discourage the spirit of enterprize, and diminish the requisite supply of metals, their price would rise until it had brought back a sufficient capital to that branch of industry.

REVENUE FROM CULTIVATION OF LAND. 243

I have mentioned fisheries as a source of employment for capital, and a means of affording a revenue.
Very large capitals are engaged in the whale, the
cod, and the herring fisheries, besides those smaller
ones which supply the country with fresh fish. But
as the sea in which these fisheries are carried on is
not susceptible of becoming private property, they
yield no rent. There are however some considerable inland river fisheries which belong to individuals, and bring in a rent. No fewer than
forty-one different salmon fisheries upon the river
Tweed are rented for several thousands a-year;
and I am informed that the Duke of Gordon lets a
salmon fishery on the Spey for 7000*l.* a-year. In
the Scotch fisheries it is very common to take four
or five score of salmon at a draught. In England
there are also considerable salmon fisheries in the
Tyne, the Trent, the Severn, and the Thames.

We have already noticed the manner in which a
revenue is obtained from manufactures; what further observations we have to make on this branch
of industry we shall defer till we enter on the subject
of trade, with which it is so naturally connected.

CAROLINE.

And will that be the subject of our next conversation?

MRS. B.

No; we have yet many general remarks to make

M 2

244 REVENUE FROM CULTIVATION OF LAND.

upon revenue. And it will be necessary also, before we turn our attention to trade or commerce, that you should understand the nature and use of money, without a knowledge of which it would be extremely difficult to render the subject clear and perspicuous.

CONVERSATION XIV.

ON THE REVENUE OF THOSE WHO DO NOT EMPLOY THEIR CAPITAL THEMSELVES.

RENT, OR INCOME DERIVED FROM LETTING LAND. — INTEREST OF MONEY, OR INCOME DERIVED FROM LOANS. — CAUSES OF THE DIFFERENT RATE OF INTEREST YIELDED BY LAND OR BY MONEY. — CAUSES OF THE FLUCTUATIONS OF INTEREST. — RATE OF INTEREST IN INDIA, IN CHINA, AND IN AMERICA. — OF USURY. — GOVERNMENT LOANS, OR INCOME DERIVED FROM THE FUNDS. — OF UNPRODUCTIVE LABOURERS, OR THOSE WHO DERIVE AN INCOME FROM THE EXPENDITURE OF OTHERS.

CAROLINE.

I THINK I now understand very well how an income is derived from agriculture and manufactures; and also how it is produced by trade; but there are many men of property who follow

246   ON REVENUE FROM CAPITAL LENT.

none of these occupations; how, therefore, can
their capital yield an income?

MRS. B.

When a man possesses a very large property, he
frequently will not be at the trouble of employing
it himself; but will engage some other person to
do it for him. You have seen that a landed proprietor who does not farm his own estate derives a
revenue from the farmer in the form of rent.

CAROLINE.

But I allude to men of fortune without landed
property, who live upon their income, although
their capital is not employed.

MRS. B.

Reflect a moment, and you will be convinced
that no capital can yield an income without being
employed. If, therefore, the owner does not invest it in some branch of industry himself, another
person must do it for him. A capitalist under
such circumstances may be supposed to say, " I
" am possessed of an ample stock of subsistence
" for labourers, and of materials for workmanship,
" but I will engage some other person to take
" charge of so troublesome an undertaking as that
" of setting the people to work, and collecting the
" profits derived from their labours."

ON REVENUE FROM CAPITAL LENT. 247

CAROLINE.

This person must be handsomely remunerated for the time and pains he bestows on the management of a capital which is not his own.

MRS. B.

No doubt; a considerable share of the profits derived from the use of capital must go to him who takes charge of it: but when a man's property is very large, he would rather lose that share than be at the trouble of managing it himself. Thus you see that the employer and the proprietor of capital are frequently different persons.

CAROLINE.

Yet I do not recollect ever to have heard of a man of fortune making use of an agent to employ his capital,

MRS. B.

He does not engage an agent on his own account, but he lends his capital to some person who invests it either in agriculture, manufactures, or trade, and who pays him so much per cent. for the use of it. This is called lending money at interest.

CAROLINE.

Is it then simply *money* that is lent; or *capital* consisting of produce ?

M 4

248 ON REVENUE FROM CAPITAL LENT.

MRS. B.

It eventually comes to the same, for money gives the borrower a command over a proportional share of the produce of the country. If the money would not purchase the things which the borrower wanted, it would not answer his purpose; but it will procure him either materials or implements for work, maintenance for labourers, stock for farming, or merchandize for trade. In a word, it will enable him to exert his industry in whatever way he chuses.

CAROLINE.

I should have imagined that it would have been more advantageous to the capitalist to have engaged an agent at a stipulated salary, for the purpose of undertaking the use of his capital?

MRS. B.

Your plan would probably not answer so well; for if, instead of lending his capital at interest, a man of property paid an agent to employ it for him, the agent would be less cautious what risks he engaged in, as he would not be a sufferer by losses.

CAROLINE.

But is not the loan of capital at interest liable to the same objection? If the employer of capital be ruined, the proprietor of it must share the same fate.

ON REVENUE FROM CAPITAL LENT. 249

MRS. B.

This not unfrequently happens; yet there is less risk incurred in this mode than if the employer of capital could injure the proprietor without being himself involved in the same fate; and it would be so if he acted as clerk or agent, as he would lose only his salary, although the proprietor might be utterly ruined.

Prudent men seldom lend capital without good security. If the loan is made to a merchant, it is usual to require other merchants, or men of property, to become responsible for the payment. If to a man of landed property, the capital is lent upon the security of his estate; that is to say, if the loan be not repaid according to agreement, the lender has the right to seize that particular property, upon the security of which the capital was advanced. This is called lending money upon the security of mortgage.

CAROLINE.

That must be the best kind of security, for the land cannot be made away with. It is making fixed capital responsible for circulating capital.

The man who borrows capital with a view to employ it, must necessarily expect to make greater profits than will pay the interest of the loan, otherwise he would be no gainer by it.

M 5

250 ON REVENUE FROM CAPITAL LENT.

MRS. B.

Certainly. The average profits of the use of capital may be estimated at about double the interest of money. Legal interest, that is to say, the highest rate which the law allows to be given, is 5 per cent., and the usual profits of trade are about ten per cent.

CAROLINE.

Therefore the lender and the borrower, or in other words the proprietor and employer of capital, commonly divide the profits arising from it equally between them; the one making as much by his property as the other by his industry.

The landed proprietor who lets his land to a farmer, I conceive to be situated in the same manner as the man who lends his capital at interest, neither of them chusing to undertake the employment of their capitals themselves, but procuring some other person to do it for them; and the rent the farmer pays for the use of the land is similar to the interest paid for the use of capital?

MRS. B.

It is so; and the advantages derived from letting land are analogous to those that result from the loan of capital. We have observed that if the farmer, instead of paying a rent, received a certain stipend for his labour, and reserved the whole of

ON REVENUE FROM CAPITAL LENT. 251

the produce for the landlord, he would certainly be less attentive to the cultivation of the land than if his gains resulted from the value of the produce raised.

There is, however, one essential difference between borrowing capital and renting land. The man who borrows capital to be employed in trade or manufactures, requires nothing more to enable him to prosecute his business. Whilst the farmer who borrows land cannot undertake the cultivation of it without the assistance of another capital, which he must either possess or borrow for that purpose.

CAROLINE.

Then there is another difference. The landed proprietor and the farmer do not divide the profits arising from the cultivation of the land equally between them, as is usually, you say, the case with the lender and borrower of capital; for the farmer makes greater profits by the use of the land than the proprietor by the rent.

MRS. B.

There are several reasons for this difference. In the first place you must recollect that the profits of capital vary with the degrees of risk to which it is exposed; and then consider that an income derived from the rent of land, is much more secure than any other kind of revenue. For

M 6

252 ON REVENUE FROM CAPITAL LENT.

if the farmer ruin himself, he cannot make away with the land : he may be obliged to quit his farm, but then his stock is liable to seizure for the payment of rent.

Another considerable advantage attached to landed property is, that in proportion as agriculture improves, the produce of the land increases: this augments the profits of the farmer, and enables the landlord to raise his rent. And lastly we must call to mind the observations we made on the origin of rent; and we shall find that in proportion as agriculture extends, and new and inferior lands are taken into cultivation, the rent of land rises. If you weigh all these advantages, you will no longer be surprized that a landed proprietor should be satisfied with making between three and four per cent. of his capital, instead of lending it at five per cent. interest, with more or less risk of loss, and a certainty that the capital will not improve.

CAROLINE.

The real profits, therefore, to be derived from the loan of capital perfectly secure, is between three and four per cent., and whatever is received above that sum may be considered as an indemnification for the risk to which it is exposed?

MRS. B.

If you take the improvable nature of rents, as

ON REVENUE FROM CAPITAL LENT. 253

well as their perfect security into the calculation, some deduction may be allowed in consideration of the certain prospect of future increase; the profits to be derived from the loan of capital, even when the security is perfect, may therefore be estimated somewhat higher than that which is afforded by the rent of land.

We must now make a few observations upon the interest of money.

The interest of money, or price paid for the loan of capital, was formerly much higher than it is at present. It has gradually diminished for some centuries past, in the same proportion as national wealth has increased.

CAROLINE.

And why should that be the case?

MRS. B.

As the capital of a country becomes larger, the profits to be derived from it diminish, and the lower the profits to be made by the use of capital, the lower the rate of interest which the borrower can afford to pay for it.

CAROLINE.

Then it seems that as a nation grows rich, the individuals who compose it become poor?

MRS. B.

Oh no; have you forgotten the observations we made upon the wages of labour, and upon the origin of rent? As a nation advances in opulence, that is to say, when its capital increases in a still greater ratio than its population, the demand for labour, and consequently its wages, rise, and leave smaller profits to the capital of their employers. On the other hand, as a country improves in wealth and population, inferior land is taken into cultivation, and rents rise.

CAROLINE.

It is then the landed proprietor and the labourer who are gainers by national opulence, and the employers of capital who are the losers by it?

MRS. B.

No; they also are eventually gainers. The man who employs capital, whether it be his own, or borrowed at interest, is a productive labourer of a superior description, and in proportion as capital, and consequently the demand for the employers of capital increases, the better is he remunerated: this additional remuneration arises from the greater quantity of capital at his command; for though the rate of his profits be reduced, let us suppose from ten to eight per cent., he finds himself compensated for that difference from the additional quantity of

ON REVENUE FROM CAPITAL LENT. 255

capital he has to employ. In our conversation on the wages of labour, you may recollect the colonists whom we supposed to be supplied with labourers by a shipwrecked crew. Do you think they had any cause to regret the change that took place, when these labourers had produced them an additional capital, although it obliged them to pay higher wages? And in regard to the borrowers of capital, the diminution of profit is compensated by the lower rate of interest.

CAROLINE.

National opulence diffuses itself, then, on all ranks of people; and, like the sun, spreads its rays all round, from the palace of the sovereign to the cottage of the peasant!

MRS. B.

When capital is allowed to follow its natural course, this will always be the result. During the reign of the Emperor Augustus, the interest of money at Rome fell from ten to four per cent., owing to the great influx of wealth from the conquered provinces. In India, where the proportion of capital to the number of labourers is comparatively small, wages are extremely low, and the profits of capital and interest of money exorbitantly high. The common rate of interest is twelve per cent., but I have heard that it is not unusual to make as much as twenty, or even thirty per cent.

256 ON REVENUE FROM CAPITAL LENT.

interest. In China, interest is six per cent. per month, or thirty-six per cent. a-year.

CAROLINE.

And is interest low in America, where labourers are scarce and wages high?

MRS. B.

No, it is not; on account of the great profits made by agriculture. In a country not yet fully peopled, where there is so great a choice of fertile land, that scarcely any of an inferior quality is brought into cultivation, and consequently where little or no rent is paid, the cultivator can afford to give high wages, and yet make great profits; and wherever great gains can be made by the use of capital, high interest will be given for the loan of it. Therefore, though capital has been increasing in America more rapidly than in any other country; yet as immediate and advantageous employment is found for every accession of capital by the cultivation of new and fruitful lands, the interest of money does not fall.

In all old established fully peopled countries the low interest of money is almost invariably a sign of prosperity; for it indicates an increasing capital, a low rate of profit to those who employ it, and high wages to the labouring poor.

There are circumstances, however, in which

ON REVENUE FROM CAPITAL LENT. 257

the interest of money may fall independantly of an augmentation of capital. This happens when the market, that is to say, the means of disposing of the produce of the country, is suddenly contracted. The home market then becomes over stocked, the price of goods falls so low as to leave very little profit, and if this state of things is of long continuance, the interest of money will sink in proportion to the diminution of profits. On the other hand, there are circumstances which sometimes produce a rise in the interest of money without indicating any diminution of prosperity, but are in fact to be considered as proofs of an opposite nature. This happens when the market is suddenly enlarged, a circumstance which is frequently occasioned by the opening of a new commercial intercourse with foreign countries, or the introduction of any new source of industry at home. A greater demand for our produce in other countries occasions a greater demand for capital, and a consequent rise in the rate of interest; but in this case the rise is only temporary, because the increased industry of the country rapidly produces an augmentation of capital equal to the demand, and a proportional fall in the interest of money.

CAROLINE.

But I thought that the interest of money was fixed by law, and incapable of fluctuation?

258   ON REVENUE FROM CAPITAL LENT.

MRS. B.

The legal interest is 5 per cent.; it may fall below that rate, though in this country it cannot rise above it without becoming usury. In former times, to receive any remuneration for the loan of money was regarded much in the same light as usury is at present; that is to say, as taking an unfair advantage of the borrower.

CAROLINE.

Such an opinion could have been entertained by those only who understood nothing of the re-productive nature of capital; for had they been aware of the profits to be made by the employment of money, they could not have considered it as unfair to pay for the use of it.

MRS. B.

Our forefathers had no pretensions to a knowledge of political economy; it is a science of later date. The prejudice against lending money at interest appears not to have prevailed in very ancient times, but to have originated in the darkness of the middle ages; for the interest of money was legally instituted both amongst the Grecians and the Romans. It must have been an established practice in the time of Solon, since it is upon record that he reduced the legal interest to 12 per cent. The Bramins in India are said to have taken

ON REVENUE FROM CAPITAL LENT. 259

$2\frac{1}{2}$ per cent. monthly so far back as 3000 years, and yet legal interest was not established in Europe until the year 1546.

Macpherson in his history of commerce makes the following observations on the unpopularity of receiving interest for the loan of money. " In the " year 1251," he observes, " the consequence of the " clamour and persecution raised against those who " took interest for the use of money was so violent, " that they were obliged to charge it much higher " than the natural price, (which if it had been let " alone would have found its level,) in order to " compensate for the opprobrium, and frequently " the plunder which they suffered; and thence the " usual rate of interest was, what we should now " call most exorbitant and scandalous usury." And what we now call exorbitant and scandalous usury proceeds in a great measure from a similar prejudice, which prevents the interest of money, like all other pecuniary interests, from finding its natural level, and stamps with criminality, and the odium of usury, any bargain in which money is lent at a higher interest than 5 per cent., however great the risk incurred by the lender. Why should there be a limit to the terms on which money may be borrowed, any more than to the borrowing, or I should rather say, to the hiring any other commodity?

260 ON REVENUE FROM CAPITAL LENT.

CAROLINE.

Would not such unlimited freedom of interest afford too great encouragement to capitalists to supply prodigals and thoughtless youths with money, and thus facilitate their means of squandering it?

MRS. B.

Men of this description find no difficulty in borrowing of usurers, provided they are able to give security for the payment, and without such security they would not obtain the loan of money either from men of respectability or from crafty usurers. The only difference now is, that they must pay a higher price for the loan, because the lender requires to be remunerated, not only for the use of the money, and the risk he incurs, but also for the ignominy and criminality attached to the proceeding; this necessarily takes it out of the hands of men of honourable character, and throws it into those of men who, having no value for reputation, are much more likely to take undue advantage of the distress of men who are in urgent want of money, and of the unguarded thoughtlessness of prodigal youth.

There is yet another means by which a man of property may derive an income from his capital without employing it himself: it is by lending it to a borrower who is distinguished from all others by the singularity of his dealings — who borrows not

ON REVENUE FROM CAPITAL LENT. 261

only without any intention of making profits by the use of the capital; but also, in general, without any prospect of repaying the principal of the debt.

CAROLINE.

Without any prospect of repaying the debt! And where can they find men weak enough to lend capital on such terms?

MRS. B.

This extraordinary borrower is no other than the government of the country. When government makes a loan, that is to say, borrows capital, it is for the purpose of spending it as soon as procured; and the proprietors of this capital, or, as they are usually denominated, the public creditors or stockholders, scarcely ever expect that the debt should be repaid. Yet notwithstanding this circumstance men are willing to lend their money to government even upon lower terms than to other borrowers. This arises from two causes; the first, that the security of government for the punctual payment of the interest is better than that of any individual; and the second, that the public creditor has an indirect means of getting back his capital whenever he pleases, without being repaid by government.

CAROLINE.

In what way?

262 ON REVENUE FROM CAPITAL LENT.

MRS. B.

By selling his right to receive the interest to any individual who wishes to invest his capital in the funds, and who will then stand in the place of the original creditor.

CAROLINE.

And can he always sell that right for the sum he originally lent to government?

MRS. B

Not always exactly; he will sometimes get more and sometimes less, according to the state of the market. If there are many creditors or stock-holders desirous to sell, and but few capitalists wishing to buy, he will get less; if many buyers and few sellers, he will obtain more: in the latter case the stocks are said to be high, or rising; in the former, to be low, or falling.

CAROLINE.

But since government spends the capital borrowed instead of deriving any profit from it, by what means is the interest paid?

MRS. B.

It is paid by taxes levied expressly for that purpose.

CAROLINE.

If then government spends what it borrowed, the capital no longer exists, and the stock-holder remains possessed of only an imaginary or fictitious capital.

MRS. B.

He remains possessed of the right to receive an annual payment, or annuity, equal to the stipulated interest, till the government pays him back the principal. And this annuity (where the government can be depended upon) will always sell for its value to such persons as have capital that they wish to lend at interest. It is thus that the stock-holder is enabled to realize this fictitious capital, whenever he chuses, by selling his stock. The capital is, therefore, not lost to the individual; but it is entirely lost to the country. The stock may be sold, but the sale does not re-create the capital that has been spent; it merely transfers to the seller capital already existing in the hands of the buyer, and which would equally have existed whether the stock were sold or not. So long, however, as it can be exchanged for real capital, and in the mean-time produces a substantial income to the possessor, it affords him all the enjoyments that can be derived from wealth.

CAROLINE.

And is it not very injurious to the prosperity of a country that the government should spend its capital?

264 ON REVENUE FROM CAPITAL LENT.

MRS. B.

No doubt; but under some circumstances it is an unavoidable evil. In cases of urgent danger during a war, it is sometimes necessary to raise larger sums of money, and with more expedition, than can be obtained by taxes; recourse is then had to loans, which, if not paid off, accumulate by repetitions, and become at length a heavy national debt, which is a great burden to the country, owing to the taxes that must be raised in order to pay the interest.

We may return to this subject at some future time; let me now ask you whether you fully understand how those who do not employ their capital themselves derive an income from it?

CAROLINE.

Through the agency of others, who, if the capital consists in land, pay them rent, if in money, pay them interest.

MRS. B.

Very well; take care, however, not to be misled by the term *money*, for no man's capital really consists in money. It must consist either in lands or saleable produce, rude or manufactured; capital is merely *estimated* in money. And you cannot, as I said before, have clear ideas on this subject until the nature and use of money have been explained to you.

ON REVENUE FROM CAPITAL LENT. 265

We have now examined all the modes by which men derive a revenue from their capital; there yet remains to be noticed a class of men who are maintained by the revenue of others.

CAROLINE.

Do you mean labourers, who are maintained by wages, and bring a profit to their employers?

MRS. B.

No; these, whom we have distinguished by the name of *productive labourers,* are maintained by the *capital* of others; whilst the class of men to whom I now allude are maintained by the *income* of others. They are labourers, it is true; but of this peculiar description that their labour is totally unproductive; they consume without re-producing: their labour, therefore, can add nothing to the future wealth of the country, and hence they are called *unproductive labourers.*

CAROLINE.

I think I guess what description of people you mean; are not menial servants unproductive labourers?

MRS. B.

Yes, they are; for their labour, however useful, does not augment the riches of the country. A productive labourer is paid out of the value of the

N

266   ON REVENUE FROM CAPITAL LENT.

work he produces: this work remains with his
employer, and may be either accumulated or exchanged for other commodities; but the labour of
the menial servant, so far from increasing the revenue of his master, is an expense to him, his
wages being necessarily paid with the produce of
some other labour.

CAROLINE.

There is no doubt an essential difference between these two kinds of labourers: keeping a
number of workmen is a source of wealth, whilst
keeping a number of servants is a source of expense.

MRS. B.

The one is the employment of capital; the other
the expenditure of income: but the class of unproductive labourers is far from being confined to
menial servants; it extends to all the servants of the
public: actors, singers, dancers, and all those who
are maintained by the productive labour of others,
are of this description.

CAROLINE.

Is it not to be regretted that these people
cannot be compelled to a more useful mode of
employment?

MRS. B.

Their labour though of an unproductive nature,

16

ON REVENUE FROM CAPITAL LENT. 267

is generally useful. Servants, for instance, by relieving the productive labourer of much necessary
work, enable him to do more than he could otherwise accomplish. Thus a man engaged in the employment of a considerable capital can spend his
time to greater advantage, both to himself and to
the community, than in cleaning his own shoes and
cooking his own dinner.

CAROLINE.

The use of servants is evidently attended with
some of the benefits of the division of labour.

MRS. B.

You will probably be surprised to hear that
many of the most valuable ranks of society are in-
cluded in the class of unproductive labourers. The
divine, the physician, the soldier, ministers of
state, and magistrates, are of this description.

CAROLINE.

I did not imagine that the class of unproductive
labourers had been so respectable. And although
their labour is of an unproductive nature, they are,
I think, in many instances more valuable members
of society than some of the productive labourers.
A magistrate, who faithfully administers justice; a
physician, who restores health; a clergyman, who
teaches religion and morals; are certainly of more

N 2

268 ON REVENUE FROM CAPITAL LENT.

essential benefit to society, than the confectioner or the perfumer, or any of those productive labourers who are employed in the fabrication of luxuries.

MRS. B.

No doubt they are. I do not, however, consider luxuries as wholly devoid of advantage. In a future conversation we shall treat of the subject of expenditure; we shall then have an opportunity of examining how far luxury is beneficial, and under what circumstances it is prejudicial to the welfare of society.

CONVERSATION XV.

ON VALUE AND PRICE.

OF THE VALUE OF COMMODITIES. — OF THE DIS-
TINCTION BETWEEN EXCHANGEABLE VALUE AND
PRICE. — OF UTILITY CONSIDERED AS ESSENTIAL
TO VALUE. — OF THE COST OF PRODUCTION, OR
NATURAL VALUE OF COMMODITIES. — OF THE
COMPONENT PARTS OF THE COST OF PRODUC-
TION, RENT, PROFIT, AND WAGES. — OF THEIR
IMPERFECTION AS A MEASURE OF VALUE. — OF
SUPPLY AND DEMAND. — OF THE COMPONENT
PARTS OF THE EXCHANGEABLE VALUE OF COM-
MODITIES. — HIGH PRICE OF COMMODITIES
ARISING FROM SCARCITY. — LOW PRICE ARISING
FROM EXCESSIVE SUPPLY. — LOW PRICE ARISING
FROM DIMINUTION OF COST OF PRODUCTION.

MRS. B.

BEFORE we proceed to the subject of trade, it
is necessary that you should understand what
is meant by the value of commodities.

270   ON VALUE AND PRICE.

CAROLINE.

That cannot be very difficult; it is one of the first things we learn.

MRS. B.

What is learnt at an age when the understanding is not yet well developed, is not always well learnt. What do you understand by the value of commodities?

CAROLINE.

We call things valuable which cost a great deal of money; a diamond necklace, for instance, is very valuable.

MRS. B.

But if, instead of money, you gave in exchange for the necklace silk or cotton goods, tea, sugar, or any other commodity, would you not still call the necklace valuable?

CAROLINE.

Certainly I should; for, supposing the necklace to be worth 1000*l.*, it is immaterial whether I give 1000*l.* in money, or 1000*l.* worth of any thing else in exchange for it.

MRS. B.

The value of a commodity is therefore estimated by the quantity of other things *generally* for which it will exchange, and hence it is frequently called exchangeable value.

ON VALUE AND PRICE. 271

CAROLINE.

Or, in other words, the *price* of a commodity.

MRS. B.

No; *price* does not admit of so extensive a sig-nification. The price of a commodity is its ex-changeable value, estimated in *money only*. It is necessary that you should remember this distinction.

CAROLINE.

But what is it that renders a commodity valu-able? I always thought that its price was the cause of its value; but I begin to perceive that I was mistaken: for things are valuable independently of money; it is their real intrinsic value which induces people to give money for them.

MRS. B.

Certainly; money cannot impart value to com-modities; it is merely the scale by which their value is measured; as a yard measures a piece of cloth.

CAROLINE.

I think the value of things must consist in their utility, for we commonly value a commodity accord-ing to the use we can make of it. Food, clothing, houses, carriages, furniture, have all their several uses.

272 ON VALUE AND PRICE.

MRS. B.

That is very true; yet there are some things of the most general and important utility, such, for instance, as light, air, and water, which, however indispensable to our welfare, have no exchangeable value; nothing is given for them, nor can any thing be obtained in exchange for them.

CAROLINE.

No one will give any thing for what is so plentiful, and so readily obtained that every one may have as much as he requires, without making any sacrifice; but as light, air, and water, are essential even to our existence, surely they should be esteemed valuable.

MRS. B.

In political econony we can consider as valuable such commodities only as are susceptible of receiving a value in exchange; for this purpose the commodity must neither be produced in so unlimited a manner, nor so easily obtained that it may be had for nothing. It must, on the contrary, be in such request that men are willing to give something for it. Thus clothes, houses, furniture, though certainly less useful than light, air, and water, have exchangeable value.

Nature works for us gratuitously; and when she supplies us with articles in such abundance that no

ON VALUE AND PRICE. 273

labour is required to procure them, those articles have not exchangeable value: but no sooner does the labour of man become necessary to procure us the use and enjoyment of any commodity, than that commodity acquires a value; either a price is paid for it in money, or other things are given in exchange for it. Light, air, and water are the free and bountiful gifts of nature, but if man constructs a lamp, we must pay for the light it diffuses: if we are are indebted to his labours for a ventilator, or even a fan, we pay for the air they procure us; and when water is conveyed through pipes into our houses, raised by pumps, or brought to us in any manner by the art of man, a price is paid for it.

CAROLINE.

Workmen must of course be paid for the labour they bestow, whether it be in the production of a commodity, or merely in its conveyance. But it appears to me, Mrs. B., that it is *labour* rather than *utility* that constitutes value, for however we may enjoy the utility, it is the labour we pay for.

MRS. B.

That labour, you will observe, is valuable only if it gives utility to an object. Were a man·to construct or fabricate commodities which had neither utility, curiosity, or beauty, the labour he bestowed upon them would give them no value, and

274 ON VALUE AND PRICE.

if he exposed them for sale, he would find no purchasers.

CAROLINE.

That is true; but the words beauty and curiosity, which you have just used, have raised another
objection in my mind, to utility being essential to
value. I recollect your defining wealth to be
every article of utility, convenience, or luxury;
wealth, no doubt, always implies value, but there
are many articles of luxury that are perfectly devoid of utility, and which are valued either for their
beauty, their curiosity, or their rarity. What, for
instance, is more valuable than diamonds? and yet
they are of no use.

MRS. B.

When we say that utility is essential to value,
the expression is used in its most enlarged sense.
Those who wear diamonds find them useful to gratify
their vanity or pride, or to support their rank in life.
The utility of luxuries must generally be considered
in this point of view. I should, however, tell you,
that Adam Smith distinguishes two kinds of value;
the one arising from utility, the other from what can
be obtained in exchange. He says, " The word
" *value*, it is to be observed, has two different
" meanings: it sometimes expresses the utility
" of some particular object, and sometimes the
" power of purchasing other goods which the pos-
" session of that object conveys. The one may be

ON VALUE AND PRICE. 275

" called *value in use*, the other *value in exchange.*
" The things which have the greatest value in use,
" have frequently little or no value in exchange;
" and, on the contrary, those that have the greatest
" value in exchange, have frequently little or no
" value in use. Nothing is more useful than water,
" but it will purchase scarce any thing; scarce
" any thing can be had in exchange for it. A dia-
" mond, on the contrary, has scarce any value in
" use, but a very great quantity of other goods may
" frequently be had in exchange for it."

Later writers on political economy, whose opinion
I have followed, have rather gone farther than
differed in opinion from Adam Smith, by tracing
all value to the same source, *utility,* a doctrine
which leads to the conclusion that it is the application of the labour of man to commodities which
gives them *exchangeable value.*

The exchangeable value of a commodity estimated in money, we have said, constitutes its *price.*
This generally corresponds with the cost of production of the commodity, that is to say, to the
expense that has been bestowed on a commodity in
order to bring it to a saleable state. You can tell
me now, I suppose, why this book-case is more
valuable than that table?

CAROLINE.

Because more workmanship has been bestowed

276   ON VALUE AND PRICE.

upon it, therefore more labour must be paid for. But, Mrs. B., the money which this book-case cost does not all go to the workmen who made it; the materials of which it is made must be paid for: the upholsterer who sold it derives a profit from it.

MRS. B.

It was his capital which purchased the raw materials, which furnished the tools, and set the journeymen to work; without this aid the book-case could not have been made. The price of commodities is the reward not only of those who prepared or fabricated them, but also of every productive labourer who has been employed in bringing them to a saleable state, for each of these concurred in giving value to the commodity.

We have formerly observed that no work can be undertaken without the use of capital, as well to maintain the labourer as to supply him with the implements to work with, and the materials to work upon. Subsisting upon this maintenance, and working with these implements, he is to transform the useless trunk of a tree into a useful piece of furniture, which acquires value in proportion as it acquires utility. The profit of capital is, therefore, a component part of the value of a commodity, as well as the wages of labour. There remains yet a third component part of the value of a commodity, which a little reflection will, I think, enable you to discover.

ON VALUE AND PRICE. 277

CAROLINE.

Agricultural produce must, besides the wages of labour, and profit of capital, pay the rent of the land on which it is raised. But this will not be the case with manufactured goods.

MRS. B.

The raw materials for manufactures are all, or almost all, the produce of land, and consequently must defray the expense of rent, the same as corn or hay. But rent does not enter into the price of commodities in the same manner as the profit of capital, or the wages of labour, because, as you may recollect, rent is the *effect*, not the *cause* of the high price of commodities. Dr. Smith observes, that " high or low wages are the causes of high or low " price; high or low rent is the effect of it. It is " because high or low wages or profit must be " made, in order to bring a particular commodity " to market, that its price is high or low. But it " is because its price is high or low, a great deal " more, or very little more, or no more than what " is sufficient to pay those wages and profit that it " affords a high rent, or a low rent, or no rent at all."

Let us now observe how the value of a commodity resolves itself into these three component parts. Take, for instance, a load of hay; its price pays, first, the wages of the labourer who cut down the grass and made it into hay; then the profits of the

278   ON VALUE AND PRICE.

farmer who sells it; and, lastly, the rent of the field
in which it grew. This, therefore, constitutes the
whole cost of production of the load of hay; and
may be called its *natural value*.

CAROLINE.

Pray let me try whether I could trace the various
payments made to the several persons concerned in
the production of a loaf of bread. — Its price must
first pay the wages of the journeyman baker who
made it; then the profits of capital of the master
baker who sells it; next the wages of the miller
who ground the corn, and the profits of the master
who employs him; afterwards the wages of the
several husbandmen who cultivated the field of
corn; the profits of the farmer; and lastly, a portion of the rent of his farm.

MRS. B.

Extremely well. Thus you see that the value of
a commodity is composed of three parts, *rent,
profit,* and *wages;* the rent of the proprietor of the
land, the profits of the several employers of capital,
and the wages of the various labourers who give it
value by rendering it useful, whence it becomes an
object of desire, and consequently a saleable commodity.

It sometimes happens that the proprietor of
land, and farmer, and even the labourer, are united

ON VALUE AND PRICE. 279

in one individual. We have already observed, that in many parts of America the cultivators of the land are both proprietors and labourers, and reap the reward of rent, profit, and wages.

CAROLINE.

And in this country a cottager who possesses a little garden cultivated by his own hands, and of which he brings the produce to market, likewise concentrates in himself all the advantages of proprietor, capitalist, and labourer; for he sells his vegetables for the same price as a market gardener, who has to deduct from the price the rent of the garden and the wages of the labourer.

MRS. B.

But he is not, therefore, the greater gainer, for if he has no rent to pay, it is because he has laid out a capital in the purchase of the land; and if he pays no wages, it is because he works himself, and employs that labour which might otherwise bring him wages: then some capital is used to purchase garden tools, manure, or whatever may be requisite for the culture of his garden.

CAROLINE.

I think I now understand perfectly well how rent, profit, and wages enter into the value of every commodity. I may say, for instance, so much rent,

280 ON VALUE AND PRICE.

profit, and wages has been expended in the production of this carp t, and therefore I must pay a sum of money for it, if I wish to purchase it; but how am I thence to infer what sum of money it is worth?

MRS. B.

By applying the same scale or measure to estimate the value of money, that you have applied to estimate the value of the carpet. Examine what quantity of rent, profit, and wages was bestowed upon the production of the money, and you will be able to ascertain how much of it should be given in exchange for the carpet, or in other words, what the carpet is worth in money. I paid 20 guineas for this carpet; I conclude therefore that the cost of production of the carpet is equal to the cost of production of 20 guineas.

CAROLINE.

But it would be impossible to calculate with any degree of accuracy the quantity of rent, profit, and wages which a commodity cost, and still less that of the gold or silver for which it is sold.

MRS. B.

Nor is it necessary to enter into this calculation; it is by long experience only that the world forms an estimation of the relative value of different commodities, sufficiently accurate for the purposes of

ON VALUE AND PRICE. 281

exchange. The calculations to which we have been alluding, though true in principle, are by no means susceptible of being brought into common use.

CAROLINE.

Yet when barter was first introduced, one savage might say to another: It is not just to offer me a hare, which is the produce of a day's hunting, in exchange for a bow which I have spent three days in making; I will not part with it unless you give me also the fruit which you gathered in the woods yesterday, and the fish you caught the day before; in short, I will not exchange the produce of my toil and trouble, for less than the produce of an equal share of your toil and trouble.' And surely this is much more clear and simple reasoning than to say that the bow is worth so much money?

MRS. B.

To a savage unacquainted with money it certainly is; but I believe that in the present times people understand better the value of a commodity estimated in money.

CAROLINE.

But if it were practicable to calculate with precision the quantity of rent, profit, and wages which had been expended on the production of commodities, *that*, I suppose, would constitute an accurate measure of their value.

282   ON VALUE AND PRICE.

MRS. B.

No; because there are other circumstances, which, as we shall presently observe, affect the value of commodities. Besides, it would be impossible to calculate with any degree of accuracy the cost of production of a commodity, since rent, profit, and wages are all liable to vary in their own value; and we cannot adopt as a *fixed* standard, a measure which is itself subject to change. If we were to measure a piece of cloth by a yard measure, which lengthened at one season of the year and shortened at another, it would not enable us to ascertain the length of the piece of cloth. Now rent varies much according to the situation of the land, and the nature of the soil: profit, according to the abundance or scarcity of capital; but nothing fluctuates more than the wages of labour; it differs not only in different countries, but even in the same town, according to the strength, the skill, and the ingenuity of the labourer. A skilful artisan may not only do more work, but may do it in a superior manner, and he will require payment in the articles of his workmanship, not only for the labour he has bestowed on them, but also for the pains he has taken, and the time he has spent in acquiring his skill; the wages of a superior workman are for this reason much higher than those of a common labourer. Since therefore neither the quantity nor the quality of the labour bestowed on

ON VALUE AND PRICE. 283

a commodity can be determined by the number of days or hours employed in producing it, time is not a measure of the value of labour; we must take into account the degrees of skill and attention which the work may require, as also the healthy, pleasant or unpleasant, easy or severe nature of the employment, all of which are to be paid accordingly.

CAROLINE.

Thus the bow which employed the savage during three days, might be worth twice the labour of the other savage during the same period of time; for much less skill is required to be a huntsman, than to be a fabricator of bows and arrows.

MRS. B.

On the other hand, we find that eight hours of the labour of a coal-heaver will be paid much higher than the same number of hours of a weaver's labour, because although the latter requires more skill, the first is much more severe and unpleasant labour. But the weaver will receive greater wages than a farmer's labourer, because the work of the latter is both more healthy and requires less skill.

Now since it is impossible to enter into a calculation of all the shades of these various difficulties, rent, profit, and labour can never form an accurate standard of value.

284 ON VALUE AND PRICE.

CAROLINE.

They have at least enabled me to acquire a much more clear and precise idea of value than I had before.

MRS. B.

Your idea of value is however yet far from being complete; for there are, as I have just observed, other circumstances to be considered independantly of the cost of production, which materially influence the value of commodities. In a besieged town, for instance, provisions have frequently risen to twenty or thirty times their natural value, and have increased proportionally in price.

CAROLINE.

Their increased price in this case is owing merely to the scarcity, not to any increase of value, for were they as plentiful as usual they would sell at the usual price.

MRS. B.

Their high price is the consequence of their increased value, for they would not only sell for a greater sum of money, but also exchange for a greater quantity of any commodities, except such as are convertible into food.

CAROLINE.

Unless perhaps it were gunpowder, or any kind of ammunition, which in a besieged town might be as much in request as food.

ON VALUE AND PRICE. 285

MRS. B.

Certainly; in that case ammunition would rise in value as well as provisions.

Plenty and scarcity are then circumstances which considerably affect the value of commodities. Tell me whether you understand the meaning of the words, plenty, and scarcity?

CAROLINE.

Yes, surely; when there is a great quantity of any thing, it is said to be plentiful; — when very little, it is scarce.

MRS. B.

If there was very little corn in a desert island, should you say there was a scarcity of corn there?

CAROLINE.

No; because as there would be no one to eat it, none would be wanted; and scarcity implies an insufficiency.

MRS. B.

And when a few years ago there was a scarcity of corn in this country, do you think that the whole of the island produced only a small quantity?

CAROLINE.

No, not positively a small quantity, but a smaller quantity than was required to supply the whole of the population of the country with bread.

286 ON VALUE AND PRICE.

MRS. B.

Plenty and scarcity are therefore relative terms: a scarcity neither implies a small quantity, nor plenty a large one; but the first implies an insufficiency, or less than is wanted; the last as much, or perhaps more than is required. When there is plenty, the supply of the commodity being at least equal to the demand, every one who can pay the cost of its production will be able to purchase it. If, on the contrary, the commodity is scarce, some of these must go without it, and the apprehension of this privation produces competition amongst those who are desirous of buying the commodity, and this raises its value above the cost of production.

CAROLINE.

This then is the cause of the rise in the price of provisions in a besieged town?

MRS. B.

Yes; or during a famine, or in any case of scarcity. Whenever, on the contrary, the supply exceeds the demand, the price will fall below the natural value of the commodity.

You see, therefore, that the *natural value* and *exchangeable value* do not always coincide.

The exchangeable value consists of the natural value, subject either to augmentation or diminution, in proportion as the commodity is scarce or plentiful.

ON VALUE AND PRICE. 287

CAROLINE.

When you say that the supply exceeds the demand, you do not, I suppose, mean that there is more of the article than the whole of the population can consume or use; but more than can be consumed by those who can afford to pay its natural *price?*

MRS. B.

Certainly. Those, therefore, who have the commodity to dispose of, rather than allow a surplus to be left unsold, will lower its price, so as to render it attainable to a class of people who could not otherwise afford to purchase it. Hence the demand is increased, and becomes by degrees proportioned to the redundant supply.

To illustrate this let us suppose that, by the breaking out of a continental war, our foreign trade should meet with such obstructions, that great part of the manufactured goods we had prepared for exportation will remain at home and overstock the market. The supply in this case exceeding the demand, the goods will fall in price below their natural value, in order to attract a greater number of purchasers; the consumption will thus be increased, but the manufacturers and dealers, having been obliged to sell the goods for less than they cost to produce, will be losers instead of gainers by their industry.

288　ON VALUE AND PRICE.

CAROLINE.

I recollect that callicoes and English muslins were much cheaper during the last war than they are at present; and the shopkeepers then said that, at the price at which they sold them, they did not pay for the workmanship, independently of the materials.

MRS. B.

The cheapness of these goods, although it arose from plenty, so far from being a sign of prosperity, entailed ruin on the manufacturers and their labourers.

CAROLINE.

But you observed that if the price of a commodity would not defray all the expenses of rent, profit, and wages, it would not be produced?

MRS. B.

In the case we have alluded to, the fall in price did not take place till after the production of the commodities; and the expense of labour having been already bestowed on them, it is better to sell them at any price than to lose entirely their value. But the manufacturers would in future take care to fabricate a smaller quantity, in consequence of which many of their labourers would be deprived of work, and part of their capital be thrown out of employ.

Plenty and cheapness are really advantageous

ON VALUE AND PRICE. 289

only when they arise from a diminution of the cost of production. Thus when the use of any new machinery, or other improvement in the process of labour, enables farmers or manufacturers to produce commodities at less expense, the reduction of price is beneficial both to the producer and the consumer; to the former, because cheapness increases the number of purchasers; to the latter, because he obtains the commodity at less expense.

CAROLINE.

But when nature gives us a superabundant supply of corn, the fall in price it occasions is not, I suppose, attended with disadvantage?

MRS. B.

No, not in general; because the farmer, if not a gainer, is at least usually repaid, by the abundance of his crops, for the reduction of price; but if (from whatever cause) he should be under the necessity of selling below the cost of production, the low price is no longer a benefit; for the evil arising from the check given to industry far surpasses the immediate advantage of cheapness of corn. The farmers and their labourers would be the first sufferers; but it is probable that, in the end, the whole community would severely feel the effects the following season.

O

290 ON VALUE AND PRICE.

CAROLINE.

True; for farmers would grow cautious, and cultivate less wheat, in order that it might not sell below its natural value; and, whilst they would be endeavouring exactly to proportion the supply to the demand, the season might chance to be less productive than usual, so as to occasion a scarcity of corn, which would be followed by a rise in the price of bread above the expense of its production.

MRS. B.

Thus, you see, when the supply equals the demand, the commodity is sold for its natural value, the producer making just the usual rate of profit. If the supply exceed the demand, it is sold below that value, the competition of producers or dealers, to dispose of their goods, lowering the price. If the supply is less than the demand, the competition of purchasers raises the price of the commodity above its natural value, and the dealers make extraordinary profits.

CAROLINE.

It must then be the interest of the farmer that corn should sell above its natural value; and the interest of the people that it should sell below it?

MRS. B.

If we excend our views beyond the present moment, it will appear that the interest of the pro-

ON VALUE AND PRICE. 291

ducer and consumer of any commodity are the same; and that it is for the advantage of both that the price and natural value should coincide. If the consumer pay less for a commodity than its cost of production, the producers will take care to diminish the quantity in future, in order that competition may raise the price; for they could not, without exposing themselves to ruin, continue to supply the public with a commodity which did not repay them. If, on the other hand, the consumers pay more for an article than its natural value, the producers will be encouraged by their great profits to increase the supply, and the price will consequently fall until it is reduced to the natural value.

CAROLINE.

I do not understand why the producers of a commodity should increase the supply, if the consequence is to lessen their profits?

MRS. B.

We are arguing under the supposition that competition is free and open, and in that case, you know, capital will immediately flow towards any branch of industry that affords extraordinary profits. If, therefore, the original producers of the profitable commodity did not increase the supply, they would soon meet with competitors, which

292 ON VALUE AND PRICE.

would compel them to lower their price without increasing their sale.

" Price," Mr. Buchanan observes, with great happiness of expression, " is the nicely poized balance " with which nature weighs and distributes to her " children their respective shares of her gifts, to " prevent waste, and make them last out till re- " produced."

We have dwelt a long time upon the subject of value; and we may now conclude, that though a fluctuation in the exchangeable value of commodities may be occasioned by various circumstances, it will seldom deviate much from the natural value, to which (when the employment of capital is left open) the exchangeable value will always tend to approximate.

CONVERSATION XVI.

ON MONEY.

OF THE USE OF MONEY AS A MEDIUM OF EXCHANGE. — OF COINING. — USE OF MONEY AS A STANDARD OF VALUE. — OF THE VARIATION OF THE EXCHANGEABLE VALUE OF GOLD AND SILVER. — IN WHAT MANNER IT AFFECTS THE PRICE OF COMMODITIES. — OF NOMINAL AND REAL CHEAPNESS. — WHAT CLASSES OF PEOPLE ARE AFFECTED BY THE VARIATION IN THE VALUE OF GOLD AND SILVER. — HOW FAR MONEY CONSTITUTES A PART OF THE WEALTH OF A COUNTRY. — OF THE EXPORTATION OF MONEY. — OF THE MEANS BY WHICH THE VALUE OF THE PRECIOUS METALS EQUALIZES ITSELF IN ALL PARTS OF THE CIVILIZED WORLD.

MRS. B.

HAVING obtained some knowledge of the nature of value, we may now proceed to examine the use of money.

o 3

294 ON MONEY.

Without this general medium of exchange, trade could never have made any considerable progress; for as the subdivisions of labour increased, insuperable difficulties would be experienced in the adjustment of accounts. The butcher perhaps would want bread, at a time that the baker did not want meat; or they might each be desirous of exchanging their respective commodities, but these might not be of equal value.

CAROLINE.

It would be very difficult, I believe, at any time to make such reckonings exactly balance each other.

MRS. B.

In order to avoid this inconvenience, it became necessary for every man to be provided with a commodity which would be willingly taken at all times in exchange for goods. Hence arose that useful representative of commodities, *money*, which, being exclusively appropriated to exchanges, every one was ready either to receive or to part with for that purpose.

CAROLINE.

When the baker did not want meat he would take the butcher's money in exchange for his bread, because that money would enable him to obtain from others what he did want.

ON MONEY.

MRS. B.

Various commodities have been employed to answer the purpose of money. Mr. Salt, in his Travels in Abyssinia, informs us, that wedges of salt are used in that country for small currency, coined money being extremely scarce. A wedge of rock-salt, weighing between two and three pounds, was estimated at 1-30th of a dollar.

CAROLINE.

How extremely inconvenient such a bulky article must be as a substitute for money; the carriage of it to any distance would cost almost as much as the salt was worth.

MRS. B.

A commodity of this nature could be used for the purpose of money in those countries only where very few mercantile transactions take place, and where labour is very cheap. Tobacco, shells, and a great variety of other articles, have been used at different times, and in different countries, as a medium of exchange; but nothing has ever been found to answer this end so well as the metals. They are the least perishable of all commodities; they are susceptible, by the process of fusion, of being divided into any number of parts without loss, and being the heaviest, they are the least bulky of all bodies. All these properties render them peculiarly

296   ON MONEY.

appropriate for the purposes of commerce and
circulation.

CAROLINE.

The use of metals as money must be very ancient,
for mention is made in history of the iron coin of
the Greeks, and the copper coin of the Romans.

MRS. B.

Nor are gold and silver coins of modern date;
but they were scarce before the discovery of the
American mines. The first gold coins were struck
at Rome, about 200 years before Christ. Those
of silver about 65 years earlier. Previous to that
period the *as*, which was of copper, was the only
coin in common use.

CAROLINE.

It is said in the Bible that Abraham gave 400
shekels of silver for the purchase of the field of
Machpelah, to bury Sarah in. Was that, do you
suppose, coined money?

MRS. B.

No; I believe there was no coined money of so
ancient a date as the time of Abraham. The metals were originally used for the purpose of money
in bars; and you may recollect that Abraham
weighed the silver for the purchase; which would
have been unnecessary had it been coined. Before

ON MONEY. 297

the invention of coining, the use of the metals as a medium of exchange was attended with great inconvenience; it being necessary not only to weigh, but also to assay the metal, to ascertain both its quantity and its degree of purity.

The invention of coining superseded this inconvenience; for coining money is affixing to a piece of metal a particular stamp or impression, which declares that it is of a certain weight and quality. Thus the impression on a guinea signifies that it is a piece of gold of a certain fineness, weighing 107 grains nearly.

CAROLINE.

Money must also be of great use in fixing the value of commodities; before its introduction the butcher and the baker might dispute which was worth most, the joint of meat or the loaf of bread which they wished to exchange.

MRS. B.

Yes, money became useful not only as a medium of exchange, but also as a common measure of value. You will learn hereafter that it is not, any more than labour, a very accurate measure, when the values of one period are compared with the values of another distant period; but for the common purposes of traffic it answers sufficiently well.

Previous to the invention of money, men were much at a loss how to estimate the value of their

o 5

298   ON MONEY.

property. In order to express that value they were
necessarily obliged to compare it to something else,
and having no settled standard, they would naturally
choose objects of known and established value. Accordingly we read both in Scripture and in the ancient poets, of a man's property being worth so many
oxen and so many flocks and herds. Dr. Clarke
informs us, that even at the present day the Calmuc
Tartars reckon the value of a coat of mail from six
to eight, and up to the value of fifty horses. In
civilized countries every one estimates his capital by
the quantity of money it is worth; — he does not
really possess the sum in money, but his property,
whatever be its nature or kind, is equivalent to
such a sum of money.

CAROLINE.

For instance, a man who is worth a capital of
20,000*l.* may perhaps not be possessed of 20*l.* in
money; but his property whether land or commodities, if sold, would bring him 20,000*l.*

When gold is brought into this country, pray
how is it paid for? Something must be given in
exchange for it; and yet that something cannot be
money?

MRS. B.

Certainly not. A bullion merchant would derive
no advantage from a trade in which he would be
employed in exchanging a certain weight of gold

ON MONEY. 299

and silver in one country, for a similar weight of gold and silver in another country, he would lose not only all the profits of trade, but the expenses of the freight, &c.; so that in fact he would be exchanging 100*l.*, for 90*l.*, or 95*l.*

We pay for gold and silver in woollen cloths, hardware, callicoes, and linens, and a variety of other commodities.

CAROLINE.

Then we purchase gold with goods just as we purchase goods with gold?

MRS. B.

Exactly; those who take our goods in exchange for gold bullion, buy goods with gold; only as the gold is not coined, it may rather be called an exchange of commodities than a purchase.

CAROLINE.

And if the mines should prove less productive than usual, or any circumstance should render gold scarce, and thus raise its exchangeable value, we must export a greater quantity of goods to exchange for the same quantity of gold?

MRS. B.

Undoubtedly. The natural value of gold bullion, like that of any other commodity, may be estimated

o 6

300 ON MONEY.

by the rent, profit, and labour bestowed upon it;
and its exchangeable value fluctuates according to
the proportion of the supply to the demand. This
fluctuation, however, can be discovered only by the
greater or smaller quantity of goods for which the
same quantity of gold will exchange. For as gold
and silver may be bought with any kind of goods,
they are not susceptible of a standard of value like
that of other commodities which is estimated in one
particular article — money.

CAROLINE.

As gold and silver are the standard of value of
all other commodities, all other commodities, I conceive, must be affected by an alteration in the
exchangeable value of gold and silver?

MRS. B.

And this is the reason why money is not an accurate standard of the value of commodities. For
if money by its plenty diminish in value, it enhances
the price of commodities, and renders them dearer.
Whilst if money by its scarcity increase in value,
it lowers the *price* of commodities, that is to say,
their *exchangeable value estimated in money,* and
renders them cheaper.

To illustrate this by an example : let us suppose
the supply of bread to be exactly equal to the
demand, so that its exchangeable and natural value

ON MONEY. 301

should coincide; in what manner would a scarcity of money affect it?

CAROLINE.

A deficiency of any article raises its exchangeable value, and consequently its price, above its natural value: thus a deficiency of gold or silver would make a smaller quantity exchange for the same quantity of goods as before; and therefore a loaf of bread would sell for less money, or, in other words, would be cheaper.

MRS. B.

Yes; and not only bread, but meat, clothes, furniture, houses; in short, every thing would be cheaper, in consequence of the scarcity of the precious metals.

CAROLINE.

It would appear then that a scarcity of money is advantageous to a country by rendering things cheap?

MRS. B.

When the cheapness of commodities arises from that plenty which results from a reduction of the cost of production, it is very advantageous; but not when it proceeds from a scarcity of money. In the latter case, the supply not being increased, commodities are cheaper, without any alteration in their general exchangeable value. They may,

302 ON MONEY.

therefore, be considered rather as nominally than really cheaper. If, for instance, a loaf of bread should sell for a penny, though there should not be a single loaf more in the country than when it sold for a shilling, the cheapness would not make bread more plentiful.

CAROLINE.

But if the price of bread were so low as a penny, though the supply should not be increased, the labouring classes would increase their consumption of it so considerably as to produce a scarcity, if not a famine, before the next harvest. This *nominal,* or I would call it *false,* cheapness, must therefore be prejudicial instead of being beneficial to a country.

MRS. B.

The consequence you have drawn from it is erroneous; for the labouring classes would not be able to purchase a greater quantity of bread than usual, owing to the scarcity of money. The wages of labour would not be exempted from the general fall in price which this scarcity would produce: the labourers, as well as the bread they eat, would be paid in pence instead of shillings, and their power of purchasing bread would neither be increased nor diminished.

CAROLINE.

True; I did not consider that. I suppose then

ON MONEY. 303

that if the contrary case occurred, that is, if the quantity of money were considerably augmented, either by the discovery of a mine in the country, or by any other means, a general rise in the price of commodities would be the consequence?

MRS. B.

Undoubtedly; but without producing any scarcity. Therefore though commodities would rise in price, their value would not be increased, and the commodities being the same in quantity, the public would be equally well supplied; but as money fell or became depreciated in value from its excess, fewer commodities would be given in exchange for the same sum; or more money must be paid for the same commodity. A loaf of bread might cost two shillings instead of one, but as the wages of labour would at the same time be doubled, the labourer would suffer no privation from the increase of price. You now see the propriety of making the distinction between the *value* and the *price* of a commodity.

It is very possible for the price of a commodity to rise, whilst its value falls. A loaf of bread may rise in price from one to two shillings; but money may be so depreciated by excess that *two* shillings may not procure so much meat, butter, and cheese as *one* shilling did before; therefore a loaf of bread would no longer exchange for so much of those commodities, and its exchangeable value compared with other things generally would have fallen; while its *price* or exchangeable value estimated in *money only* would have risen.

CAROLINE.

And when the price alters, how can we distinguish whether it is the goods or the money which changes in value?

MRS. B.

There is no point so difficult to ascertain as a variation of value, because we have no fixed standard measure of value; neither nature nor art furnishes us with a commodity whose value is incapable of change; and such alone would afford us an accurate standard of value.

CAROLINE.

How useful such a commodity would be; for we cannot estimate the value of any thing without comparing it with the value of something else; and if that something else is liable to variation, it is but of little assistance to us: it is supporting the earth by the elephant, and the elephant by the tortoise; but we still remain in the same dilemma. When a man says he is worth 500 acres of land, we can form scarcely any judgment of his wealth, unless he tells us what the acres are worth; his land may be situated in the most fruitful parts of

ON MONEY. 305

England, or it may be in the wilds of America, or the deserts of Arabia; and if he values his land in money, and says my acres are worth, or would sell for 1000*l.*, we can form some notion of their real value, but not an accurate one; for we do not know what is the real value of the money, whether it is plentiful or scarce, cheap or dear; nor can we ever learn it unless we had some invariable standard by which to measure it.

MRS. B.

Now supposing money to be depreciated in value 25 per cent., and that the expense of manufacturing a piece of muslin, from some improvement in the process, fell from four to three shillings a-yard, at what price would the muslin sell?

CAROLINE.

It would retain its original price of four shillings, though it would really be cheaper; for the diminution of the value of money would exactly counterbalance the diminution of the cost of production of the muslin.

MRS. B.

Very well. And if, on the contrary, money should become scarce at the same time as the cost of production of a commodity diminished, then these two causes, acting in conjunction instead of opposition, the commodity would be both nominally and really cheaper.

306 ON MONEY.

CAROLINE.

The muslin in that case would fall from four to two shillings a-yard.

MRS. B.

In order still further to reduce the price of the muslin, we may suppose the supply to exceed the demand, so as to oblige the manufacturer to sell it below its cost of production; and thus the price might fall so low as one shilling or even sixpence a-yard.

But of all these reductions of price, that which proceeds from a diminished cost of production is the only one from which general advantage is derived. That arising from the depreciation of money producing merely a nominal cheapness; and that which results from an excess of supply being decidedly an evil, inasmuch as it creates distress and discourages industry.

CAROLINE.

It appears then, from what you have said, that an increase or diminution of money in a country does not really affect the pecuniary circumstances of any one?

MRS. B.

I beg your pardon; all classes of men are temporarily affected when the change is abrupt; because the due level is not immediately ascertained, and until that takes place the pressure falls un-

ON MONEY. 307

equally. But independently of this, there are many classes of people who would be very sensibly and permanently injured by an alteration in the exchangeable value of money.

Let us suppose, for instance, that the proprietor of a field lets it for a long lease at a rent of 20*l.* a-year; and that some years afterwards, money having risen in value, and he being in want of hay for his horses, purchases the crop of hay for 15*l.* In this case the landlord will continue to receive 20*l.* a-year for the rent, and yet pay but 15*l.* for the produce, so that the farmer will lose 5*l.*, besides the profits of his capital. Is not this a very serious injury?

CAROLINE.

No doubt; and this would be the case with all leases; for it is immaterial to whom the farmer sells his crops; if the market price has fallen he must be a loser.

MRS. B.

Yes. Were money raised to double its former value, the rent would purchase double the quantity of commodities that it did before; for 100*l.* in money would exchange for a quantity of goods which was reckoned worth 200*l.* previous to the alteration; so that rent, though nominally the same, would in reality be doubled, and it would be so much unjustly taken out of the pocket of the tenant to put into that of the landlord.

308   ON MONEY.

CAROLINE.

This evil, however, admits of a remedy when a new lease is made?

MRS. B.

True; but should the old one have several years to run the farmer may be ruined first; and though it is true it does not violate any law, it is a manifest infraction on the security of property, which we have observed to be the foundation of all wealth, and the strongest motive for its accumulation. There is no more active and steady stimulus to industry than the certainty of reaping the fruits of our labour.

CAROLINE.

Then I suppose that when money is depreciated in value, in consequence of being more plentiful, the case would be reversed; the farmer would be benefited and the landlord would be the loser; for the rent would not be really worth so much as it was before?

MRS. B.

Undoubtedly. Another class of people who are materially affected by an alteration in the value of money, are the unproductive labourers. Their pay is generally a regular stipend, not liable to the same variation as the wages of productive labourers. The pay of the army and navy, of all the officers under government, and of the learned professions, is fixed; those persons must therefore suffer all the

ON MONEY. 309

evil, or enjoy all the benefit arising from an alteration in the value of money.

CAROLINE.

The higher classes of the unproductive labourers might be able to support the hardship resulting from a depreciation of the value of money; but how can the common sailor or soldier do so? It is absolutely necessary that their pay should enable them to procure a suitable subsistence.

MRS. B.

They are usually paid, partly in money and partly in provisions and clothing, and are not therefore such sufferers by a depreciation of money as they would be if paid entirely in currency. It has nevertheless been found necessary of late to augment the pay of both army and navy.

CAROLINE.

The value of money has then fallen?

MRS. B.

Yes, it has; but I must defer explaining the reason of this fall till our next interview. A third class of people who are considerably injured by a depreciation of the value of money, are those who have lent money at interest for a long period of time, persons who live on annuities, and parti-

310   ON MONEY.

cularly the stockholders in the public funds. Not
only is the interest they receive depreciated, but
also the value of their capital. The interest they
receive for their stock remains nominally the same,
whatever diminution may have taken place in the
value of money; and their income being thus apparently stationary, they partake in the general
disadvantage of the rise of prices, without being
enabled to avail themselves of the compensation
arising from the greater abundance of money.
Professional men, and all those who receive sala-
ries, have ultimately the remedy of an increase of
pay; but the stockholder has no resource: his
income wastes away, and he perceives his means of
procuring his accustomed enjoyments gradually
diminish, without being able to trace the source
from whence the evil springs; for as his income
remains nominally the same, he is not aware of any
diminution of wealth.

CAROLINE.

How very much I have been mistaken in my
idea of money! Instead of being the only, or at
least the principal article which (as I thought) constituted wealth; it seems, on the contrary, to be
the only one which is unworthy of that title, since
it does not contribute to the riches of a country.
An excess of money renders other things dear; a
deficiency of it makes them cheap; but it appears

15

ON MONEY.

to me that a country is not one atom the richer for all the money it possesses. Money therefore, I think, cannot be called wealth, but merely its representative, like the counters at cards; and its chief use seems to consist in its affording us a convenient medium of exchange, and a useful, though imperfect standard of value.

MRS. B.

Money cannot with justice be compared to counters, for it is not, like them, a sign or representative of value, but really possesses (or ought to possess) the value for which it exchanges. A banknote, which has no intrinsic value, is simply a sign of value; but when you purchase goods for a guinea, you give a piece of gold of equivalent value in exchange.

In order to judge whether money forms any part of the wealth of a nation, let us refer to our definition of wealth. I believe we said that every article, either of utility or luxury, constituted wealth. Now I leave you to judge whether money, considered either as a medium of exchange, or as a standard of value, is not eminently useful; since by facilitating the circulation of commodities it indirectly contributes to their multiplication.

CAROLINE.

That is true certainly with regard to the money

312 ON MONEY.

actually required for circulation; but should it exceed that sum, the surplus would be of no value to us.

MRS. B.

The same might be said of a superfluous quantity of any kind of wealth; more tables and chairs, or a greater quantity of gowns and coats than are wanted, would be equally useless, and would equally be depreciated in value.

CAROLINE.

But then we could export such commodities, and exchange them for goods which we did want.

MRS. B.

And why should we not do the same with money? When we have more money than is required for the purpose of circulation, we should export it, by purchasing foreign goods; without this resource, a superfluity of money is perfectly useless, and will no more contribute to the production of wealth, than a superfluous number of mills would contribute to the production of flour.

CAROLINE.

I had always imagined that the more money a country possessed, the more affluent was its condition.

ON MONEY.

313

MRS. B.

And that usually is the case. The error lies in mistaking the cause for the effect. A great quantity of money is necessary to circulate a great quantity of commodities. Rich flourishing countries require abundance of money, and possess the means of obtaining it; but this abundance is the *consequence*, not the *cause* of their wealth, which consists in the commodities circulated, rather than in the circulating medium. Specie, we have just said, constitutes wealth, so far as it is required for circulation; but if a country possess one guinea more than is necessary for that purpose, the wealth which purchased that guinea has been thrown away.

CAROLINE.

Yet what a common observation it is, that plenty of money animates the industry of a country, and encourages commerce; and this seems to be proved by the miserable and barbarous state of Europe previous to the discovery of the American mines.

MRS. B.

The discovery of America was certainly a very efficient cause in rousing the industry of Europe from the state of stagnation into which it was sunk by ignorance and barbarism But had America possessed no mines, I doubt whether the advantages we have derived from our connection with that

P

314   ON MONEY.

country would not have been equally great: we could easily find a substitute for the specie with which she supplies us, but never for the abundance and variety of wealth which she is incessantly pouring in upon us. The increase of European comforts, of affluence, of luxury, is attributed to the influx of the treasures of the new world — and with reason; but those treasures are the sugar, the coffee, the indigo, the tobacco, the drugs, &c. which America exports, to obtain which we must send her commodities that have been produced by the employment of our poor. Gold and silver, though they have greatly excited our avarice and ambition, have eventually contributed but little to stimulate our industry.

It is not to the multiplication of the precious metals that we are indebted for our improved agriculture, our prosperous commerce, and the variety and excellence of our manufactures; nor do I believe that it was their scarcity which deprived our ancestors of these advantages. It was because they were ignorant and barbarous, and that we are comparatively enlightened and civilized; — comparatively I may indeed say, for error is still active in retarding the progress of improvement, and this is no where more evident than in the anxiety of governments to prevent the exportation of specie, although it is now above thirty years since Adam Smith fully proved the impolicy of this prohibition.

ON MONEY.

CAROLINE.

If the exportation of specie be prohibited, the only use that can be made of a superfluous quantity of it, is to melt it down and re-convert it into bullion.

MRS. B.

But melting the coin is, in this country, equally illegal. A superfluous quantity of money, therefore, (were these laws never infringed) would be necessarily added to the circulation, and depreciate the value of the whole.

How different is the situation of a country where no such prohibitory laws exist! There, no sooner does money accumulate so as to occasion a depreciation of its value, or, in other words, an advance in the price of commodities, than the merchants of that country export specie, and purchase with it foreign goods; while at the same time foreign merchants send their goods to the country where prices have risen, and exchange them, not for other goods, which are dear, but for money, which is cheap.

CAROLINE.

That is to say, they will sell, but not purchase?

MRS. B.

Precisely. — it is thus that a country is drained of its superfluous specie; as this traffic goes on, money rises in value, commodities fall in price, and foreign

P 2

316 ON MONEY.

merchants again exchange their goods for commodities of the country, instead of receiving payment for it in specie.

No apprehension need therefore be entertained of ill consequences arising either from the melting down or exporting the coin of the country. This exportation will take place secretly whenever there is a superfluity, however severe the law may be against it; the only difference is, that instead of being carried on in an open and regular manner by merchants of respectability, it is thrown into the hands of men of despicable character, who are tempted by extraordinary profits to engage into this illicit traffic.

Could Spain and Portugal, countries which receive all the precious metals imported from America to Europe, have carried into effect the absurd restrictive laws, by which they attempted to keep their gold and silver at home, those metals would eventually have become of little more value to them than lead and copper.

If you have understood what I have said, you will now be able to tell me what effect will be produced in the mercantile transactions of a country, which is not shackled by restrictive laws, when a scarcity of money produces a fall in the price of commodities.

CAROLINE.

In that case the very reverse will happen of what

ON MONEY. 317

we before observed. Foreign merchants will come and buy goods, and instead of offering merchandize in exchange, will bring money in payment; for they will be willing to make purchases, but not sales at a cheap market.

MRS. B.

It is thus that the value of gold and silver equalizes itself in all parts of the civilized world; wherever there is a deficiency, it flows in from every quarter; and wherever there is a redundancy, the tide sets in an opposite direction. It is the regular diffusion of the precious metals, and their constant tendency to an equality of value, which renders them so peculiarly calculated for a general standard. Were money as liable to variation of value as the commodities for which it serves as a medium of exchange, it would be totally unfit for a standard.

CONVERSATION XVII.

Subject of MONEY continued.

OF THE DEPRECIATION OF GOLD AND SILVER. —
OF THE ADULTERATION AND DEPRECIATION OF
COINED MONEY — OF BANKS. — OF PAPER MO-
NEY — EFFECTS OF PAPER MONEY WHEN NOT
PAYABLE IN SPECIE ON DEMAND. — OF THE PRO-
PORTION OF CURRENCY TO THE COMMODITIES TO
BE CIRCULATED BY IT.

CAROLINE.

I HAVE been reflecting much upon the subject
of our last conversation, Mrs. B.; and it has
occurred to me that though there may be no permanent excess and depreciation of specie in any
particular country, yet it must gradually decrease
in value throughout the world: for money is very
little liable to wear; a great quantity of the precious metals is annually extracted from the mines,
and though a considerable portion of it may be
converted into plate and jewellery, yet the greater

ON MONEY. 319

part, I suppose, goes to the mint to be coined, and this additional quantity must produce a depreciation of value?

MRS. B.

An increase of supply will not occasion depreciation of value, if there should at the same time be a proportional increase of demand, and we must recollect that the consumable produce of the earth increases as well as that of the mines — the commodities to be circulated as well as the medium of circulation; and it is not the actual quantity of money, but the proportion which it bears to the quantity of commodities for which it is to serve as a medium of exchange, that regulates the price of those commodities.

Let us suppose the price of a loaf of bread to be one shilling; and say, if 1000 more loaves of bread be produced every year by agriculture, and such an additional number of shillings be obtained from the mines as will be necessary to circulate them, the price of a loaf will then remain the same, and the value of money will not, by this additional quantity of specie, be depreciated.

CAROLINE.

But, Mrs. B., you do not consider that when the thousand additional loaves are eaten, the additional shillings will remain.

320　　ON MONEY.

MRS. B.

The greater part of these loaves will be eaten by those who will not only reproduce them, but probably increase the number the following year.

CAROLINE.

In that case it would be very possible that the progress of agriculture and manufactures should keep pace with, or even precede that of the mines.

MRS. B.

If the quantity of the precious metals annually extracted from the mines be exactly what is required for the arts, and for the additional specie necessary to circulate the increasing produce of the land, there will be no change in the value of money, and commodities will continue to be bought and sold at their former prices. If less gold and silver be extracted than is requisite for these purposes, goods will fall in price; and if, on the contrary, a greater quantity be produced, goods will rise in price, the fluctuations in the price of commodities gradually and constantly conforming to the variations of the scale by which their value is measured.

Dr. Adam Smith was of opinion that for many years past the supply of gold and silver did not exceed the demand; but several later writers conceive that he was mistaken on this point. I am very far from being a competent judge of such a

ON MONEY.

question, but I confess that I feel inclined to favour the opinion of a general depreciation.

Previous to the discovery of America the exchangeable value of money was certainly much greater than it has been since that period. Some notion may be formed of the difference of the value of money in ancient and in modern times from the amount of the revenue which Xerxes, King of Persia, derived from his wealthy and extensive empire, and which enabled him to maintain his mighty fleets and armies; it is said in history to have amounted to only three millions sterling.

CAROLINE.

The prodigality and extravagance of the Romans was then in fact still greater than it appears, since the immense sums they expended upon luxuries were then more valuable than they would be at the present times.

MRS. B.

As the wealth of the Romans arose in a great measure from the spoliation of the countries they conquered, gold and silver formed an essential part of their plunder; specie, therefore, might possibly be of less value there than in other parts of the world at the same period.

Independently, however, of the increase of quantity which produces a depreciation in the value of the precious metals themselves, there are causes

P 5

322 ON MONEY.

quite foreign to this, which have considerable effect on the value of the money into which they have been coined. One of these is the adulteration of the coin. A pound sterling, or twenty shillings, originally weighed a pound of silver; hence its denomination. But sovereigns, in making new coinages, frequently found it convenient to adulterate the metal by mixing it with alloy. It was a means of increasing the value of their treasures, by paying their debts with a much less quantity of the precious metals, and thus defrauding their creditor-subjects, who in the first instance were not aware of the change.

In the year 1351, Edward the Fourth, distressed by the debts he had incurred in his chimerical attempts to conquer France, adopted this mode of paying his creditors with less money than he borrowed of them. He ordered a pound of silver to be coined into 266, instead of 240 pennies. Having experienced the beneficial effects of this expedient, he soon after coined 270 pennies out of the same pound. By this imposition, not only the creditors of the crown, but all other creditors were defrauded of about a tenth of their property; being compelled to receive in payment money of less value than that they had lent. Considerable inconvenience was also experienced from the alteration in the standard of value; as soon as it was discovered, it produced a general rise in the price of commodities, and the poor were greatly distressed by the enhancement of prices of the necessaries of live.

ON MONEY. 323

CAROLINE.

But did not wages rise in the same proportion?

MRS. B.

Eventually they did, no doubt; but after such a revolution in prices as an event of this nature produces, a length of time is required to restore the due level; and the rich always resist the rise of wages as long as they can. In the instance I have mentioned it does not appear that the labouring class made any effort to obtain a compensation by a rise of wages, until a dreadful pestilence, which originated in the east, extended its ravages to England, and carried off the greater part of the lower classes. The survivors then took advantage of the scarcity of hands to raise their terms; but the king, instead of allowing the remedy to pursue its natural course, considered this attempt of the labourers to raises their wages as an unwarrantable exaction; and in order to prevent it, enacted the *statute of labourers*. This statute ordained that labourers should receive no more than the wages which were paid previous to the adulteration of the coin.

It would be difficult to conceive a law more calculated to repress the efforts of industry. But Edward, urged by the weight of his accumulated debts, continued to depreciate the value of the coin; endeavouring to conceal the fraud by the introduction of a new silver coin called a *groat*, but in value

324 ON MONEY.

only $3\frac{1}{4}d.$: and in 1358 he made 75 groats, or 300 pennies, out of a pound of silver.

CAROLINE.

What a prodigious depreciation in the course of so short a period of time ! and have similar expedients been resorted to by successive sovereigns?

MRS. B.

Yes; so repeatedly that 20 shillings, or a pound sterling, instead of containing, as formerly, a pound of silver, now weighs rather less than four ounces of that metal.

CAROLINE.

But this is but a partial depreciation, which affects only the coin of Great Britain. Have other countries also adopted so unjust and pernicious a measure ?

MRS. B.

It is so tempting an expedient for sovereigns, that it has been resorted to in almost all countries where money is used. In the time of Charlemagne the French livre weighed a pound, of 12 ounces. Phillip the First adulterated it with one-third of alloy. Phillip of Valois practised the same fraud on gold coin, and it has been repeated by successive sovereigns till the depreciation of the French louis is even greater than that of our pound sterling, and their livre is now worth not more than ten-pence.

ON MONEY. 325

As far back as the time of the Romans this surreptitious mode of obtaining wealth had been discovered, and was practised. The Roman *as,* which originally contained a pound of brass, was in the course of time diminished to half an ounce.

CAROLINE.

But now that the world must be fully aware of the imposition, I should think that governments would not venture to have recourse to such expedients.

MRS. B.

This country has increased so much in wealth, that in the present times less difficulty is experienced in raising taxes, and the facility of making loans has induced government to give the preference to that mode of obtaining money during a time of war, or whenever any remarkable expenses are incurred.

Of late years a new mode of augmenting the currency of the country has been invented; by substituting for the precious metals a more convenient and more economical medium of exchange, under the form of *paper money.*

CAROLINE.

Paper money! What value can there be in money made of paper?

326   ON MONEY.

MRS. B.

None whatever intrinsically, yet it has been found
to answer most of the purposes of specie. — You
remember that money was first invented to avoid
the inconvenience of barter. When a commodity
is sold for money, it is under a confidence, on the
part of the seller, that he will be able with the
money to purchase any other commodity of equal
value that he may want. It is of no consequence
to him of what material the money be made, provided it have this quality.

CAROLINE.

True; but paper can never have that quality:
who would part with any thing of value for a bit
of paper?

MRS. B.

Suppose I were to give you a paper containing
my promise to pay you 100*l.* in money whenever
you demanded it; would you not consider the promise so formally given, nearly of the same value as
the money itself?

CAROLINE.

Yes; because I have perfect confidence in you;
but a stranger would not.

MRS. B.

Suppose that instead of my promise to pay you
100*l.*, I should give you a piece of paper contain-

II

ON MONEY. 327

ing a promise to the same effect of some of the wealthiest and best known merchants in London?

CAROLINE.

My confidence in the value of such paper would be in proportion to the reliance I could place on the promise of such merchants.

MRS. B.

Exactly so. Such confidence is the foundation of all banking establishments, which are in general a partnership of wealthy and respectable merchants, in whom the public repose so great a confidence that they are willing to take their promissory note, commonly called a *bank-note,* instead of money.

CAROLINE.

A bank-note then is a written engagement, or promise, to pay the sum, whatever it be, that is specified in the note?

MRS. B.

It is; and these notes become current as a medium of exchange; having no intrinsic value, they are merely the sign or representative of wealth; but are received by the public under the persuasion that they will be paid in money by the bank whenever required.

CAROLINE.

This is indeed an excellent invention; what a

328   ON MONEY.

saving of expense! The establishment of a bank
of paper money appears to me very similar to the
discovery of a mine of gold in the country: or indeed the bank has even some advantages over the
mine, for it is certain of being productive, and yet
it is attended with much less expense. Is the invention of paper money quite of modern date?

MRS. B.

There is, I believe, no vestige of any thing of
the kind in ancient history; unless we should consider, as such, a species of stamped leather used as
money by the Carthagenians; and as they had also
coined money, it is possible that their stamped leather might be considered merely as a sign or representative of real value, analogous to our paper
money.

CAROLINE.

The leather was probably a species of parchment,
the substance commonly used for writing on, before the invention of paper, and the impression
stamped on it might signify the sum of money
which the piece of leather was to represent, or pass
for.

MRS. B.

These are points upon which, in the imperfect
state of our knowledge of Carthagenian currency,
it would be difficult to determine; it is fortunate,
therefore, that they are questions more of curiosity
than of utility.

ON MONEY. 329

The first bank we are distinctly acquainted with was established at Amsterdam in the year 1609 *; but this institution was rather of a different kind from what I have been describing. It issued no paper, but received the deposit of coined money, an account of which was taken in the books of the bank; and through the medium of these books, transfers of property were made from one individual to another, as occasion required, without the money being once removed from the strong chests in which it was originally deposited.

CAROLINE.

There does not seem to be any economy in this species of bank; whilst those that issue bank notes, by the substitution of a cheap circulating medium, render that of gold and silver superfluous, and enable it to be sent abroad to purchase foreign commodities.

MRS. B.

And, should foreign countries adopt the same economical expedient, and send us their super-fluous specie . . . . . ?

CAROLINE.

True, I did not consider that. If paper mo-ney were generally adopted, every country would be overstocked with specie; for though the estab-

* It is said, however, that a bank was established at Venice at least two centuries before.

330   ON MONEY.

lishment of a bank in any one country may force
the superfluous money into others, this cannot happen
pen if banks are set up in every country. They
are far therefore from being attended with the
advantages I at first imagined.

MRS. B.

By issuing paper money, so much is, in fact, added
to the circulation throughout the civilized world;
and inasmuch as it supersedes the use of the precious
metals, and therefore lessens the demand, it must
to a certain degree lessen their value. The immediate
mediate effect of opening a new bank is certainly to
drive some portion of the specie out of the country
try in which the bank is established. It does not,
however, force out the whole quantity which the
paper represents, for independently of the general
excess to which we have alluded, a bank must keep
a certain quantity of specie in reserve to be enabled
to fulfil the promise of paying its notes on demand.

CAROLINE.

You do not mean to say that a bank will keep a
fund of specie, like that of Amsterdam, equal to
the value of its notes, for that purpose; for if so,
no saving would result from the use of paper
money?

MRS. B.

Certainly not. The profits of the bank arise
from the employment of the capital thus saved,

ON MONEY.

which consists of the difference between the amount of notes issued and the specie reserved in the bank. It is so improbable that every person possessed of notes should apply at once for payment, that there is no necessity for providing a fund equal to the amount of the notes in circulation in order to fulfil the engagement. Banks discover from experience what is the proportion of specie requisite to enable them to answer the average demand made upon them; and they regulate the quantity of notes they issue accordingly: for if they failed in their engagement to pay them in cash on demand, they would become bankrupt.

CAROLINE.

Yet I understand that the Bank of England no longer pays its notes in specie?

MRS. B.

That is true; but it is owing to an act of parliament having been passed purposely to grant this privilege to the Bank of England for a specified time.

CAROLINE.

And if a Bank of England note can no longer be exchanged at pleasure for specie, in what does its value consist?

MRS. B.

In the expectation that it will one day be paid in gold, or something equivalent to gold: this opinion renders bank notes still current: were such confidence

332 ON MONEY.

destroyed, their value would be reduced to that of the paper of which they are made.

CAROLINE.

But since the Bank of England is not obliged to pay its notes in cash, it is at liberty to issue any quantity however great. In short, it seems to have discovered the philosopher's stone, for though it may not have found the means of making gold, it possesses a substitute which answers the purpose equally well.

MRS. B.

Excepting that, as it has no intrinsic value, it cannot be exported in case of excess; and you may recollect our observing, that no use could be made of any superfluous quantity of money but to exchange it for foreign goods. An excess of currency produced by an over-issue of bank notes must therefore remain in the country, and cause a depreciation in the value of money, which would be discovered by a general rise in the prices of commodities, and would be attended with all the evils enumerated in our last conversation.

CAROLINE.

And is there not great danger of a bank issuing an excess of notes when it is not restricted by the obligation of paying them in specie?

ON MONEY. 333

MRS. B.

A very considerable risk is certainly incurred by such an exemption.

When a bank issues more notes than are required for the purpose of circulation, its effect in depreciating the value of the currency, and raising the price of commodities, is at first very trifling, because as soon as that effect is perceived, the coined money begins to disappear. Notwithstanding the prohibition of law, it never fails to make its escape out of the country. It is either clandestinely sent abroad, or privately melted, and exported in bullion. As long therefore as an over-issue of notes serves to replace the coin which it forces out of the country, there is but little augmentation of the circulating currency; but if after the specie has disappeared, the bank still continue to force an additional quantity of notes into circulation, the excess will be absorbed in it, the value of the currency will be proportionally depreciated, and will produce a corresponding rise in the price of commodities.

CAROLINE.

But is it known whether the Bank of England has materially increased its issuo of notes since it has been exonerated from the obligation of paying them in cash?

MRS. B.

Of that there is no doubt; but it is the opinion

334 ON MONEY.

of many people that the supply of notes has not exceeded the demand; — that the paper mine (as you call it) has increased its produce only in proportion to the increase of the produce of the country, and the peculiar exigencies of the times, political circumstances having deranged the natural order of things, and rendered, during the late revolutions of Europe, a more than usual quantity of currency necessary.

CAROLINE.

But was it not during the late war that all our gold coin disappeared, and was supposed to be melted down or exported? And was there not a general rise in the price of provisions and all commodities at the same period?

MRS. B.

That is true; and the question is very much disputed whether these circumstances were owing to the war, and the taxes it entailed upon us, or to an over issue of bank notes. England was under the necessity of paying her troops on the Continent, and of subsidizing foreign sovereigns; this, some people are of opinion, was a sufficient reason to account for the disappearance of our specie, and to render an additional issue of bank notes necessary. Then the rise in the price of provisions they attributed to the difficulty of importing foreign agricultural produce, which naturally raised the price of

ON MONEY. 335

the home supply. Foreign commodities also became dear from their scarcity, and this enhanced the price of such goods as would serve as a substitute for them at home.

CAROLINE.

And commodities of English manufacture, so far from rising in price, were, I recollect, much cheaper during the last war. Now if the currency were depreciated, it should produce a general rise in the price of all commodities. I begin therefore to think that the bank may not have issued more notes than were required.

MRS. B.

The rise of price produced by a depreciation of the value of money is general, but not universal; for other circumstances may not only counter-balance the effect of the depreciation of currency, in regard to particular commodities, but even render them cheaper notwithstanding. You must recollect that there are other causes which affect the price of goods.

CAROLINE.

True, the proportion of the supply to the demand; but we have just been observing, that during a war there is a deficiency of supply, which increases instead of counteracting the effect of the depreciation of currency, as it would make commodities still dearer.

336 ON MONEY.

MRS. B.

During a war there is generally a deficiency of foreign commodities, and there may also be of agricultural produce for our own consumption; but of English manufactures intended for exportation, there must, as we have before observed, be a redundancy, owing to the difficulty of exporting them. Supposing, therefore, that a depreciation of the value of money should produce a general rise in the value of commodities of 10 per cent., whilst on the other hand the excess of the supply occasioned a reduction of value of English manufactures of 20 per cent., at what rate would such goods sell?

CAROLINE.

Ten per cent. must be added on account of the depreciation of money, and 20 per cent. deducted on account of the excess of supply; the goods would therefore sell 10 per cent. lower than before. The cheapness of our own manufactures, then, affords no proof against a depreciation of the currency. This makes me again waver in my opinion, Mrs. B., and I feel at a loss which side of the question to adopt.

MRS. B.

The strongest argument in favour of a depreciation of the currency is, that guineas no longer passed for the same value as gold bullion, which is the natural standard of the value of coined money.

ON MONEY. 337

CAROLINE.

Was the gold then adulterated, and an ounce of gold coined into more than $3l.$ $17s.$ $10\frac{1}{2}d.$?

MRS. B.

No; but gold bullion partook of the general rise of commodities, and instead of selling for $3l.$ $17s.$ $10\frac{1}{2}d.$ it sold for four, and even once as high as $5l.$ an ounce.

CAROLINE.

But why did not guineas rise in the same proportion? I cannot conceive how they can be less valuable than a similar weight of the gold of which they are made.

MRS. B.

The coined and the uncoined gold remain in reality of the same value, but as it is not lawful for a guinea to pass for more than a pound-note and a shilling, the guineas are compelled to share the fate of the paper currency; and if that be depreciated, all the coined money of the country, whether gold or silver, must be so likewise.

CAROLINE.

Then, if it were not illegal, every one would melt his depreciated guineas and shillings, and convert them into gold and silver bullion?

338 ON MONEY.

MRS. B.

Certainly. It is this which causes our specie to disappear, and transports it to foreign countries, where it is freed from the shackles of a depreciated paper currency, and enabled to fetch its real value in exchange for goods; it is this also which, as we before observed, brings foreign goods to be sold at our market, because it is dear; and sends our money to purchase goods at foreign markets, because they are cheap.

CAROLINE.

But if an ounce of gold rises in price from $3l.$ $17s.$ $10\frac{1}{2}d.$ to $5l.$, is it not rather the value of the bullion that has risen than the currency that has fallen?

MRS. B.

Gold bullion, like every other commodity, rises in *price* only, not in *value;* and that rise is owing to the depreciation of the currency in which its price is estimated; were there no depreciation, bullion and guineas would both be worth $3l.$ $17s.$ $10\frac{1}{4}d.$ an ounce.

CAROLINE.

This then I think seems to decide the point of depreciation.

MRS. B.

You must recollect that when I undertook to assist you in acquiring a knowledge of the principles of political economy, we agreed to confine

ON MONEY. 339

our inquiries to such points as were well established. We cannot, therefore, venture to decide upon questions which are yet in dispute.

It is very easy to acquire some knowledge of the principles of a science, but extremely difficult to know how to apply them. I would particularly caution you against hasty conclusions or inferences; the errors arising from the misapplication of sound principles, are scarcely less dangerous than those that proceed from total ignorance.

Let us now conclude our observations on currency, which we may henceforth consider as consisting not merely of specie, but of coined and of paper money.

CAROLINE.

Pray is it necessary that the value of the currency of a country should be equal to the value of the commodities to be circulated by it?

MRS. B.

By no means. The same guinea or bank-note will serve the purpose of transferring from one individual to another several hundred pounds worth of goods in the course of a short time. There are besides many expedients for economising money, the most remarkable of which is an arrangement made amongst bankers. Their clerks meet every day after the hours of business to exchange the draughts made on each other for the preceding day.

340 ON MONEY.

If, for instance, the banking-house A. has draughts to the amount of 20,000*l.* on the banking-house B., the latter has also, in all probability, draughts upon the former, though they may not be to the same amount; the two houses exchange these draughts as far as they will balance each other, and are thus prevented the necessity of providing money for the payment of the whole. By this economical expedient, which is carried on amongst all the bankers in London east of St. Paul's, I understand that about 200,000*l.* performs the function of four or five millions.

CAROLINE.

And what do you suppose to be the proportion of the money to the value of the commodities to be circulated by it?

MRS. B.

That, I believe, it would be impossible to ascertain. Mr. Sismondi, in his valuable Treatise on Commercial Wealth, compares these respective quantities to mechanical powers, which, though of different weights, balance each other from the equality of their momentum; and, to follow up the comparison, he observes that though commodities are by far the most considerable in quantity, yet that the velocity with which currency circulates compensates for its deficiency.

ON MONEY. 341

CAROLINE.

This is an extremely ingenious comparison, and I should suppose the analogy to be perfectly correct; for the less money there is in circulation the more frequently it will be transferred from one to another in exchange for goods.

MRS. B.

Perfectly correct is rather too strong a term. The analogy will only bear to a certain extent, otherwise, whatever were the proportions of currency and of commodities, they would always balance each other, and the price of commodities would never be affected by the increase or diminution of the quantity of currency.

CONVERSATION XVIII.

ON COMMERCE.

DIFFERENCE OF WHOLESALE AND RETAIL TRADE. — GENERAL ADVANTAGES OF TRADE. — HOW IT ENRICHES A COUNTRY. — ADVANTAGES OF RETAIL TRADE. — GREAT PROFITS OF SMALL CAPITALS EXPLAINED. — ADVANTAGES OF QUICK RETURN OF CAPITAL TO FARMERS AND MANUFACTURERS. — ADVANTAGES OF ROADS, CANALS, &c. — DIFFERENCE OF THE HOME TRADE, FOREIGN TRADE, AND CARRYING TRADE — OF THE HOME TRADE: IT EMPLOYS TWO CAPITALS AT HOME, AND PUTS IN MOTION DOUBLE THE QUANTITY OF HOME INDUSTRY. — IT RETURNS CAPITAL QUICKER.

MRS. B.

WE mentioned commerce as one of the modes of employing capital to produce a revenue; but deferred investigating its effects until you had acquired some knowledge of the nature and use of money. We may now, therefore, proceed to exa-

ON COMMERCE. 343

mine in what manner commerce enriches individuals, and augments the wealth of a country.

Those who engage their capitals in commerce or trade act as agents or middle-men between the producers and the consumers of the fruits of the earth; they purchase them of the former, and sell them to the latter; and it is by the profits on the sale that capital so employed yields a revenue.

There are two distinct sets of men engaged in trade: merchants, who purchase commodities (either in a rude or a manufactured state) of those who produce them: this is called wholesale trade; and shopkeepers, who purchase goods in smaller quantities of the merchants, and distribute them to the public according to the demand: this constitutes the retail trade.

CAROLINE.

Trade will no doubt bring a revenue to those who employ their capital in it; but I do not conceive how it contributes to the wealth of the country: for neither merchants nor shopkeepers produce any thing new; they add nothing to the general stock of wealth, but merely distribute that which is produced by others. It is true that mercantile men form a considerable part of the community; but if their profits arc taken out of the pockets of their countrymen, they may make fortunes without enriching their country.

ON COMMERCE.

MRS. B.

Trade increases the wealth of a nation, not by raising produce, like agriculture, nor by working up raw materials, like manufactures; but it gives an additional value to commodities by bringing them from places where they are plentiful to those where they are scarce; and by providing the means of a more extended distribution of commodities, it gives a spur to the industry both of the agricultural and manufacturing classes.

CAROLINE.

Do you mean to say that the merchant and tradesman encourage farmers and manufacturers to increase their productions, by finding purchasers for them?

MRS. B.

Yes. It would be impossible, you know, for every town or district to produce the several kinds of commodities required for its consumption; different soils and climates, and various species of skill and industry are requisite for that purpose. Some lands are best calculated for corn, others for pasture; some towns are celebrated by their cotton manufactures, others for their woollen cloths. Every place has, therefore, an excess of some kind of commodities and a deficiency of others; which renders a system of exchanges necessary, not only between individuals (as we observed in treating of the origin of barter), but between towns and countries to the most distant regions of the earth.

ON COMMERCE. 345

Now it is the business of merchants to exchange the surplus produce of one place for that of another. A man who deals in any particular commodity makes it his business to find out in what parts that commodity is most abundant, and will be sold at the lowest price; and in what parts it is most scarce, and will fetch the highest price, and then to ascertain the least expensive mode of conveying it from the one to the other market.

CAROLINE.

In this they consult their own interest; since to purchase at the cheapest and sell at the dearest market will give them the greatest profits.

MRS. B.

No doubt; but it is wisely and beneficially ordained that by consulting their own interest they are at the same time favouring that of the community. When merchants hasten to send their goods to a market where they will sell at a high price, they supply those who are in want of such goods: the higher the price, the more urgent is the demand; it is a deficiency that has rendered them dear, and by furnishing the market with an ample supply, merchants not only satisfy the wants of the purchasers, but ultimately lower the price of the commodity.

Do you think that manufacturers would be able

346   ON COMMERCE.

to dispose of an equal quantity of goods without
the intervention of mercantile men? In such a case
Manchester would be reduced to distribute its
cottons merely within its own precincts and environs, instead of supplying, as it now does, not
only the demand of all England, but even that of
the most remote provinces of America.

Trade encourages industry, in the second place,
by rendering commodities cheaper. The merchant,
by dealing in large quantities, is enabled to bring
goods to market at a less expense of conveyance,
and can therefore afford to sell them on lower
terms than if the consumer were obliged to send for
them to the places where they are produced.

CAROLINE.

Yet things may generally be bought at the lowest
price where they are produced or manufactured?

MRS. B.

True; but if you add the charges of a private
conveyance, they will cost you much dearer. Had
we no means of procuring coals, than by sending
a waggon to Newcastle, though we should pay less
for them there than in London, they would, from
the expense of carriage, cost us more. Merchants
who deal in large quantities have a regular system
of conveyance for their goods, which considerably
diminishes the charges. The coals are by them

ON COMMERCE. 347

transported in ships to the different sea-ports, and thence conveyed in barges to the inland parts of the country wherever water-carriage is practicable.

CAROLINE.

It would, to be sure, not only be very expensive, but extremely inconvenient, were we obliged to send to distant parts for the commodities they produce. If, for instance, it were necessary to send to Sheffield to purchase a set of knives and forks; to Leeds for a coat, and to Norwich for a shawl; — or, without going so far, were it requisite to send into the country for corn, meat, hay, in short, every thing which the country produces, these things would cost us much more than if we bought them of shopkeepers.

But admitting that trade, by facilitating the distribution of commodities, promotes their consumption, I cannot understand how that can conduce to the wealth of a country: it increases its comforts and enjoyments, but it seems to me, to encourage expenditure, rather than production.

MRS. B.

To increase the comforts and enjoyments of a country is the ultimate aim of national wealth; and whilst trade promotes consumption, by rendering commodities cheaper, it does not engender prodigality in the consumer, but encourages industry in

348   ON COMMERCE.

the producer, to augment the supply. A reduction of price brings a commodity within the reach of a greater number of persons, which increases the demand for it; the man who could afford to wear only a linen frock, will, when commodities are cheaper, be able to wear a coat. He who could allow himself but one coat in the year, can now without extravagance wear two.

This increasing demand for commodities spurs the industry of the farmer and manufacturer, and they enrich themselves by furnishing the requifite supplies. With their wealth their consumption also augments; for the wants of men increase with their means of satisfying them; and when they add to their income, they usually add also to their expenditure. The farmer has more to satisfy the desires of the manufacturer; and the manufacturer produces more to supply the demands of the farmer: so that each is enabled to give and receive a greater quantity of things in exchange. These exchanges, it is true, are made through the agency of merchants, and by the means of money, but they are effectually exchanges of commodities, as really as if the manufacturer supplied the farmer with clothing in exchange for provisions. The increase of saleable commodities affects in a similar manner all classes of people. The proprietor of land improves his fortune by the increasing value of his rents, which the prosperous state of agriculture enables

ON COMMERCE.

the farmer to pay ; and the labourer betters his condition by the rise in the rate of wages resulting from the increased demand for labour. The whole may be summed up by saying, that, the quantity of commodities being increased, a larger portion will fall to the lot of every consumer who has any share in their production.

CAROLINE.

I now begin to understand the general advantages resulting from commerce. The retail trade carried on by shopkeepers must be attended with the same happy effects. It would be extremely inconvenient to the rich, and impracticable for the poor, to purchase the commodities they wanted in such large quantities as are disposed of by merchants and wholesale dealers. Were there no such trade as a butcher, for instance, every family would be obliged to purchase a whole sheep or a whole ox of the farmer.

MRS. B.

Retail trade is one of the most useful subdivisions of labour. Nothing can be more desirable than that the poor, who are maintained by daily or weekly wages, should be able to purchase their provisions in as small quantities as possible.

CAROLINE.

Yet I have often regretted the high price which

350　　ON COMMERCE.

the lower orders of people are obliged to pay for fuel, candles, grocery, and various little articles with which they are supplied by the chandlers' shops; whilst the higher ranks, who can afford to purchase the same goods in larger quantities, obtain them of more extensive dealers, at a cheaper rate.

MRS. B.

You must consider that were there no small shopkeepers, the lower classes would be reduced to the utmost distress; and these petty dealers cannot afford to sell their pennyworths, without being paid for the additional labour and trouble such kind of traffic requires. Their profits cannot be exorbitant, otherwise competition would in time reduce them to their natural standard.

CAROLINE.

But by selling very small quantities at a higher price, they must make more than the usual rate of profit; and how do you reconcile this to the common level of profit in all employment of capital?

MRS. B.

By reckoning whatever gains they make above the usual profits of capital, as *wages*, that is to say, the reward of their personal labour. The smaller is the capital which a man employs, the greater is the proportion which his wages will bear to the

ON COMMERCE. 351

profits of his capital. A man who sells oranges in the streets has laid out perhaps a capital of 20 or 30 shillings on the goods in which he deals, the usual profits of trade on such a sum is two or three shillings a year; but if he did not carry about oranges for sale, he would work as a labourer, and get perhaps two shillings a day wages; these two shillings a day, or 626 shillings a-year, the man must make by the sale of his oranges, in addition to the usual profits of trade; the whole of his gains go however under the name of profits, because the distinction can be made only in theory.

CAROLINE.

But all tradesmen and mercantile men devote their time and attention to their business: should not, therefore, a portion of their gains be considered as the reward of their personal labour, which must be valuable in proportion to the extent and importance of the concern in which they are engaged.

MRS. B.

No doubt; yet it will bear but a small proportion to their profits, compared with that of petty dealers. A merchant who makes in trade an income of 5000l. a-year, were he to engage himself as clerk, would probably not obtain a salary of above 500l.; his wages would therefore be equal to only one-tenth of his profits, whilst those of the

352 ON COMMERCE.

man who sold oranges would be above 200 times the amount of the profits of his capital.

Another advantage resulting to the farmer and manufacturer, from the disposal of their goods to merchants, is the quick return of the capital they have employed in their production; for they receive the price of their goods from the merchant much sooner than they would, were they obliged to collect it gradually from the consumers.

Let us suppose a cotton manufacturer who devotes a capital of a thousand pounds to the employment of as many labourers as it will maintain, and sells their work to a wholesale dealer for 1100*l.* With this money he immediately sets his men and his mills to work again; whilst, if he retailed the goods himself, though instead of 1100*l.* he might perhaps get 1200*l.* or even 1300*l.* for them; yet, as the money would come in very slowly, he and his workmen would necessarily be kept a long time out of employ.

CAROLINE.

To the farmer such delays would prove ruinous, if he could not sell his crops in time to proceed with the necessary cultivation of the farm for the ensuing season.

MRS. B.

In order to avoid such extremities, both the farmer and manufacturer would be obliged to divide their capital into two parts, and employ the

ON COMMERCE. 353

one in raising or manufacturing commodities, and the other in disposing of them. To the occupations of agriculture or manufactures, they would find it necessary to add that of trade, a complication which would be equally injurious to each of the concerns. Commerce is one of the economical divisions of labour; if it sets apart a certain number of men, for the purpose of circulating and distributing the produce of the earth, it is in order that those who are engaged in raising and manufacturing that produce should be able to devote the whole of their capital, their time, and their talents, to their respective employments. It is worthy of observation, too, that none of these divisions are enforced by law, but exist under the choice of the parties, and have been adopted from a view to their general interest.

But although it is advantageous to separate commerce from other branches of industry, it is desirable that its operations should be facilitated as much as possible, both in order that the agriculture and manufactures should not be deprived of too many labourers, and that commodities should be brought to market with the least possible expense. Good and numerous roads and navigable canals are extremely conducive to this end, as they enable the produce of the country to be conveyed with ease and expedition to the several markets; for ease and expedition economise time and labour,

354   ON COMMERCE.

and economy of time and labour is productive of
cheapness.

CAROLINE.

Were there no roads, the farmer being without
means of sending his crops to market would not
produce more than could be consumed by his
family, and perhaps some few customers in his
neighbourhood, and he must be content to clothe
himself with the fleeces of his flocks and the skins
of his herds, for he would be unable to procure
manufactured articles. Nor would the manufacturers be better off, as the market for the disposal
of their goods would be equally limited.

MRS. B.

Neither towns nor manufactures could exist in
such a state of things, because they could not be
supplied with the produce of the country, which is
still more necessary to their existence, than the
workmanship of the towns is to the farmer. It is
the surplus produce of the country which pays for
the workmanship of the towns, and the surplus
workmanship of the towns that pays for the produce of the country. The greater, therefore, the
intercourse between town and country, the greater
is the encouragement given to the industry of both.

History teaches us that in all old settled countries no material improvement has taken place in
the cultivation of the lands without a considerable

ON COMMERCE. 355

advance in the state of manufactures and commerce; and Adam Smith even goes so far as to say, that " through the greater part of Europe the com- " merce and manufactures of cities, instead of being " the effect, have been the cause and occasion of " the improvement and cultivation of the country."

But as the forms of governments, and the man- ners and customs of our barbarous ancestors, have constantly interfered with and restricted the pro- gress of wealth and civilization of Europe, the natural order of things has frequently been re- versed, and towns have arisen, not from the surplus wealth of the country, but as citadels and fortresses in which the people found shelter from the oppres- sion of their superiors, and the incursions of their warlike neighbours. We must look to America for the natural effect of the progress of wealth and civilization, and we shall there behold the habita- tions of farmers scattered over the face of the country, and towns built only after cultivation was far advanced.

CAROLINE.

In expatiating on the advantages of facility of conveyance it must not, however, be forgotten, that the land which is converted into roads is taken from tillage; and could we calculate the quantity of corn and hay which the roads, in a state of culture, might have produced, it would perhaps be found that some of them have occasioned more loss than gain.

356 ON COMMERCE.

To take land from cultivation for the purpose of roads appears to me very analogous to taking la_ bourers from agriculture for the purpose of trade.

MRS. B.

The result is in both cases similar; for there can be no doubt but that the general effect of roads and canals is to increase the produce of the country. If we are indebted to merchants for the advantages of trade, roads and canals are the instruments with which they carry it on. Deprived of such means, their operations would be very circumscribed; there would be no trade but at sea-ports, and along the course of rivers.

The charges of conveyance from Liverpool to Manchester on the Duke of Bridgewater's canal is six shillings a ton, whilst the price of land carriage is forty shillings.

CAROLINE.

If there had been a river from one of those towns to the other the expense of carriage would have been still less than that of the canal.

MRS. B.

I beg your pardon; a river is seldom uniformly navigable, and is always more or less circuitous in its course; and where the stream is powerful, it will admit of navigation only in one direction, as is the case in some of the American rivers. Before the

ON COMMERCE. 357

Bridgewater canal was dug, the usual mode of conveyance of goods was along the Mersea and the Trevell, and the cost was twelve shillings a ton, just double that of conveyance on the canal. Macpherson observes, that " this spirited and patriotic en- " terprize of the Duke of Bridgewater is rewarded " by a vast revenue, arising from his water-carriage " and his formerly useless coal-mine; and the sur- " rounding country is benefited a pound at least in " every shilling paid to the Duke."

CAROLINE.

This reminds me of a circumstance that occurred during a tour in Wales; we were admiring a neat fountain which supplied a village with water, and were informed by the landlord of the inn, that he had constructed it, and had had the water conveyed from a distant spring, whence the people of the village had formerly been under the necessity of fetching it. A trifling sum was annually paid by each family for liberty to use this water, and the landlord thought it necessary to make many apologies for not allowing it them free of expence, and talked much of the money he had laid out in the enterprize. My father assured him that he was convinced the speculation was still more beneficial to the village than it was to himself; that as the inhabitants had the option of fetching water for themselves, the payment proved that it was because

358 ON COMMERCE.

they could turn the time and labour they bestowed on the conveyance of water to better account; and upon inquiry we found the village had been in an improving state ever since the erection of this fountain. It had not only become more opulent, but had acquired habits of cleanliness, which had proved very beneficial to the health of the people.

MRS. B.

There are three species of commerce in which merchants engage their capitals. The *home trade*, *foreign trade*, and the *carrying trade*.

The home trade comprehends all the internal and coasting trade of a country. The foreign trade is that in which we exchange our commodities for those of foreign countries; and the carrying trade consists in conveying the commodities of one foreign country to another. Let us at present confine our observations to the home trade.

CAROLINE.

The home trade, I conclude, must be the most advantageous to the country, because it encourages the industry of our own people.

MRS. B.

But what difference is there whether our labourers are employed to work for us, or for foreigners? for if we export English goods, we receive an equal

15

ON COMMERCE. 359

amount of foreign goods in exchange; so that foreign labourers work equally for us in return.

It is true, however, that the home trade possesses over the foreign trade the advantage of employing a greater quantity of our own capital. As trade consists in an exchange of commodities, two capitals must be employed in the purchase of the different commodities to be exchanged; in the home trade both these capitals are our own, and both of them are employed in the purchase of British goods, the produce of British labourers; thus affording the means of maintaining and continuing their industry.

In the foreign trade, only one of the capitals engaged is our own; the other is foreign. When, for instance, the hardware of Birmingham is exchanged for the cotton goods of Manchester, the country benefits by the profits of the capitals of both the parties concerned in the exchange. But if the Birmingham merchant sends his goods to France, to be exchanged for cambrics, this country will benefit only by the profits of one of the parties, those of the French merchant enriching his own country.

CAROLINE.

And it must be desirable that the second capital should bo English instead of foreign, not only on account of the capitalist, but also of the labourers whom it employs.

360   ON COMMERCE.

MRS. B.

Another advantage of the home trade is that it affords a quicker return of capital, which is a further means of promoting industry. The nearer is the market at which the merchant disposes of his goods, the sooner will his capital be returned to him, and the sooner will he be able to take other goods from the hands of the farmer or manufacturer. If a London merchant trades with Sheffield or Manchester, his capital may be returned to him in the course of a few weeks; if with America or the East Indies, it may be a year or two, or more, before he gets it back. The greater the vicinity of the market, therefore, the greater the number of sales and purchases he will be able to make in a given time. A capital of 1000*l*., for instance, might in the home trade be returned once a-month, and enable the merchant, during the course of the year, to purchase 12,000*l*. worth of goods; whilst, if he sent his merchandize to India, two years would probably elapse before he got his capital returned. In the first case, therefore, the 1000*l*. capital would afford 24 times more encouragement to industry than it would in the latter.

CAROLINE.

You do not thence mean to infer, that in the first case the profits would be twenty-four times greater?

ON COMMERCE. 361

MRS. B.

Certainly not. Competition is, you know, perpetually tending to equalize the profits of capital, in whatever way it is employed. Profits will consequently be proportioned to the slow return of capital; and must, therefore, be reckoned annually, and not calculated upon every time the capital is returned.

CAROLINE.

The period of the return of capital applies, then, not so much to the home or foreign trade, as to the distance of the market; for capital might be returned quicker in trading with Calais or Dunkirk than with Edinburgh or Cork?

MRS. B.

It is very true; and how much it is to be regretted that jealousies and dissensions should so frequently impede and restrict the trade between neighbouring nations, which would otherwise be carried on with such great and reciprocal advantage! But we shall reserve till our next interview the observations we have to make on foreign trade.

CONVERSATION XIX.

ON FOREIGN TRADE.

ADVANTAGES OF FOREIGN TRADE. — IT EMPLOYS THE SURPLUS OF CAPITAL, AND DISPOSES OF A SURPLUS OF COMMODITIES. — OF BOUNTIES. — EFFECTS OF RESTRICTIONS ON FOREIGN TRADE. — EXTRACT FROM SAY'S POLITICAL ECONOMY. — EXTRACT FROM FRANKLIN'S WORKS.

CAROLINE.

AT our last interview, Mrs. B., you were regretting that any restraint should be imposed on our trade with foreign countries; but since you have explained to me the superior advantages arising from the home trade, I should have supposed that every measure tending to discourage foreign commerce, and promote our own industry, would be extremely useful.

MRS. B.

You would find it difficult to accomplish both

ON FOREIGN TRADE. 363

those objects; for in order to encourage our own industry we must facilitate the means of selling the produce of our manufactures, and extend their market as much as possible. On the other hand, if we prohibit exportation, we limit the production of our manufactures to the supply which can be consumed at home. No measure tending to the discouragement of foreign trade can, therefore, be said to promote the industry of the country.

CAROLINE.

But foreign trade cannot be both advantageous and disadvantageous to a country?

MRS. B.

It is never disadvantageous, but only less beneficial than the home trade. It is only after the demand at home is supplied, that our surplus produce is sent to foreign markets. When we have more capital to dispose of than is required in the home trade, instead of leaving it useless and the labourers it would employ idle, we set them to work for foreign markets. If, for instance, the woollen manufacturers of Leeds, after having supplied the whole demand of England for broad cloths, have any capital left, they will use it in the preparation of woollen goods for exportation.

R 2

364 ON FOREIGN TRADE.

CAROLINE.

Why not rather employ it in the fabrication of other commodities which may be consumed at home?

MRS. B.

If there were a deficiency of capital in any other branch of industry at home, the redundancy would naturally be drawn to that branch; but if all the trade, that is, all the exchanges that could be made at home, have been made, we send the residue of our commodities to foreign markets for sale.

CAROLINE.

Yet it appears a great hardship on the poor to send goods abroad, which so many of them are in want of at home.

MRS. B.

The poor are first supplied with whatever they can afford to purchase; and without the means of purchase you must recollect that there can be no effectual demand. It is not to be expected that farmers and manufacturers should labour for them merely from charitable motives, and were they so disposed, they would not long possess the means of continuing their benevolence. It would be very wrong, therefore, to consider this surplus produce as taken from the poor; for it would not have been produced had there been no demand for it in foreign countries.

ON FOREIGN TRADE. 365

CAROLINE.

That is very true. In all employment of capital men labour with a view to profit; they work, therefore, only for those who will pay them the value of their produce. And it is easy to conceive that those who have no further want of English commodities may yet wish to procure foreign goods. The English merchant will therefore say, " Since there is no more demand for the goods I deal in, I will export the remainder, which will be purchased abroad, and I shall get foreign commodities in exchange; — though my countrymen do not require any more cotton goods, I know that they will purchase wines, coffee, sugar, &c."

MRS. B.

Very well. Let us examine now what would be the effect of confining the employment of commercial capital to the home trade. If the inhabitants of the West Indian islands, Jamaica, for instance, were to prohibit the exportation of coffee and sugar, and the planters were obliged to trade only within the island, the consequence would be, that the demand for coffee and sugar would be very insignificant, and that an inconsiderable part only of the capital of the colony would find employment. The same effect would take place in Russia, if foreign merchants were not allowed to purchase the hemp and flax so abundantly produced in that country. If in Peru and

R 3

366   ON FOREIGN TRADE.

Chili the exportation of indigo, bark, and other
drugs was prohibited, the Europeans, who purchase them, would not be the only sufferers; the
Americans would be impoverished for want of employment for their capital.

CAROLINE.

All this is very clear, I admit. But what security
have we that merchants will not employ their capital in foreign commerce, before the demand for it
in the home trade is fully supplied?

MRS. B.

That security is derived from the natural distribution of capital according to the rate of profit. If
foreign commerce employed more capital than the
country could spare, the demand for it at home
would raise the profits of the home trade, and the
temptation of these increased profits would soon restore that portion of capital which had been unne-
cessarily withdrawn from it.

CAROLINE.

What an excellent criterion the rate of profit
affords of the employment of capital most advantageous to the community! When foreign commerce then offers greater profits than the home
trade, it proves that there is a greater demand for
capital in that branch of industry?

ON FOREIGN TRADE.

MRS. B.

Yes; it proves that the country possesses a surplus quantity of produce either agricultural or manufactured, which cannot be disposed of in the home market; and if the owners of this surplus were prevented from exchanging it for foreign commodities, it would not in future be produced, and those who produced it would be thrown out of employment.

The first commodities a country usually exports is agricultural produce, which she exchanges for manufactured goods; this is still the case with America, on account of its being a newly settled nation; it is also the case with Poland and Russia, those countries having made slower progress in wealth and population than the other communities of Europe. When nations are considerably advanced in wealth and population, all the food they can raise is required at home, and manufactures are established in order to employ the increased numbers of people; in the course of time they find it expedient to export manufactured goods in return for corn, the home supply, which was at first so redundant, being no longer sufficient to maintain the increased population. And it is at this point that England is now arrived.

CAROLINE.

I am surprised that foreign commerce with dis-

368   ON FOREIGN TRADE.

tant countries should ever offer sufficient profits to afford a compensation to the merchant for the disadvantages arising from the slow return of capital.

MRS. B.

If it did not, no merchant would engage in it. The greater the distance of the market to which he sends his goods the greater must be the profits on their sale, to make up not only for the tardy return of his capital, but also for the charges of conveyance of the goods. Freight and insurance from sea risks are both to be deducted from the profits of the merchant in foreign trade.

CAROLINE.

Then since we are obliged to sell our goods at such high prices in distant markets, I wonder that we should find purchasers for them: would it not answer better for those countries to produce them at home?

MRS. B.

You may be assured that no nation will purchase from abroad what may be procured of the same quality and for less expense at home. But all countries are not equally capable of producing the same kind of commodities, either rude or manufactured. The gifts of nature are still more diversified in the different climates of the earth, than the habits and dispositions of men. It would

ON FOREIGN TRADE. 369

be impossible for us at any expense to produce the wines of Portugal, on account of the coldness of our climate. We can procure them only by an exchange of commodities: the Portuguese take our broad cloth in return: this, it is true, they might manufacture at home; but as our climate is peculiarly favourable to pasturage, and our workmen particularly skilful in manufactures, broad cloths could not be made in Portugal equally good at the same expense, including the charges of freight and insurance; and whilst the Portuguese can purchase them of us for less than they can fabricate them at home, it is certainly their interest to procure them in exchange for commodities the culture or fabrication of which is more suited to the nature of their climate and the habits of the people.

But the difference of price of our manufactured goods at home or abroad is not so great as you would imagine; in articles of small bulk it is very trifling. I recollect some years since purchasing an English pocket-book at Turin for nearly the same price that it would have cost in London.

CAROLINE.

How then was the expense of conveyance defrayed; and what compensation was there for the slow return of capital?

R 5

370 ON FOREIGN TRADE.

MRS. B.

These expenses probably did not more than counterbalance the high rent and taxes paid by London shopkeepers, which I believe are comparatively insignificant at Turin. There might, perhaps, also be some bounty on the exportation of such goods, which would enable the merchant to sell them at a lower price.

CAROLINE.

Pray what is a bounty on goods?

MRS. B.

It is a pecuniary reward given by government for the exportation of certain goods. Governments, so far from partaking of your prejudices against foreign trade, often think it right to encourage the exportation of their manufactures by such artificial measures.

CAROLINE.

A bounty, then, on any commodity has the effect of inducing merchants to export more of it than they would otherwise do, as it raises their profits. But in consequence of this, capital will be drawn into this trade beyond its due proportion?

MRS. B.

Certainly; a bounty often tempts merchants to

ON FOREIGN TRADE. 371

invest capital in a trade which otherwise would not answer; that is, to export goods which would not yield a profit, after paying the expenses of conveyance, without such encouragement; and this capital, were it not artificially drawn out of its natural course, would flow into channels which would yield profits, without any expense to government.

CAROLINE.

Here then my apprehension of foreign trade is well-founded; for more capital is drawn into it than is required to preserve the equality of profits.

MRS. B.

That is sometimes the case; but it may also be unduly drawn from one branch of foreign commerce to another. The effect of bounties, however, is generally counteracted by the nations with whom we trade. Alarmed at our thus forcing our goods upon them, and dreadfully apprehensive of its interfering with the sale of their own manufactures, they immediately lay a duty on the commodity on which we grant a bounty, and oblige it to pay, on entering their territory, a sum at least equivalent to that which we bestow on it on quitting our own.

CAROLINE.

What a pity that either party should interfere to check and restrain the natural course of commerce!

R 6

372   ON FOREIGN TRADE.

The disease, however, seems to call for the remedy; as it is sometimes expedient to take one poison as an antidote to another.

MRS. B.

If we are so generous, or so foolish, as to enable foreigners to purchase our commodities at a cheaper rate, by paying a part of the price for them, are we not doing them a service, and ourselves an injury? and is it wise in them to endeavour to counteract such a measure?

CAROLINE.

True; I did not consider it in that point of view. It is really laughable to see two nations, the one strenuously endeavouring to injure itself, whilst the other studiously avoids receiving a benefit; and thus, by the mutual counteraction of each other's artifice, they leave the trade to follow its natural course.

I am now perfectly satisfied of the advantage of obtaining, by means of foreign commerce, such articles as cannot be produced at home; but I confess I do not feel the same conviction with regard to commodities which might be produced at home, though with some additional expense.

MRS. B.

Why should it not be the interest of a country

ON FOREIGN TRADE.

as well as that of an individual to purchase commodities wherever they can be procured cheapest? It might be very possible, as it has been observed by an ingenious writer *, for England to produce at a great expense of labour the tobacco which we now import from Virginia: and the Virginians, with no less difficulty, might fabricate the broad cloths with which we furnish them. But if our climate is better adapted to pasturage, and that of Virginia to the culture of tobacco, it is evident that the exchange of these commodities is a mutual advantage.

CAROLINE.

But are not the goods exchanged in trade of equal value? If we send the Virginians a thousand pounds worth of broad cloths, they will send us only a thousand pounds worth of tobacco in return. It may be a convenient measure, and the exchanging merchants will each make their profits; but I cannot perceive how the country can derive any accession of wealth from such traffic.

MRS. B.

Recollect that we said trade gives an additional value to commodities by bringing them from places where they are plentiful to those where they are scarce. When we ship off 1000*l.* worth of broad

---

* Sir Francis Divernois.

374   ON FOREIGN TRADE.

cloths for Virginia, and the Virginians export
1000*l.* worth of tobacco for England, the commodities exchanged are of equal value; but they
each acquire an additional value during the transport; the tobacco was not worth so much in Virginia as it is when it arrives in England, because,
not being cultivated here, it is more scarce and in
greater demand with us.   The broad cloth was not
worth so much in England as it is when it reaches
Virginia, because, not being fabricated in that
country, it is more scarce and in greater demand
there.

CAROLINE.

Very true; but if we both cultivated tobacco and
fabricated broad cloths; and if the Virginians did
the same, each country would be supplied at home,
and the expense of conveyance of the two cargoes
exchanged would be saved.

MRS. B.

If we could raise tobacco at as little expense as it
is done in Virginia, and the Virginians could manufacture broad cloths as cheap as they can purchase
them of us, your argument would be just; but that
is not the case.   To make this clear to you, let us
examine what quantity of labour is bestowed upon
the production of these several commodities.   If the
broad cloth which we send to Virginia cost us the
labour of one man we will say for 1000 days, while

15

ON FOREIGN TRADE. 375

the tobacco which we receive in exchange would
have cost us 2000 days' labour to produce at
home, do we not save a thousand days' labour?
and is not the advantage to the Virginians similar,
if the tobacco which cost them 1000 days' labour
to raise, will exchange for English broad cloth
which they could not have manufactured under
2000 days' labour?

CAROLINE.

By such an exchange, then, each country saves
1000 days' labour?

MRS. B.

Yes; and to save is to gain; for the thousand
days' labour thus economised are employed in the
production of some other commodity, which is so
much clear gain to each country.

CAROLINE.

Then each country procures the commodity it
wants at half the expense which would have been
required to produce it at home?

MRS. B.

Just so. To put the question in other words,
we may say, if by the employment of 50,000l. in
the Virginia trade we can obtain as much tobacco
as would require 100,000l. if cultivated at home,

376 ON FOREIGN TRADE.

there is 50,000*l.* economised, which will be employed in producing something else. The advantages of foreign commerce, it is true, are seldom carried so far as a saving of half the expenses of production; but they must always exist in a greater or less degree; for it is evident that no nation will purchase from abroad what can be produced equally cheap and good at home.

CAROLINE.

When goods are equally good and cheap I certainly prefer buying them of shops in the neighbourhood rather than at a distance, because it is more convenient; but why merchants should feel the same preference I do not clearly see: provided the goods they receive in their warehouses are of the same quality and price, I should think it would be immaterial to them from whence they came?

MRS. B.

They, like you, find advantages in dealing with their neighbours; it enables them to ascertain better the character of the persons of whom they make their purchases; it affords them the means of protecting themselves against imposition, and of applying a legal remedy in case of necessity. As long as profits are equal, therefore, (independently of risk) a merchant will always prefer employing his capital in the home trade; and it is only

ON FOREIGN TRADE. 377

superior profits that can tempt him to enter on a trade in which he is exposed to greater risks. You may recollect we formerly observed that the chances of gain must always be proportioned to the chances of loss.

CAROLINE.

I confess that before this explanation I never could comprehend how foreign trade could be a mutual advantage to the countries engaged in it, for I imagined tnat what was gained by the one was lost by the other.

MRS. B.

All free trade, of whatever description, must be a mutual benefit to the parties engaged in it; the only difference that can exist with regard to profit is, that it may not always be equally divided between them. An opposition of interests takes place, not between merchants or countries exchanging their commodities, but between rival dealers in the same commodity; and it is from that circumstance probably that you have been led to form such an erroneous idea of commerce. Do you not recollect our observing, some time since, that competition amongst dealers to dispose of their commodities renders them cheap, whilst competition amongst purchasers renders them dear. When you make any purchase, are you not sensible that the greater

378   ON FOREIGN TRADE.

the number of shops in the same neighbourhood dealing in the same commodity, the more likely you are to purchase it at a low price ?

CAROLINE.

Yes, because the shopkeepers endeavour to undersell each other.

MRS. B.

It is therefore the interest of the dealer to narrow competition, whilst it is that of the consumer to enlarge it. Now which do you suppose to be the interest of the country at large?

CAROLINE.

That of the consumers; for every man is a consumer, even the dealers themselves, who, though they are desirous of preventing competition in their own individual trade, must wish for it in all other species of commerce.

MRS. B.

No doubt; it is by free and open competition alone that extravagant prices and exorbitant profits are prevented, and that the public are supplied with commodities as cheap as the dealer can afford to sell them.

CAROLINE.

But in regard to luxuries, Mrs. B., may we not be allowed to encourage those of our own produc-

ON FOREIGN TRADE. 379

tion in preference to those brought from foreign
countries?

MRS. B.

The commercial state of France during Bona-
parte's system of prohibition will furnish a very
satisfactory answer to your question. The West
Indian produce, which the French were prohibited
from purchasing, consists chiefly of certain luxuries
of which they could not endure to be deprived; so
that, for instance, they were employed, at an immense
expense of capital, in extracting a sacharine juice
from various fruits and roots to answer in an inferior
degree the purpose of sugar; they cultivated bitter
endives, the root of which supplied them with a
wretched substitute for coffee; their tea was composed of indigenous herbs of a very inferior flavour
to that of China. In a word, labour was multiplied
to produce commodities of inferior value; or they
would have been altogether deprived of a variety of
comforts to which they had been accustomed, and
which, besides the pleasure derived from the enjoyment of them, we have observed to be one of the
strongest incitements to industry.

But the privation of the consumers of luxuries is
but a trifling evil compared with the consequences
of such restrictions upon the labouring classes;
for its effect is to increase the difficulty of raising
produce, and, consequently, to diminish the quantity of capital, the fund upon which the poor
subsist.

380 ON FOREIGN TRADE.

Mr. Say, who witnessed all the pernicious effects of this system, thus expresses himself: " C'est un " bien mauvais calcul que de vouloir obliger la " zone temperée à fournir des produits à la zone " torride. Nos terres produisent péniblement en " petite quantité, et en qualité médiocre, des ma- " tieres sucrées et colorantes, qu'un autre climat " donne avec profusion; mais elles produisent, au " contraire avec facilité, des fruits, des céréales " que leur poids et leur volume ne permettent " pas de tirer de bien loin. Lorsque nous con- " damnons nos terres à nous donner ce qu'elles " produisent avec désavantage aux dépends de ce " qu'elles produisent plus volontiers; lorsque nous " achetons fort cher, ce que nous payerions a fort " bon marché, si nous le tirions des lieux ou il " est produit avec avantage, nous devenons nous " mêmes victimes de notre propre folie. Le comble " de l'habilité est de tirer le parti le plus avantageux " des forces de la nature; et le comble de la dé- " mence est de lutter contre elles; car c'est em- " ployer nos peines à detruire une partie des " forces qu'elle voudroit nous prêter."

CAROLINE.

The prohibition of foreign commodities has then an effect precisely the reverse of that of machinery; for it increases instead of diminishing the quantity of labour; and produces inferior, instead of more perfect commodities.

ON FOREIGN TRADE. 381

MRS. B.

And consequently the wealth, prosperity, and enjoyments of a country so situated, instead of augmenting would decline. Let us hear what Dr. Franklin says on the subject of restrictions and prohibitions.

" Perhaps, in general, it would be better if go-
" vernment meddled no further with trade than to
" protect it, and let it take its course. Most of the
" statutes or acts, edicts, arrets, and placards, of
" parliaments, princes, and states, for regulating,
" directing, or restraining of trade, have, we think,
" been either political blunders, or jobs obtained
" by artful men, for private advantage, under pre-
" tence of public good. When Colbert assembled
" some wise old merchants of France, and desired
" their advice and opinion how he could serve and
" promote commerce: their answer, after consult-
" ation, was in three words only, ' *Laissez nous*
" *faire.*' It is said by a very solid writer of the
" same nation, that *he* is well advanced in the
" science of politics who knows the full force of
" that maxim, *pas trop gouverner*, which perhaps
" would be of more use when applied to trade than
" in any other public concern. It were, therefore, to
" be wished that commerce were as free between all
" the nations in the world, as between the several
" counties of England. So would all, by mutual
" communication, obtain more enjoyment. Those

382   ON FOREIGN TRADE.

"counties do not ruin each other by trade,
"neither would the nations. No nation was ever
"ruined by trade, even seemingly the most disad-
"vantageous. Whenever desirable superfluities
"are imported, industry is thereby excited and
"superfluity produced."

CAROLINE.

Well, I abandon the exclusive use of English
luxuries; but the very argument you have used
against them makes me think that it must be ad-
visable to rely on home produce for the necessaries
of life. Were we dependant on foreign countries
for a supply of corn, what would become of us if
those countries, in time of war, prohibited its exportation?

MRS. B.

Your question will lead us into a discussion on
the corn-trade, which it is too late for us to enter
upon to-day; we will, therefore, reserve it for our
next meeting.

CONVERSATION XX.

Continuation of FOREIGN TRADE.

ON THE CORN TRADE — CONSEQUENCES OF DEPEND-
ING UPON A HOME SUPPLY OF CORN IN COUNTRIES
OF GREAT CAPITAL AND POPULATION. — IT PRO-
DUCES HIGH PRICES IN ORDINARY SEASONS, AND
GREAT FLUCTUATION OF PRICES IN TIMES OF
SCARCITY AND OF ABUNDANCE — WHY THIS IS
NOT THE CASE IN NEWLY SETTLED COUNTRIES.
— PROPRIETY OF FREE TRADE IN GENERAL. —
DANGER OF INTRODUCING A NEW BRANCH OF
INDUSTRY PREMATURELY — EXTRACT FROM MI-
RABEAU'S MONARCHIE PRUSSIENNE ON THE AD-
VANTAGES OF FREE COMMERCIAL INTERCOURSE.

MRS. B.

WHEN we last parted, you expressed a wish
that we should raise all our corn at home,
in order to be completely independant of the casualties attending a foreign supply.

384 ON FOREIGN TRADE.

CAROLINE.

Yes; for were we at war with those countries which usually furnished us with corn, they would withhold the supply. Or, should they experience a dearth, they would no longer have it in their power to send us corn.

MRS. B.

We occasionally import corn from different parts of America, from the shores of the Baltic, and those of the Mediterranean seas. Now it is very improbable either that we should be in a state of warfare with those various countries at the same period of time, or that they should all be afflicted with a dearth of produce in the same season. There is much greater chance of a scarcity prevailing in any single country than in every part of the world at once; and should we depend wholly on that country for our supply, where would be our resource in case of a deficiency?

CAROLINE.

Under such circumstances it would certainly be right to import corn; I object only to doing so habitually, and not depending, in ordinary times, on the produce of our own country.

MRS. B.

If we apply to corn countries only in seasons of distress, we shall find it very difficult to obtain

ON FOREIGN TRADE. 385

relief. Those countries raise corn expressly for the nations which they usually supply with that article: but they will have but little to spare for a new customer, who, from a dearth at home, is compelled to seek for food abroad; and we could obtain it only by outbidding other competitors. The supply, therefore, would be both scanty, and at a price which the lower ranks of people could ill afford to pay; so that there would be great distress if not danger of a famine.

CAROLINE.

To prevent such a calamity we have only to raise so large a quantity of corn at home as will afford a plentiful supply in years of average produce; then in seasons of abundance we have the resource of exportation, and in bad seasons we might still have a sufficiency.

MRS. B.

It is impossible to raise at all times a sufficiency, without having often a superfluity. This is particularly the case with corn, as it is the most variable of almost all kinds of agricultural produce. If, therefore, we wish to raise such a quantity as will always secure us against want, we must in common seasons have some to spare, and in abundant years a great superfluity.

Now the more corn-land we cultivate, the higher

s

386   ON FOREIGN TRADE.

will the price of corn be in average seasons. You
start, Caroline; but paradoxical as this may appear, if you reflect upon the causes which occasion
the regular high price of corn, independently of
the variations of supply and demand, you will understand it.

The more corn is grown in a country, the greater
will be the quantity of inferior land brought into
cultivation, in order to produce it; and the price
of corn, you know, must pay the cost of its production on the worst soil in which it is raised *,
otherwise it would cease to be produced. If,
therefore, in order to insure a home supply, we
force an ungrateful soil, at a great expense of capital, to yield a scanty crop, we raise the price of
all the corn of the country to that standard, and we
thus enable the landed proprietors to increase their
rents. — By enhancing the price of the first necessaries of life we raise the rate of wages, in order to
enable the labouring classes to live; and we raise
the price of all manufactured goods, the produce
of their labour.

CAROLINE.

This is indeed a long catalogue of ruinous consequences.

MRS. B.

Nor is this all; when the home supply proves

* See Conversation on Rent.

ON FOREIGN TRADE. 387

superabundant, what is to become of it ? The unnatural high price at which it usually sells in our
market, owing to the forced encouragement given
to agriculture, renders it unsaleable in foreign
markets until the price is fallen so low as to be
ruinous to farmers.

CAROLINE.

I cannot easily bring myself to look upon a
superfluity of the necessaries of life as a calamity;
— if it is injurious to the farmer, what an advantage it is to the lower classes of people !

MRS. B.

The advantage is of a very temporary nature.
The farmer who cultivates poor land in hopes of a
remunerating price, must be ruined if he continues
to cultivate at the low price occasioned by superfluity: he will therefore throw up the inferior lands,
and the consequence will be that less corn will be
produced in succeeding years than is requisite for
the supply; and the superfluity will be succeeded by
dearth or famine. Thus the price of corn will be
continually fluctuating between the low price of a
glutted market and the high price of scarcity.

A redundance of the necessaries of life is in some
respects attended with more pernicious consequences than the excess of any other species of commodity. If the market were overstocked with tea and

s 2

388   ON FOREIGN TRADE.

coffee, those articles would fall in price, and would not only be more freely consumed by the people accustomed to enjoy them, but the reduction of price would bring them within reach of a lower and more extensive class of people. Now this cannot happen with bread, because it is already the daily and most common food of the lowest ranks of society; and though in seasons of great plenty they may consume somewhat more than usual, the difference will not be very considerable; they will rather avail themselves of the cheapness of bread to devote a larger share of their wages to other gratifications; they will eat more meat, drink more spirits, or wear better clothes. The superabundance of corn will therefore remain in the granary of the farmer, instead of supplying him with the means of carrying on the cultivation of his land; the labourers who raised that corn will probably be driven to the parish for want of work, and the consequences which will ensue to the community who would have been fed by the fruits of their industry, it is easy to conceive.

CAROLINE.

But do you then regard a low price of corn, under all circumstances, as an evil?

MRS. B.

On the contrary, I consider it in general as

ON FOREIGN TRADE.

389

highly advantageous; it is attended with injurious consequences only when it will not remunerate the farmer. But when corn can be raised at a small expense, it can afford to be sold at a low price. It is this which renders it desirable to bring only good land under tillage, and not to force poor soils to yield scanty and expensive crops.

Countries that have plenty of good land and but little capital find no branch of industry so advantageous as the productions of agriculture; and the exportation of corn, we have observed, is their first attempt at foreign commerce. Thus America, being a newly settled country, and as yet but thinly inhabited, has great choice of fine soils, and can raise corn at a very small expense of production; accordingly we find that she not only feeds her own population, but regularly exports corn.

Old established countries, on the contrary, such as England, whose population is too great to be maintained by the produce of her good soils, will find it answer better to import some portion of the corn they consume, and to convert their inferior lands into pasture. This would not only lower the price of bread, but also that of meat, milk, butter, and cheese, the supply of which would be increased by the conversion of corn land into pasture. When the home crops proved abundant, they would import less; when scanty, they would import more. Thus without difficulty they would proportion the

s 3

390   ON FOREIGN TRADE.

supply to the demand, and keep both bread and
wages steadily at moderate prices.

CAROLINE.

But with the additional expenses of freight and
insurance, can we import corn from America
cheaper than we can produce it at home?

MRS. B.

In ordinary seasons we certainly can; but not at
the present price of corn.

CAROLINE.

And do you suppose that the present low price
of corn, and the distressed state of agriculture, are
owing to our producing too much corn at home?

MRS. B.

I have no doubt but that it is one of the causes,
but it is connected with many others, which render
the question so complicated and intricate that we
must leave it to wiser heads than our own to unravel it.

The system of growing a home supply of corn,
in countries where great capital affords the means
of maintaining a very large population, is attended
not only with the disadvantage of keeping the price
of corn high, in average seasons, but likewise occasions greater fluctuations of price, in times of dearth

ON FOREIGN TRADE. 391

or abundance, than if those casualties were diminished by a free corn-trade with other countries. It would perhaps be difficult to say whether we have suffered most from a high or a low price of corn, within these last twenty years; but we have acquired sufficient experience of the evils arising from both these extremes to think, that the wisest measures we could pursue, would be to adopt such as would prevent great fluctuations of price.

Nothing is more injurious to the interests of the labouring classes than great and sudden fluctuations in the price of bread: they are either distressed by unexpected poverty, or intoxicated by sudden prosperity; but if that prosperity is the effect but of one fruitful season, it gives rise to expenses they are unable to maintain. It is but a gleam of sunshine on a wintry day, and the buds it untimely developes are nipped by the succeeding frost.

CAROLINE.

Well, Mrs. B., I see that you will not allow of any exception in favour of the corn trade, and that I must consent to admit of the propriety of leaving all trade whatever perfectly free and open.

MRS. B.

That is certainly the wisest way. Instead of struggling against the dictates of reason and nature, and madly attempting to produce every thing at

392 ON FOREIGN TRADE.

home, countries should study to direct their labours to those departments of industry for which their situation and circumstances are best adapted.

CAROLINE.

Yet you must allow me to observe, that there are numerous instances of our having established flourishing manufactures of goods which we formerly procured entirely from foreign commerce; such, for instance, as china-ware, muslins, damask linen, and a variety of others. Now does not this imply that we may sometimes direct our labour to a new branch of industry with greater advantage than by importing the goods from foreign countries?

MRS. B.

It certainly does; and it shews also, that as soon as we are able to cultivate or fabricate the commodities we have been accustomed to procure from foreign parts as cheap as we can import them, we never fail to do so. But the period for the introduction of any new branch of industry should be left to the experience and discretion of the individuals concerned in it, and not attempted to be regulated or enforced by government. James I. attempted to compel his subjects to dye their woollen cloths in this country, instead of sending them to the Netherlands, as had been the usual practice; but the English-dyed woollen cloths proved both

ON FOREIGN TRADE. 393

of worse quality and dearer than those of the Netherlands, and James was obliged to abandon his plan. Had the sovereign not interfered, dyers would have established themselves in this country as soon as the people had acquired sufficient skill to undertake the business; but the discouragement produced by an unsuccessful attempt probably retarded the natural period of adopting it.

If it were possible for a country both to cultivate and manufacture all kinds of produce with as little labour as it costs to purchase them from other countries, there would be no occasion for foreign commerce; but the remarkable manner in which Providence has varied the productions of nature in different climates, appears to indicate a design to promote an intercourse between nations, even to the most distant regions of the earth; an intercourse which would ever prove a source of reciprocal benefit and happiness, were it not often perverted by the bad passions and blind policy of man.

CAROLINE.

And independently of the diversity of soils, climates, and natural productions, I do not suppose that it would be possible for any single country to succeed in all branches of industry, any more than for a single individual to acquire any considerable skill in a great variety of pursuits?

s 5

394 ON FOREIGN TRADE.

MRS. B.

Certainly not. The same kind of division of labour which exists among the individuals of a community, is also in some degree observable among different countries; and when particular branches of industry are not formed by local circumstances, it will generally be found the best policy to endeavour to excel a neighbouring nation in those manufactures in which we are nearly on a par, rather than to attempt competition in those in which by long habit and skill they have acquired a decided superiority. Thus will the common stock of productions be most improved, and all countries most benefitted. Nothing can be more illiberal and short-sighted than a jealousy of the progress of neighbouring countries, either in agriculture or manufactures. Their demand for our commodities, so far from diminishing, will always be found to increase with the means of purchasing them. It is the idleness and poverty, not the wealth and industry of neighbouring nations, that should excite alarm.

CAROLINE.

A tradesman would consider it more to his interest to set up his shop in the neighbourhood of opulent customers than of poor people who could not afford to purchase his goods; and why should not countries consider trade in the same point of view?

ON FOREIGN TRADE. 395

MRS. B.

Mirabeau, in his " *Monarchie Prussienne,*" has carried this principle so far, that it has made him doubt whether the trade of France was injured by the revocation of the edict of Nantz, which drove so many skilful manufacturers and artificers out of the country.

" Il est en general un principe sûr en commerce ; " plus vos acheteurs seront riches, plus vous leur " vendrez; ainsi les causes qui enrichissent un " peuple augmente toujours l'industrie de ceux qui " ont des affaires à negocier avec lui. Sans doute " c'est une demence frénétique de chasser 200,000 " individus de son pays pour enricher celui des " autres; mais la nature qui veut conserver son " ouvrage ne cesse de reparer par des compensa- " tions insensibles, les erreurs des hommes, et les " fautes les plus désastreuses ne sont pas sans " rémédes. La grande verité que nous offre cet " exemple mémorable, c'est qu'il est insensé de " detruire l'industrie et le commerce de ses voisins, " puisqu'on anéantit en même tems chez soi même " ces trésors. Si de tels efforts pouvoient jamais " produire leur effet, ils dépeupleroient le monde, " et rendroient trés infortunée la nation qui auroit " eu le malheur d'engloutir toute l'industrie, tout " le commerce du globe, et de vendre toujours " sans jamais acheter. Heureusement la Provi- " dence a tellement disposé les choses que les

s 6

396 ON FOREIGN TRADE.

" delires des souverains ne sauroient arrêter en-
" tierement ses vues de bonheur pour notre espêce."

CAROLINE.

The more I learn upon this subject, the more I feel convinced that the interests of nations, as well as those of individuals, so far from being opposed to each other, are in the most perfect unison.

MRS. B.

Liberal and enlarged views will always lead to similar conclusions, and teach us to cherish sentiments of universal benevolence towards each other; hence the superiority of science over mere practical knowledge.

CONVERSATION XXI.

Subject of FOREIGN TRADE *continued.*

OF BILLS OF EXCHANGE. — OF THE BALANCE OF TRADE. — CAUSE OF THE *REAL* VARIATION OF THE EXCHANGE. — DISPROPORTION OF EXPORTS AND IMPORTS. — CAUSE OF THE *NOMINAL* VARIATION OF THE EXCHANGE. — DEPRECIATION OF THE VALUE OF THE CURRENCY OF THE COUNTRY.

MRS. B.

I HOPE that you are now quite satisfied of the advantages which result from foreign commerce?

CAROLINE.

Perfectly so; but there is one thing that perplexes me. In a general point of view I conceive that trade consists in an exchange of commodities; but I do not understand how this exchange takes place between merchants. The wine merchant, for instance, who imports wine from Portugal, does

398 ON FOREIGN TRADE.

not export goods in return for it; his trade is confined to the article of wine?

MRS. B.

There are many general merchants who both export and import various articles of trade. Thus the Spanish merchant, the Turkey merchant, and the West Indian merchant, import all the different commodities which we receive from those countries, and generally export English goods in return. It is, however, the countries, rather than the individuals, who *exchange* their respective productions; for both the goods exported and imported are in all cases bought and sold, and never actually exchanged.

CAROLINE.

But since the merchants of the respective countries do not literally exchange their goods, they must each of them send a sum of money in payment; and these sums of money will be nearly equivalent. If the London merchant has 1000*l.* to pay for wines at Lisbon, the Lisbon merchant will have nearly the same sum to pay for broad cloth in London. It is to be regretted, therefore, that the goods should not be actually exchanged, or that some mode should not be devised of reciprocally transferring the debts, in order to avoid so much useless expense and trouble.

ON FOREIGN TRADE. 399

MRS. B.

Such a mode has been devised, and these purchases and sales are usually made without the intervention of money, by means of written orders called *bills of exchange.*

CAROLINE.

Is not then a bill of exchange a species of paper-money like a bank-note?

MRS. B.

Not exactly; instead of being a promissory note, it is an order addressed to the person abroad to whom the merchant sends his goods, directing him to pay the amount of the bill, at a certain date, to some third person mentioned in the bill. Thus when a woollen merchant sends broad cloths to Portugal, he draws such a bill on the merchant to whom he consigns them; but instead of sending it with the goods to Portugal, he disposes of it in London : that is to say, he inquires whether any person wants such a bill for the purpose of discharging a debt in Portugal. He accordingly applies to some wine merchant who owes a sum of money to a mercantile house at Lisbon for wines imported from that country, and who finds it convenient to avail himself of this mode of payment, in order to avoid the expense of sending money to Portugal. He therefore gives the woollen merchant the value

400 ON FOREIGN TRADE.

of his bill, and having his own name or that of his correspondent in Portugal inserted in the bill as the third person to whom the amount of the bill is to be paid, transmits it to his correspondent in Portugal, who receives the money from the person on whom it is drawn.

CAROLINE.

The same bill then is the means of paying for both commodities, the broad cloth and the wine; and it supersedes the necessity of transmitting two sums of money for that purpose. A bill of exchange is a most convenient and economical contrivance, and I feel very much inclined to avail myself of it. A friend of mine at York owes me a sum of money for purchases I have made for her in London; and my sister Emily is indebted about the same sum to a glover at York. I might, therefore, draw a bill of exchange on my friend, which Emily would buy of me, and forward it to the glover at York for the purpose of discharging her debt for the gloves; and he would receive the money from my friend on whom it was drawn. It is, if I understand you right, by such transfers of debts that commodities are really exchanged between merchants?

MRS. B.

I am glad to see that you understand the use of

ON FOREIGN TRADE. 401

a bill of exchange so well. It will therefore be evident to you that if, when two countries are trading together, the value of the goods exported and imported be equal, the amount of the bills of exchange in payment of those goods will be so likewise; and the debts will be mutually settled without the necessity of transmitting money.

CAROLINE.

That is quite clear: but it must, I suppose, frequently happen, that the value of the goods exported and imported is not equal, and in that case the bills of exchange will not settle the whole of the respective debts, and some balance or sum of money will remain due from one country to the other.

MRS. B.

This is called the balance of trade. In order to explain to you in what manner such a debt is settled, let us take, for example, our trade with Russia: — if, in trading with that country, our exports and imports are exactly equal in value, the exchange between Russia and England is said to be at par, or equal.

But if the value of our imports should have exceeded our exports, so that, for instance, we should have received more hemp and tallow *from*, than we have sent broad-cloths and hard-

402 ON FOREIGN TRADE.

ware *to* Russia, there will be a greater amount of bills drawn by Russian merchants on England, than by English merchants on Russia. After their reciprocal debts are settled, therefore, as far as the bills will enable them to do so, there will remain a surplus of Russian bills drawn on England, which will require to be paid in money.

CAROLINE.

Then some of our merchants will be under the necessity of sending money to Russia in payment of their debts.

MRS. B.

This every merchant endeavours to avoid, on account of the heavy expenses of freight and insurance of the money; as soon, therefore, as there appears to be a scarcity of English bills on Russia, every English merchant who is indebted to that country for hemp and tallow is eager to procure them. The competition of merchants for these bills raises their price, for they find it answer to give something more than the amount of the bill rather than send gold to Russia. The sum thus given for a bill above its amount is called a *premium*, and our exchange with Russia is, in this case, said to be *unfavourable*, or *below par*.

CAROLINE.

That is to say, that a man who owes a sum of

ON FOREIGN TRADE. 403

money to Russia, must give something more than the amount of the debt in order to pay it?

MRS. B.

Yes; and the amount of the premium given depends, of course, on the degree of scarcity of the bills.

CAROLINE.

But the exchange, I suppose, can never fall below what it would cost to transport gold to Russia; for as it is optional with our merchants to pay either in bills or money, if the premium on the bill were greater than the expense of sending money, they would prefer the latter mode of payment.

MRS. B.

Undoubtedly; and as the expense of sending gold to different countries varies according to the distance, and to the facility or difficulty of our intercourse with them, a favourable or unfavourable exchange with those countries will vary accordingly.

CAROLINE.

But the premium given for bills of exchange, after all, does not supersede the necessity of our paying the balance of debt in gold; it merely removes the difficulty from one individual to another: for those merchants who finally cannot obtain bills must transmit money in payment.

404 ON FOREIGN TRADE.

MRS. B.

I beg your pardon; an unfavourable exchange in a great measure corrects itself: but this, it is true, requires some explanation. There are merchants who make it their business to trade in bills of exchange; that is to say, to buy them where they are abundant and cheap, and sell them where they are scarce and dear. Thus bills of exchange become an article of commerce like gold, or any other commodity. Therefore when English bills on Russia are scarce, those merchants buy up the bills drawn by other countries on Russia, and supply the English market with them.

CAROLINE.

But when English bills on Russia are scarce, there may perhaps be no surplus of bills on Russia in other countries to supply the English market.

MRS. B.

Generally speaking, when there is a deficiency of bills on Russia in one country, there will be a redundancy of them in some other; for though the exportations and importation of Russia with any particular country may be unequal, her general exportations and importations will, upon the whole, nearly balance each other: because if there was a constant excess of importation, Russia would be drained of money to pay for it; if, on the contrary,

ON FOREIGN TRADE. 405

there was an excess of exportations, the money received in payment would accumulate, and depreciate the value of the currency of the country. The goods which Russia purchases, therefore, from foreign countries, must, upon the long run, be to the same amount as the goods which she sells in exchange for them; so that if there is a balance of debt due *to* Russia from one country, there must be a balance of debt due *from* Russia to another country. The bills of exchange, therefore, drawn by Russia on foreign countries, and those drawn by foreign countries on Russia, will balance each other; and it is the business of the dealers in bills to discover where there is a superfluity, and where a deficiency of these bills, with a view to buy them in the one place, and sell them in the other.

CAROLINE.

If then the bill merchants instead of supplying the English market with bills on Russia, bought up the surplus of Russian bills on England, it would equally answer the purpose of paying our debt to that country?

MRS. B.

Exactly. In our trade with Italy, for instance, we import large quantities of silk, olive oil, and various other articles, and our exportations are manufactured goods only to a trifling amount.

406 ON FOREIGN TRADE.

The exchange would, in this case, be so unfavourable as to reduce us to the necessity of exporting gold in payment for the excess of imports, did not the bill merchants come to our assistance. This useful class of men buy up the surplus of Italian bills on England, and send them for sale to Germany, France, Spain, or wherever there is a deficiency of bills on Italy, and where they will consequently sell with profit.

CAROLINE.

Thus Germany, France, or Spain, discharge our debt to Italy?

MRS. B.

Yes; provided any of those countries are in our debt; otherwise, you know they would not purchase our bills of exchange.

CAROLINE.

One would imagine that these operations of the bill merchants would invariably have the effect of counteracting the fluctuations of exchanges, and keep them constantly at par.

MRS. B.

If the business of the bill merchant could be transacted with the same celerity and regularity as that of the bankers in London, who meet together every day, after the hours of business, to settle

ON FOREIGN TRADE. 407

their respective accounts, it might influence the exchanges in the manner you suppose. But the speculations of the bill merchant embrace so wide a sphere, and so many circumstances occur in the course of trade, or of political events, by which the exchanges are affected, that no individual prudence or foresight can prevent great fluctuations.

CAROLINE.

Are then merchants often reduced to the necessity of sending abroad money in payment of foreign goods?

MRS. B.

Scarcely ever, I believe, excepting where there is a greater demand for money than for goods; for independently of the operations of the bill merchants, there is yet another means of preventing that expense. When the English merchants who export goods to Russia, find that the excess of imports over exports, produces a scarcity of their bills on Russia, which enables them to sell them to the importing merchants at a premium, such an addition to their usual profits of trade, induces them to increase their exportations, and has, in fact, the effect of a bounty; for they can now afford to export goods which, before, did not yield sufficient profits to enable them to do it. Whilst, on the contrary, our importing merchants of Russian commodities, who are obliged to purchase these bills at a premium, (which has

408   ON FOREIGN TRADE.

the effect of a duty, since it is a clear deduction
from their profits), will confine their importations
to such commodities only as will leave them their
usual profits, after deducting the premium upon
the bills with which they were to be paid.

CAROLINE.

The premiums, then, which our importing merchants lose, our exporting merchants gain. This
must undoubtedly have a considerable effect in encouraging exportation, and restraining importation,
and tend rapidly to restore the equality of the
exchange.

MRS. B.

The evil, then, of an unfavourable exchange immediately gives rise to the remedy which corrects
it, and actually tends to equalize the exports and
imports. But in order to have completely that
effect, it would be necessary that the country with
whom the exchange is unfavourable should require
as much of our productions as we do of theirs,
which is not always the case. The unfavourable
exchange, however, enables the exporting merchant to afford his goods abroad at a lower rate,
because a part of his profit is derived from the premium on the exchange, and thus more persons
abroad being able to purchase at the reduced price,
the market for the goods is enlarged, and a much
greater quantity consumed.

ON FOREIGN COMMERCE. 409

CAROLINE.

All these circumstances then together must nearly supersede the necessity of sending money to balance the account?

MRS. B.

Very nearly so, I believe, except with such countries as, having mines of their own, may be said to produce money. If Spain and Portugal were to retain all the gold and silver which they derive from their mines, it would fall so much in value in those countries that no laws could prevent its conveyance to others where its value was greater. It would be the most profitable article a Spanish or Portugueze merchant could export in payment for the goods imported; and indeed we find that they supply Europe with gold and silver, in the same manner as we supply it with the produce of our West Indian colonies, coffee and sugar. We have, in a former conversation, observed how the precious metals were diffused throughout all civilized nations, and the supply every where so proportioned to the demand, as to admit of no other variation of value than the small difference arising from the expense of bringing them from the mines to the different countries where they are wanted.

CAROLINE.

But have I not heard of the exchange having

T

410 ON FOREIGN COMMERCE.

been much below what it would cost to send money abroad?

MRS. B.

That is true; but I believe it is principally to be ascribed to another and a totally different cause, which nominally influences the exchanges to a very great extent. We formerly observed, that a depreciation of value of the currency of a country raises the price of commodities in that country. Whether the depreciation arises from an unnecessary increase of currency, from an adulteration of the coin, or from any other cause, it invariably produces this effect.

Let us suppose the currency of England to be depreciated 25 per cent.; that is to say, that a sum worth 100*l.* previous to the depreciation, is now really worth only 75*l.*, though it retains its nominal value of 100*l.* An English bill of exchange, which represents a certain portion of the currency, will partake of this depreciation, and will no longer be equal in value to a foreign bill of the same amount. It would require an English bill of 125*l.* to exchange for a foreign one of 100*l.*; therefore if before the depreciation the exchange were at par, this circumstance would make it immediately fall 25 per cent.

CAROLINE.

Would not the evil then be remedied by increasing the exports and diminishing the imports, as

ON FOREIGN COMMERCE. 411

when the unfavourable state of the exchange arises from the unequal balance of trade?

MRS. B.

Certainly not For though it is true that in both cases the exporting merchant can sell his bills at a premium, yet when this premium arises from a depreciation of the currency, it cannot be considered as any gain to him, because it is exactly balanced by the advanced price of the goods he exports, which operates as a loss.

CAROLINE.

I think I understand it. The depreciation of currency which produces the premium on the bill of exchange produces also an increase in the price of the merchandize, and these effects, resulting from the same cause, must always correspond and be felt in the same proportion. Thus if a merchant exports cloth to Hamburgh which costs him 200*l.*, whatever profits he might expect under the ordinary state of the currency must be diminished 25 per cent., in consequence of his giving 50*l.* more for his cloth than he would otherwise have done. Yet as he will sell the bill of exchange which he draws on Hamburgh for the payment of his cloth, at a premium of 50*l.*, his profits will remain precisely the same, upon the whole transaction, as if every thing had gone on in its regular way.

T 2

412 ON FOREIGN COMMERCE.

MRS. B.

You have explained it perfectly well. Remember therefore that when the exchange is unfavourable in consequence of the depreciation of the currency, it is only *nominally*, not really unfavourable; for it may take place when the exports and imports are perfectly equal. And recollect also that the difference the exchange produces in the sale or purchase of bills is neither a loss nor a gain to the parties, and that it has no effect either on exportation or importation.

CAROLINE.

But is it easy to distinguish between two causes which are so similar in their effects, and to ascertain at any time which of them it is that influences the exchange?

MRS. B.

Far from it : this has been a subject of much discussion, particularly during the late war. If it be true that the currency of the country has been increased beyond what was required, it must be considered as depreciated, and as having nominally affected the exchange.

On the other hand, as the system of warfare was remarkably unfavourable to our exportations, the balance of foreign debt was very much against us, and the expense of transmitting gold considerably increased; — so far the exchange may be said to have been *really* unfavourable. It is probable that both

ON FOREIGN COMMERCE. 413

these causes contributed to the very low rate of our exchange during the late war.

Notwithstanding all the investigation which these subjects have undergone, there still prevails, even amongst our legislators, the old popular error respecting the balance of trade. Even at this day we find persons congratulating the country, that the exports exceed the imports, and that in consequence a balance of money remains due to us, which is considered as so much gain to the country.

CAROLINE.

But do those who maintain such an opinion know, that this money would not be due to us, unless we had exported a surplus of merchandize to an equal amount?

MRS. B.

It is from that circumstance they conceive the advantage arises. They assert that since the poor are maintained by labour, the more work we perform for other countries, and the more money we receive for our work, the richer we must be.

CAROLINE.

Not if we export the fruits of their labour and receive only gold in return: for the poor are maintained not by the act of labour, but by its produce; and if all that produce were exported, and nothing but gold received in exchange, we should be much

T 3

414 ON FOREIGN COMMERCE.

in the situation of King Midas, who was starved because every thing he touched was converted into gold.

But do not the bill merchants prevent this importation of gold, by transferring the bills of exchange from one country to another? for if our balance of trade is favourable with one country, it must be unfavourable with another.

MRS. B.

No doubt they do. If it were possible to have what is called a favourable balance of trade with every country, we should accumulate a quantity of the precious metals which would answer no other purpose than to depreciate our currency.

The most advantageous trade for both parties concerned is when the exports and imports are equal, so that the balance does not preponderate on either side; for it is as injurious to one country to part with money which is wanted at home for the purposes of currency, as it is to the other to receive it when it is not wanted.

When a country receives bullion, it should not be in payment of a balance of debt, but as a commodity for which there is a demand. This demand will always take place in thriving countries, not only because gold and silver bullion are wanted by jewellers and silversmiths for the purposes of luxury; but also because, as the saleable produce of the country

ON FOREIGN COMMERCE. 415

increases, an additional quantity of currency is required for its circulation.

CAROLINE.

According to this theory of the balance of trade, it should always be against Spain and Portugal, and favourable to every other country; because it is through Spain and Portugal that all the treasures of the new world flow into Europe?

MRS. B.

True; but they are not sent immediately from those countries to the most distant parts of Europe, but are transferred through the intermediate countries. Thus France sends *Louis* to Geneva to pay for the watches she imports from that place; or to Italy, in payment of raw silks, olive oil, &c. So that the countries most distant from Spain and Portugal would constantly have what is absurdly called the balance of trade in their favour; whilst the intermediate countries would have it favourable with those which were nearer Spain than themselves, and unfavourable with those which were more distant.

This, however, is a general principle, which, though true in theory, requires modification, if applied to practice. A great variety of circumstances occasion fluctuations in the regular distribution of the wealth of America. However

T 4

416 ON FOREIGN COMMERCE.

extraordinary it may appear, it is not very long since we sent considerable quantities of specie to Spain and Portugal, to maintain our troops in those countries: so much does war reverse the natural order of things. Instead of exporting our manufactures to bring back gold, we were obliged to drain our circulation to send money in order to support our troops, whilst our manufacturers were either starving, or became members of that very army which caused their ruin.

CAROLINE.

But if Spain, from the abundance of her gold and silver, imports such large quantities of manufacured goods, is it not a check to her industry at home?

MRS. B.

It certainly is; though not so much as you would imagine, because she does not obtain the gold and silver of America free of cost: she obtains it partly in the form of a tax imposed by the mother country, or rent for the royal mines; and the rest by payment in produce or manufactured goods. But these goods not necessarily manufactured in Spain or Portugal. A Spanish merchant having imported goods from England and sent them to America, receives back gold and silver in payment, which are transmitted to England, if wanted there. Spain and Portugal being the entrepôt, in conse-

ON FOREIGN COMMERCE. 417

quence of the strict regulations by which the gold
and silver are compelled to be brought to the mother
country.

The want of industry in Spain, though it proceeds in a great measure from the nature of its
religion and government, is also in part attributable
to the effect which the influx of the precious metals
has produced.

In Townsend's Travels in Spain, which abound
with philosophical observations, it is stated " that
" the gold and silver of America, instead of
" animating the country and promoting industry,
" instead of giving life and vigour to the whole
" community, by the increase of arts, of manufac-
" tures, and of commerce, had an opposite effect,
" and produced in the event weakness, poverty,
" and depopulation. The wealth which proceeds
" from industry resembles the copious yet tranquil
" stream, which passes silent, and almost invisible,
" enriches the whole extent of country through
" which it flows; but the treasures of the new
" world, like a swelling torrent, were seen, were
" heard, were felt, were admired; yet their first
" operation was to desolate and lay waste the spot
" on which they fell. The shock was sudden; the
" contrast was too great. Spain overflowed with
" specie, whilst other nations were comparatively
" poor in the extreme. The price of labour, of
" provisions, and of manufactures, bore proportion

T 5

418 ON FOREIGN COMMERCE.

" to the quantity of circulating cash. The conse-
" quence is obvious; in the poor countries industry
" advanced; in the more wealthy it declined.

" Even in the present day (1806), specie being
" about 6 per cent. less valuable in Spain than it
" is in other countries, operates precisely in the
" same proportion against her manufactures and
" her population."

We may here, I think, conclude our observations on the principles of trade; and having now
explained the different sources from which a revenue may be derived, we shall at our next meeting
make a few inquiries into the nature and effects of
expenditure.

CONVERSATION XXI.

ON EXPENDITURE.

OF THE DISPOSAL OF REVENUE. — OF THE EXPENDI-
TURE OF INDIVIDUALS. — EFFECTS OF CONSUM-
ING CAPITAL. — INCREASE OF REVENUE OF A
COUNTRY BENEFICIAL TO ALL CLASSES OF PEOPLE.
— EXCEPT IN CASES WHERE GOVERNMENT INTER-
FERES WITH THE DISPOSAL OF CAPITAL. — OF
SUMPTUARY LAWS. — OF LUXURY. — INDUSTRY
PROMOTED BY LUXURY. — PASSAGE FROM PALEY
ON LUXURY. — SUDDEN INCREASE OF WEALTH
PREJUDICIAL TO THE LABOURING CLASSES. —
PASSAGE FROM BENTHAM ON LEGISLATION. —
LUXURY OF THE ROMANS NOT THE RESULT OF
INDUSTRY. — OF THE DISADVANTAGES ARISING
FROM EXCESS OF LUXURY.

MRS. B.

I TRUST that you now understand both the
manner in which capital is accumulated, and the
various modes of employing it to produce a revenue.

T 6

420   ON EXPENDITURE.

It remains for us to examine how this revenue may be disposed of.

CAROLINE.

I have already learnt that revenue may either be spent, or accumulated and converted into capital; and that the more a man economises for the latter purpose, the richer he becomes.

MRS. B.

This observation is equally applicable to the capital of a country, which may be augmented by industry and frugality, or diminished by prodigality.

CAROLINE.

The capital of a country, I think you said, consisted of the capital of its inhabitants taken collectively?

MRS. B.

It does; but you must be careful not to estimate the revenue of a country in the same manner, for it would lead to very erroneous calculations. Let us for instance suppose my income to be 10,000*l.* a-year, and that I pay 500*l.* a-year for the rent of my house—it is plain that this 500*l.* constitutes a portion of the income of my landlord; and since therefore the same property, by being transferred from one to another, may successively form the income of several individuals, the revenue of the country cannot be estimated by the aggregate income of the people.   15

ON EXPENDITURE.

CAROLINE.

And does not the same reasoning apply to the expenditure of a country; since the 500*l.* a-year which you spend in house-rent will be afterwards spent by your landlord in some other manner?

MRS. B.

True, because spending money is but exchanging one thing against another of equal value; — it is giving, for instance, one shilling in exchange for a loaf of bread, five guineas in exchange for a coat; instead of a shilling we are possessed of a loaf of bread; instead of five guineas, of a coat; we are therefore as rich before as after these purchases are made.

CAROLINE.

If so, how is it that we are impoverished by spending money?

MRS. B.

It is not by purchasing, but by consuming the things we have purchased, that we are impoverished. When we have eaten the bread and worn out the coat, we are the poorer by five guineas and a shilling than we were before.

A baker is not poorer for purchasing a hundred sacks of flour, nor a clothier for buying a hundred pieces of cloth, because they do not consume these commodities.

422 ON EXPENDITURE.

When a man purchases commodities with a view of re-selling them, he is a dealer in such commodities, and it is capital which he lays out. But when he purchases commodities for the purpose of using and consuming them, it is called expenditure. Expenditure therefore always implies consumption.

CAROLINE.

I understand the difference perfectly. The one lays out capital with the view of re-selling his goods with profit. The other spends money with the view of consuming the goods, with loss; — that is to say, the loss of the value of the goods he consumes.

MRS. B.

Just so. Thus though the sum of money you spend will serve the purpose of transferring commodities successively from one person to another, yet the commodities themselves can be consumed but once.

Therefore the consumption of a country may, like its capital, be estimated by the aggregate consumption of its inhabitants; and the great question relative to the prosperity of the country, is, how far that consumption takes place productively, and how far unproductively.

CAROLINE.

That certainly is a very important point; for in

ON EXPENDITURE. 423

the former case it increases wealth, in the latter it destroys it.

Yet, Mrs. B., supposing a man were so prodigal as to spend not only the whole of his income, but even the capital itself, provided that it were spent in the maintenance of productive labourers, though it would ruin the individual, I do not conceive that it would injure the country; for whether a man lay out his capital in the maintenance of productive labourers with a view to profit, or whether he spend it in purchasing the fruits of their industry for the purpose of enjoyment, I can perceive no difference relative to the country; in both cases an equal number of people would be employed, and consequently an equal quantity of wealth produced.

MRS. B.

I have a strong suspicion that the difficulty you feel in understanding clearly the distinction between the employment and expenditure of capital, arises from confounding capital with money?

CAROLINE.

Indeed I think not; my notion of capital is, that it consists of any kind of commodity useful to man.

MRS. D.

Well, then, suppose that two persons are possessed of such commodities to the value of 5000*l*. each: —

424 ON EXPENDITURE.

that the one distributes them out to industrious workmen, furnishing them with food and materials to work upon, and that by the time the various commodities have been finally distributed, the workmen have fashioned them into objects of another form, but of superior value to what has been consumed. Let the other distribute his capital amongst his servants, who in return amuse their employer with theatrical representations, fireworks, or any other species of enjoyment, which, by the time the commodities have been consumed, leave no other traces than the recollection that they have existed. Can you see no difference in these two instances?

CAROLINE.

Oh yes; I see a very material difference: one of the capitals of 5000*l.* is destroyed, and the person who has consumed it thus idly is reduced to beggary. But this is not the case I put. Let the prodigal, instead of consuming his capital in the way you have described, spend it amongst tradesmen, who will furnish him with articles for his enjoyment, such as magnificent apparel, splendid equipages, sumptuous entertainments. He will then replace the capital that those tradesmen have been consuming, in order to produce these commodities, which capital will again be usefully employed in producing more.

ON EXPENDITURE.   425

MRS. B.

That is very true; and so far the prodigal has
done no harm. In spending his capital amongst
tradesmen, he has exchanged his various commodities for others of equal value, and the same quantity of capital exists as before the exchange took
place; but what is the prodigal to do with the
new stock that he has acquired?

CAROLINE.

It will be applied to the gratification of his desires: he will regale with his friends at the sumptuous feasts, he will use the equipages, and clothe
himself and his servants in the rich apparel.

MRS. B.

Then don't you see that you have only removed
the evil one step farther? He and his friends
will consume amongst servants and dependants, in
fetes and splendid entertainments, what the tradesmen furnished him with, instead of that which he
gave in exchange for it; and that as much capital
will be lost to himself and to the community in
the one case as in the other. The spending of capital is a sterile consumption of it, whilst its employment is a reproductive consumption.

CAROLINE.

But if money were not thus spent, what would

426 ON EXPENDITURE.

the tradesman do with the luxuries which he had prepared for the purpose of supplying the demand of persons who spend in order to enjoy?

MRS. B.

Such tradesmen would certainly find less employment; but you would not thence conclude that the community would be injured. You have already seen that capital cannot produce revenue unless it is consumed; if it be consumed by industrious persons, who work whilst they are consuming it, something of superior value will be produced, and that product, whatever it may be, will be exchanged against other productions; it will be distributed amongst another order of tradesmen, and will afford precisely the same amount of encouragement, though of a different kind. Whatever is saved from the extravagant consumption of the rich, is a stock to contribute to the comforts of the middling and lower ranks of society.

CAROLINE.

Yet how often has it been said that a generous and liberal expenditure, however injurious to the individual, was a source from which the middling and lower classes drew their principal means of subsistence.

MRS. B.

There is not a more fatal delusion in political

ON EXPENDITURE. 427

economy. By such wanton extravagance as we have been describing, the capital, which should annually furnish a subsistence to labourers, is wasted and destroyed, and the industrious are reduced to idleness and want. They are covered with rags, because the prodigal has clothed himself in gorgeous apparel; they wander without a home, because the prodigal has erected a palace; they must starve, because the wealth that should have fed them has been squandered in sumptuous feasts.

It is easy to comprehend that the prevalence of such conduct in a state must be followed by the gradual decay of its wealth and population.

CAROLINE.

This is a most painful reflection; but on the other hand it would not, I suppose, be possible for a country to make any progress in wealth by which the poor were not more or less benefitted?

MRS. B.

Certainly not, if things are allowed to follow their natural course. Where property is secure, there is a general tendency to accumulation of capital. The great majority are governed by good sense and prudence, and their efforts to save and better their condition more than counterbalance the occasional loss that arises from the extrava-

428   ON EXPENDITURE.

gance of spendthrifts. Besides, if expenditure were directed in too large a proportion towards the production of mere luxuries, and the number of persons employed in producing them were to be increased without at the same time augmenting the number of persons employed in producing articles of subsistence, the same quantity of provisions must be divided amongst a greater number of consumers; and as provisions, in consequence of being more scarce, would increase in price, the profits of agriculture would become so great, that the capital which had been applied to the production of luxuries would flow to the more advantageous employment of agriculture, and thus the natural distribution of capital would be restored.

CAROLINE.

The more I hear on this subject, and the better I understand it, the greater is my admiration of that wise and beneficent arrangement which has so closely interwoven the interests of all classes of men!

MRS. B.

We are accustomed to trace the hand of Providence chiefly in the natural world, but it is no less conspicuous in moral life, and cannot be more strongly exemplified than in that order of things which renders it essential to the interests of the rich not to turn the labour of the poor to the produc-

ON EXPENDITURE.

tion of superfluities until they have provided an ample supply of the necessaries of life.

But these wise dispensations are often in a great measure subverted by the folly and ignorance of man. An injudicious interference of government, for instance, may give peculiar advantages to the employment of capital in one particular branch of industry, to the prejudice of others, and thus destroy that natural and useful distribution of it, which is so essential to the prosperity of the community.

CAROLINE.

If ever the legislature could interfere with advantage, I should think it would be in some regulations respecting expenditure. I should be strongly tempted to restrain the use of luxuries, in order to induce the owners of capital to employ it in agriculture, and such homely manufactures as are suited to the consumption of the poor: such a measure could not fail to produce a more equal distribution of the comforts of life.

MRS. B.

Sumptuary laws have been instituted with that view in many countries. But after all we have said of the benefits resulting from the natural distribution of capital when unrestrained and uninfluenced by political regulations, I am surprized at

430 ON EXPENDITURE.

your wishes to compel people to employ it in one way rather than in another.

CAROLINE.

But if that one way should prove the right way?

MRS. B.

Then capital will follow that direction by its natural impulse, without requiring any foreign aid. Be assured that the only right way is to leave the use of capital to the care of those to whom it belongs; they will be the most likely to discover in what line it can be employed to the greatest advantage.

CAROLINE.

Of their own advantage they are no doubt the best judges; but are you sure that they will be equally attentive to the advantage of the poor? Sumptuary laws appear to me to afford peculiar encouragement to the production of the necessaries of life. But the principal advantage of sumptuary laws would be to repress the expenditure of revenue. And since it is so desirable that capital should not be dissipated, surely the same principles will apply to revenue; would it not be advantageous to save that also, in order to convert it into capital?

MRS. B.

Capital, you know, has arisen solely from savings

ON EXPENDITURE. 431

from revenue; but you are aware that there must be a limit to such savings.

CAROLINE.

Certainly there is a limit, because we could not live without consuming some part of it; but the less we consume, and the more we save, the better.

MRS. B.

That is pushing the principle too far: we accumulate wealth for the purpose of enjoying it; and if by a liberal though prudent expenditure, social affections are cultivated, and the happiness of mankind promoted and extended, I see no reason why we should be debarred from indulging in some of the best feelings of our nature.

The two extremes of parsimony and prodigality are perhaps equally pernicious; the one as destructive of the social and benevolent affections, the other as wasting the provision which nature has destined for the maintenance and employment of the poor.

But there is another point of view in which sumptuary laws have a dangerous tendency. By diminishing objects of desire you run some risk of giving a general check to industry.

Tell me why do the rich employ the poor?

15

432   ON EXPENDITURE.

CAROLINE.

In order to derive an income from the profits of their labour.

MRS. B.

And what use do the rich make of this income?

CAROLINE.

They either spend the whole, or they economise part in order to augment their capital.

MRS. B.

But why should they be desirous of increasing their capital?

CAROLINE.

There are so many reasons for wishing to be rich, that I scarcely know how to enumerate them. The pride of wealth is a motive with some men, the love of independence with others; the apprehension of future reverses incites a third to accumulate; the wish to increase his means of doing good stimulates the industry of another; the desire of providing for a family, and leaving them in affluence, is a powerful inducement with many; but the ambition of improving their situation in life, and of increasing their enjoyments by a more liberal expenditure, is, I think, the most general, and perhaps the strongest of all the motives for accumulating riches.

ON EXPENDITURE. 433

MRS. B.

If, then, laws be enacted which restrain a man from spending any part of his income in luxuries, you take away one of his motives for wishing to augment his capital; and a growing capital is, you know, an increase of subsistence for the poor.

CAROLINE.

I would wish to prohibit only that excess of luxury which you have censured as pernicious.

MRS. B.

It is extremely difficult to draw the line between necessaries and luxuries; these form a scale which comprehends all the various comforts and conveniencies of life, the graduations of which are too numerous and too minute to be distinct. We have considered as necessaries whatever the rate of wages of the lowest ranks of people have enabled them to command; *they* would consider as luxuries whatever they have not been accustomed to enjoy; though when they can afford it there is no excess.

Excess, I conceive, depends not so much on the quantity or nature of the luxury, as upon its relative proportion to the means of the individual. A daily meal of meat is an excess of luxury to the family of a common labourer, because they are not used to it, and their wages will not enable them to command it;

U

434   ON EXPENDITURE.

whilst a table abounding with expensive delicacies can scarcely be called excess of luxury to a man whose income is so large that such gratifications do not prevent his making considerable savings.

CAROLINE.

Since then it is impossible to define what are and what are not luxuries, no general line of prohibition can be drawn.

MRS. B.

The ruin which extravagance entails on the prodigal is his natural punishment, and serves as a warning to deter others from similar imprudence. Any attempt to prevent such partial evil by sumptuary laws, would, generally, tend to depress the efforts of industry. The desire of increasing our enjoyments, and of improving our situation in life, as it is one of the strongest sentiments implanted in our nature, so I conceive it to be essentially conducive to the general welfare. It is the active zeal of each individual exerted in his own cause, which, in the aggregate, gives an impulse to the progressive improvement of the world at large. The desire of bettering his condition is justly considered as a laudable disposition in a poor man, and it is a feeling dangerous to repress in any classes of society.

ON EXPENDITURE.
435

CAROLINE.

—— " The man of wealth and pride
" Takes up a space that many poor supply'd;
" Space for his lake, his park's extensive bounds;
" Space for his horses, equipage, and hounds:
" The robe that wraps his limbs in silken sloth,
" Has robb'd the neighbouring fields of half their growth:
" His seat, where solitary sports are seen,
" Indignant spurns the cottage from the green."

What can you reply to these beautiful lines, Mrs. B.? I fear they are but too faithful a representation of the state of society.

MRS. B.

I must first inquire whether this man of wealth and pride either spends or produces capital in order to procure these gratifications. If the former, he deserves all the censure we have bestowed upon the spendthrift. If the latter, his wealth may possibly be more increased by his industry than diminished by his luxury.

CAROLINE.

In all probability he does neither; but being possessed of a considerable property, he lives upon his income; and such an expensive style of living must greatly diminish, if not wholly absorb what he might otherwise economise.

MRS. B.

Still I cannot approve of compulsory measures

U 2

436   ON EXPENDITURE.

to lessen his expenses.   If it be desirable to stimulate and encourage the industry of man, and induce him to accumulate wealth, he must be at full liberty to dispose of it according to his inclinations.   It is unquestionably true that unless the rich impoverish themselves by spending their capital, they cannot impoverish their country.

CAROLINE.

That is not enough; the question is, what are the best means of enriching their country?

MRS. B.

One man sits down contented with his little property; brings up his children with humble views and desires, and every year lays by something to provide for their future support in life.

Another of a more ambitious character rises early and labours hard, exerting every faculty of his mind to turn his capital to the best account; he likewise makes savings from his income, but they do not prevent his growing wealth from enabling him to spend more liberally, and enjoy more freely; and none of his enjoyments is more heart-felt, than that of having raised his family in the world by the exertions of his industry.

CAROLINE.

Every man who is striving to acquire wealth is

ON EXPENDITURE. 437

certainly more or less actuated by the prospects of the various enjoyments which he hopes his increasing income will enable him to command. One wishes to become rich enough to marry; another to keep a carriage, or a country house; a third to be able to settle his children respectably in the world.

MRS. B.

Such motives are strong incitements both to industry and frugality; and these useful habits often remain when the cause which gave rise to them no longer exists; it is far from uncommon to see men retain the taste for accumulating long after they have lost the inclination for spending.

Dr. Adam Smith observes, that before the introduction of refined luxuries, the English nobles had no other means of spending their wealth, than by maintaining in their houses a train of dependants, either in a state of absolute idleness, or whose only business was to indulge the follies or flatter the vanity of their patron; and this is in a great measure the case in Russia, Poland, and several other parts of Europe, even at the present day. We find that the consumption of provisions by the household of an English nobleman some centuries ago was perhaps a hundred times greater than it is at present. But you must not thence infer that the estate, which maintained such numerous retainers, produces less now than it did in those times;

U 3

438 ON EXPENDITURE.

on the contrary, it is perhaps as much increased as the consumption of the household is diminished. The difference is, that the produce, instead of supporting a number of lazy dependants, maintains probably a hundred times that number of industrious independant workmen, part of whom are employed in raising the produce of the estate, and part in supplying the nobleman with all the luxuries he requires: it was to obtain these luxuries that he dismissed his train of dependants, that he improved the culture of his land, and that, whilst studying only the gratification of his wishes, he contributed so essentially to the welfare of his country.

Here is a passage in Paley's Political Philosophy on the subject of luxury, extremely well worth your reading.

CAROLINE *reads.*

" It appears that the business of one half of
" mankind is to set the other half at work; that is,
" to provide articles, which, by tempting the de-
" sires, may stimulate the industry, and call forth
" the activity of those upon the exertion of whose
" industry, and the application of whose faculties,
" the production of human provision depends.
" It signifies nothing to the main purpose of trade
" how superfluous the articles which it furnishes
" are, whether the want of them be real or imagin-

ON EXPENDITURE. 439

" ary; whether it be founded in nature or in
" opinion, in fashion, habit, or emulation; it is
" enough that they be actually desired and sought
" after. Flourishing cities are raised and supported
" by trading in tobacco; populous towns subsist
" by the manufactory of ribbons. A watch may be
" a very unnecessary appendage to the dress of a
" peasant, yet if the peasant will till the ground in
" order to obtain a watch, the true design of trade
" is answered; and the watchmaker, whilst he po-
" lishes the case, and files the wheels of his machine,
" is contributing to the production of corn, as
" effectually, though not so directly, as if he handled
" the spade or the plough. If the fisherman will
" ply his nets, or the mariner fetch rice from foreign
" countries, in order to procure the indulgence of
" the use of tobacco, the market is supplied with
" two important articles of provision by the instru-
" mentality of a merchandise which has no other
" apparent use than the gratification of a vitiated
" palate."

This reminds me of an anecdote in Dr. Franklin's works. He describes the admiration which
was excited by a new cap worn at church by one
of the young girls of Cape May. This piece of
finery had come from Philadelphia; and with a
view of obtaining similar ornaments, the young girls
had all set to knitting worsted mittens, an article

U 4

440   ON EXPENDITURE.

in request at Philadelphia, the sale of which enabled
them to gratify their wishes.

MRS. B.

We often hear the poor reproached for aiming
at things above their situation; but I own that I
delight in seeing them strive to ornament their
cottages, to raise a few flowers amongst the nutritious vegetables in their gardens, to deck their
room, though it be but with rows of broken china,
cups, and plates, or a few gaudy prints; it shews a
desire of creditable appearance, and of aiming at
something beyond the bare means of subsistence.

CAROLINE.

The desire of improving their condition is not,
however, in all cases a sufficient motive to rouse the
industry of the lower classes.   I once knew an easy
indulgent landed proprietor, who having no ambition to increase his income could never be induced
to raise his rents; his tenants, finding that they
could pay their landlord and maintain their families
as well as their neighbours, with much less labour,
neglected their farms, and became so idle and disorderly, that the estate was the least productive of
any in the county.

MRS. B.

The country thus suffered from the well-meant,
but ill-judged indulgence of this landlord.

ON EXPENDITURE.   441

CAROLINE.

But why was not the industry of these tenants stimulated by the desire of raising themselves in the world, which the forbearance of their landlord enabled them so easily to do?

MRS. B.

In the course of time it probably would have had that effect; but when uneducated men obtain an increase of wealth, the first use they generally make of it is to procure indulgences and exemption from labour; it is only after becoming sensible that idleness leads them back to poverty, that they think of turning their wealth to better account. Well educated people seldom require the experience of so severe a lesson, but amongst the lower classes it is not uncommon to find that a great, and especially a sudden accession of riches, terminates in ruin.

CAROLINE.

There are frequently instances of poor people being ultimately ruined by a high prize in the lottery.

MRS. B.

And the lower the state of ignorance and degradation of mind of the poor man who gains the prize, the more certain is his ruin. The different state of improvement of the lower classes in England, in Scotland, and in Ireland, are strongly ex-

U 5

442 ON EXPENDITURE.

emplified in this respect. If you were to give a guinea to a Scotch peasant, he would consider long how he could turn it to the best account; he would perhaps buy a pig, or something that would bring a future profit. An English peasant is not quite so long sighted, yet he would contrive to derive some substantial advantages from the gift of a guinea; he would probably lay it out in repairing his cottage, or in purchasing some new clothes for his children. But the Irishman, whose joy would be the greatest of the three at such an unexpected acquisition of wealth, would in all likelihood spend the whole of it in drinking whiskey with his friends, and thus disable himself for the labour of the following day.

CAROLINE.

And do you suppose that a sudden and considerable increase of wages would be attended with mischievous effects to the labouring poor?

MRS. B.

In the first instance it probably would. In manufactures it is generally found that an accidental increase of wages, arising from a sudden demand for workmen, is productive of intemperance and disorderly conduct; and this has been urged as a general objection to high wages; but this bad effect seldom takes place unless the augmentation be sudden and unlooked for, and it discontinues when

ON EXPENDITURE. 443

the high wages become regularly established. You may almost consider it as certain, that uneducated men will derive no advantage from such an augmentation of income as raises them suddenly above their accustomed habits of life. The beneficial effects, I have described to you in one of our preceding conversations as arising from increasing wealth and demand for labour, must be gradual, in order to prove useful to the lower classes.

CAROLINE.

All that you have said reconciles me, in a great measure, to the inequality of the distribution of wealth; for it proves that, however great a man's possessions may be, it is decidedly advantageous to the country that he should still endeavour to augment them. Formerly I imagined that whatever addition was made to the wealth of the rich was so much subtracted from the pittance of the poor, but now I see that it is, on the contrary, an addition to the general stock of wealth of the country, by which the poor benefit equally with the rich.

MRS. B.

Yes; every accession of wealth to a country must have not only employed labourers to produce it, but will in future employ other labourers in order that the proprietor may derive an income from it. For every increase of capital is the result of a past and the cause of a future augmentation of produce

444   ON EXPENDITURE.

therefore whatever a man's property may be, he
should be encouraged to improve it.   I will read
you an eloquent passage in Bentham's *Théorie de la
Législation* on the subject of luxury.

  " L'attrait du plaisir, la successions des besoins,
" le desir actif d'ajouter au bien être, produiront
" sans cesse, sous le regime de la sureté, de nou-
" veaux efforts vers des nouvelles acquisitions. Les
" besoins les jouissances, ces agens universels de la
" societé aprés avoir fait eclore les premieres gerbes
" de blés, éleveront peu a peu les magazins de
" l'abondance toujours croissans et jamais remplis.
" Les desirs sétendent avec les moyens ; l'horizon
" s'aggrandit, à mesure qu'on s'avance, et chaque
" besoin nouveau également accompagné de sa
" peine et de son plaisir devient un nouveau prin-
" cipe d'action ; l'opulence qui n'est qu'un terme
" comparatif n'arrete pas même ce mouvement,
" une fois qu'il est imprimé, au contraire plus
" on opére en grand, plus la recompense est
" grande, et par consequent plus est grande
" aussi la force du motif qui anime l'homme au
" travail.

  " On a vu que l'abondance se forme peu à
" peu par l'operation continue des mêmes causes
" qui ont produit la subsistence. Il n'y a donc
" point d'opposition entre ces deux buts.   Au con-
" traire plus l'abondance augmente plus on est sur
" de la substance. Ceux qui blament l'abondance

ON EXPENDITURE. 445

" sous le nom de *Luxe* n'ont jamais saisi cette con-
" sideration.

" Les intempéries, les guerres, les accidens de
" toute espéce attaquent souvent le fond de la sub-
" sistence; ensorte qu'une societé qui n'auroit pas de
" superflu et même beaucoup de superflu seroit su-
" jette a manquer souvent de necessaire; c'est ce
" qu'on voit chez les peuples sauvages. C'est ce qu'on
" a vu frequemment chez toutes les nations dans
" les tems de l'antique pauvreté. C'est ce qui
" arrive encore de nos jours dans les pays peu
" favorisés de la nature, tel que la Suéde, et dans
" ceux où le gouvernement contrarie les operations
" du commerce au lieu de se borner à le proteger.
" Mais les pays ou le luxe abonde et où l'adminis-
" tration est eclairée, sont à l'abri de la famine.
" Telle est l'heureuse situation de l'Angleterre.
" Des manufactures de luxe deviennent des bu-
" reaux d'assurances contre la disette. Une fa-
" brique de bierre ou d'amidon se convertira en
" moyen de subsistence. Que de fois n'a t'on pas
" declamé contre les chevaux et les chiens comme
" dévorant la subsistence des hommes ! Ces pro-
" fonds politiques ne s'elevent que d'un degré
" au dessus de ces apôtres du désintercssement qui
" pour ramener l'abondance des blés courent in-
" cendier les magazins."

446

ON EXPENDITURE.

CAROLINE.

We had not yet considered luxury under this point of view; I confess I was of the opinion of those who thought that dogs and horses devoured the subsistence of man, but I am much better pleased to think that the food which luxury raises for the nourishment of those animals may, in case of necessity, become nourishment for the human species; and, if a famine should take place, even the animals themselves would afford a resource.

MRS. B.

Hair powder we may consider as a kind of granary for the preservation of wheat, for though the powder would not, unless in cases of very great urgency, be converted into food, the quantity of corn annually grown for the purpose of making hair powder would, during a moderate scarcity, find its way more readily to the baker's than to the perfumer's shop.

CAROLINE.

And pray, Mrs. B., what do you think of the luxury of the Romans? We read in Pliny of a Roman lady who was dressed in jewels to the amount of 300,000*l*. I recollect, also, an account of a dish of fish having cost 64*l*.

ON EXPENDITURE. 447

MRS. B.

These are but trifling instances of profusion, in comparison of some others related of the Romans. Mark Anthony expended 60,000*l.* in an entertainment given to Cleopatra. And the supper of Heliogabalus cost 6000*l.* every night. But nothing can be said in apology for the luxuries of the Romans; they were extremely objectionable, because their wealth did not proceed from industry, but from plunder. Their extravagance and profusion, therefore, far from being a spur to industry, acted in a contrary direction; it encouraged the love of rapine in themselves, whilst it depressed the spirit of industry in the countries subject to their power, by destroying the strongest of all inducements to labour, the security of property. It has been well observed by Macpherson, that " The luxuries of " the Romans cannot be considered as the summit " of a general scale of prosperity; it was a scale " graduated but by one division, which separated " immense wealth and power from abject slavery, " wretchedness, and want."

In considering the advantages to be derived from luxury, we must, however, carefully remember, that it acts in a twofold manner; whilst on the one hand it encourages industry, on the other it increases expenditure; so far as its productive powers prevail over its prodigal effects, it is beneficial to mankind; but in the contrary case it becomes an evil, and when it en-

448 ON EXPENDITURE.

croaches on capital we have seen that it is an evil of the greatest magnitude.

The grand object to be kept in view in order to promote the general prosperity of the country, is the increase of *capital.* But it is not in the power of the legislature to promote this end in any other way than by providing for the security of property; any attempts to interfere either with the disposal of capital or with the nature and extent of expenditure, are equally discouraging to industry.

CAROLINE.

Whoever, I conceive, augments his capital by savings from his income, increases the general stock of subsistence for the labouring classes; whilst he who spends part of his capital diminishes that stock of subsistence, and consequently the means of employing the labouring classes in its reproduction.

Every man ought, therefore, to consider it as a moral duty, independently of his private interest, to keep his expenditure so far within the limits of his income that he may be enabled every year to make some addition to his capital.

MRS. B.

And the question what that addition should be, must depend entirely upon the extent of his income, and his motives for expenditure. We can only point out illiberal parsimony, and extravagant

ON EXPENDITURE. 449

prodigality as extremes to be avoided; there are so many gradations in the scale between them, that every man must draw the line for himself, according to the dictates of his good sense and his conscience, and in so doing should consult, perhaps, the moral philosopher as well as the political economist. He who has a large family to maintain and establish in the world, though more strict economy be required of him, cannot be expected to make savings equal to those of a man of a similar income, who has not the same calls for expenditure.

But however large a man's income may be, he has no apology for neglect of economy. Economy is a virtue incumbent on all; a rich man may have sufficient motives to authorize a liberal expenditure, but he can have none for negligence and waste; and however immaterial to himself the loss which waste occasions, he should consider it as so much taken from that fund which provides maintenance and employment for the poor.

THE END.

INDEX.

A

ACCUMULATION of wealth, 83.
Adulteration of the coin of the country, 322.
    its effect on wages, 323.
    has been adopted in almost all countries, 324.
Agriculture, introduction of, 19. 42.
    whether preferable to other branches of industry, 173.
    of the proportion it should bear to manufactures and commerce, 177.
    most advantageous to newly settled countries, 178.
    yields two incomes, 213.
    Metayer system of, 229.
    state of, in France, 235.
Agricultural produce, high price of, 191.
    not susceptible of unlimited increase, 192.
    causes of its high price, 194.
    and population alternately take the lead, 200.
    causes which lower its price, 202.
    high price of, necessary to proportion the consumption to the supply, 208.
    the first commodity which a country exports, 367. 389.
Alms, giving, effects of, 167, 168.
America, increase of population in, 138.
    exports corn, 367.
    agriculture of, 389.
    effect of its discovery on the industry of Europe, 313.

452   INDEX.

America, the produce of its mines how distributed throughout
       the world, 409.
Annuitants, affected by the exchangeable value of money, 310.
Art, advantages it has over the powers of nature, 175.

B

Balance of trade, 401.
       popular error respecting it, 413.
Banks, saving, advantages of, 162.
Banks, issuing notes, 327.
       of Amsterdam, 329.
       of England, 331.
       restriction of paying in specie, 332.
Barter, origin of, 62.
Benefit clubs, or friendly societies, advantages resulting from,159.
Bentham's Théorie de Legislation, extract from, on the effects
       of luxury, 444.
Bills of exchange, their use in foreign commerce, 399.
Blackstone's Commentaries, extract from, on civil liberty, 40.
Bounty, on the exportation of goods, 370.
Buchanan's edition of Adam Smith's, passage from, on price,292.

C

Canals, advantages arising from, 353. 356.
Capital, origin of, 88.
       employment of, 89. 109.
       profits derived from, 92.
       necessary for all productive enterprises, 93. 276.
       fixed and circulating, distinction of, 102.
       definition of, 113.
       of a country, 113. 420.
       effect of its increase on profit and wages, 121.
       effect of its diminution, 124.
       increase of, in Europe, 144.
       increase of, in America, 138.

INDEX. 453

Capital, various modes of employing it, 172.
    required for agriculture, 214, 215.
    lent at interest, 248.
    quick return of in the home trade, 360.
    expenditure of, 423.
    increase of, always advantageous, 448.
Cheapness, beneficial only when it arises from a low cost of
    production, 288, 289.
    only nominal when arising from scarcity of money,
    302. 306.
Circulating capital explained, 102.
Civilization, progress of, 41.
Civilized state of society, 20.
Clarke's (Dr.) Travels, extract from, on insecurity of property, 52.
Coined money, antiquity of, 296.
    advantages of, 297.
Coin, adulteration of,
Colonies, establishment of, 155.
Commerce, a mode of employing capital, 343,
    foreign, 358.
    advantages of, 362, 363.
Competition of sellers reduces prices, 378.
Consumption, distinguished from expenditure, 421,
    of a country, 422.
    productive and unproductive, 422,
Corn, unknown origin of, 43.
    - trade, 383.
    home and foreign supply of, 384.
    exportation of, 389.
    natural high price of, 194.
Cost of production of commodities, 275. 278.
    component parts of, 278.
    diminished, cause of cheapness, 288, 289.
Creditor, public, how repaid, 261.

454 INDEX.

D

Dairy, establishments of Fruitieres in Switzerland, 233
Debt, national, 264.
Demand, definition of, 119.
    for labour, on what it depends, 130.
    for the necessaries of life, 193.
    and supply, 287.
Depreciation of money, its effect on price, 332.
Division of labour, 66.
    passages from Adam Smith on, 67, 68. 71. 73.
    its effect on the moral and intellectual faculties, 77.
    its effect in the multiplication of wealth, 80.

E

Economy, 448.
Edinburgh Review, extract from, on small farms, 239.
Education of the poor, advantages of, 158.
Emigration, a resource for redundant population, 155.
    impolicy of restraining it, 156.
    under some circumstances injurious to a country, 157.
Employment of capital, 89. 109.
Exchange, bill of, its use in trade, 399.
    unfavourable, or below par, 402.
    premium on, 402.
    unfavourable, promotes exportation, 407.
    how affected by depreciation of currency, 410.
    nominal, 412.
Exchangeable value, 270. 284.
    definition of, 282.
    and natural value do not always coincide, 286.
    of money, what classes of men affected by its varia-
        tions, 306.
Expenditure, 97. 419.
    distinguished from consumption, 421.

INDEX. 455

Expenditure of capital, its consequences, 264. 423.
Exportation of corn, under what circumstances advantageous, 389.

F

Farmers, exposed to small risks, 185.
    require capital, 214.
    gentlemen, 224, 225.
Farms, small, objections to, 236.
    what size most advantageous, 238.
    size of, in Belgium and Tuscany, 238.
Fisheries, rent of, 243.
Fishing, capital required for it, 94.
Fixed capital, 102.
Foreign trade, 358.
    advantages of, 362, 363.
    advantageous to both countries engaged in it, 375.
Franklin, passage from, on prohibitions in trade, 381.
    anecdote from, on the effects of luxury, 439.
Friendly societies, or benefit clubs, 159.

G

Gardens, for cottagers, 170.
Garnier, extract from, on the employment of capital, 180.
Gold, how paid for, 298.
    - coins, antiquity of, 296.
    - bullion, the standard of value of coined money, 336.
    - bullion, high price of, 337.
    and silver, effect of its influx in Spain, 416, 417.
Goldsmith's Deserted Village, passages from, on small farms, 230.
    on inclosures, 154.
    on emigration, 156.
    on luxury, 435.
Goods, community of, 56.
Governments, origin of, 19.

456 INDEX.

Governments, errors of, in political economy, 22.
    despotic, effects of, 48, 49, 50. 52.

H

Happiness, how influenced by wealth, 98.
Home trade, 358, 359.

I

Ignorance of savages, 31.
Importation of corn, 389.
Improvement, gradual, preferable to revolution, 166.
Income, or revenue, origin of, 88.
    derived from profits, 96.
Industry, encouraged by security, 37.
    of the Swiss, 58.
    limited by extent of capital, 96. 153.
    encouraged by emancipation, 104.
        by high wages, 148.
        by piece-work, 149.
Interest of money, 247.
    diminishes, as wealth increases, 253.
    varies in different countries, 255, 256.
    low rate of, a sign of prosperity, 256.
    exceptions to this rule, 257.
    impolicy of fixing it by law, 258.
    in ancient times and countries, 258.
    in the public funds, 260.

J

Jesuits, their establishment in Paraguay, 57.

L

Labour, its effect in the production of wealth, 30.
    considered as a cause of value, 273.
Labourers, productive, 92.

INDEX. 457

Labourers, unproductive, 265.
Land, monopoly of, 210.
    mortgaged, 249.
Landed property, 37, 38.
Laws, utility of, 39.
Leases, their terms and duration, 218.
Loans, to individuals, 247.
    to government, 260, 261.
Luxury, a relative term, 433.
    its excess only pernicious, 434.
    promotes industry, 434.
    a resource in scarcity, 446.
    of the Romans, objections to,
    when beneficial, and when injurious, 447.

M

Machines, their effect in abridging labour, 75.
Machinery, objections to it, 107.
    advantages derived from it, 108.
Macpherson's History of Commerce, extract from on machinery, 110.
    on fixing the price of provisions, 128. 130.
Manufactures, their influence on population, 146.
Manufacturers, rate of their profits, 185.
Measures of value, all imperfect, 282.
Merchants, rate of their profits, 185.
Metals, used only in civilized countries, 76.
Metayer system of farming, 229.
    in Belgium and Tuscany, 238.
Mines, first worked in England, 76.
    in general, 240.
    of coal, 240.
    of metal, 241.
    great risk attending them, 241.
Mirabeau Monarchie Prussienne, passage from, on free trade, 395.

458   INDEX.

Money, lent at interest, 247.

     in general, 293.

     its use as a medium of exchange, 294.

     various articles used for this purpose, 295.

     coined, antiquity of, 296.

     advantages of, 297.

     its use as a standard of value, 297.

     not an accurate standard of value, 300.

     cheapness of commodities arising from its scarcity, 301.

     dearness of commodities arising from its abundance, 303.

     depreciation of, 305. 318.

     variation in the exchangeable value of, 306.

     has of late years fallen in value, 309. 320.

     has real value, not merely a sign, 311.

     impolicy of preventing its exportation, 312. 314.

     effects of its free exportation, 315.

     how it regulates price, 319.

     its value in ancient times, 321.

     adulteration of, 322.

     of paper, no real value, 325.

     excess of, creates depreciation, 338.

     expedients for economising it, 339. 399.

Monopoly of land explained, 210.

     defined, 210.

Moravians, their institution, 58.

Mortgage of land, 249.

N

National debt, 264.

Natural value, 278.

     of gold bullion, 299.

Nature, of the variety and profusion of her gifts, 38.

     assists the labours of man, 174.

INDEX. 459

Necessaries of life, definition of, varies in different countries, 116.

    effects of redundancy of, 387.

Nominal cheapness, 302.

    exchange, 412.

P

Paley's Moral Philosophy, passage from, on accumulation of wealth, 143.

    on agriculture, 221.

    on luxury, 438.

Paper money, no real value, 325.

    its effect in driving specie out of the country, 330.

    excess of, creates depreciation,

Pastoral life, 19. 41.

Patent, a species of partial monopoly, 211.

Piece-work stimulates industry, 149.

Poor-rates, objections to, 163.

    lowers the price of labour, 164.

Political economy, errors arising from ignorance of its principles, 7.

    advantages arising from some of its principles, 11.

    difficulties to be surmounted in this study, 14.

    definition of, 18.

Population, wages how affected by it, 118. 121.

    rapid increase of, in America, 138.

    in Europe, 139.

    great, under what circumstances advantageous, 141.

    effects of its increase beyond the means of subsistence,

    naturally increases with capital, 150.

    redundant, relieved by emigration, 155.

    and agricultural produce alternately take the lead, 200.

Poverty, 95.

Price, impolicy of the legislature interfering with it, 126.

X 2

460 INDEX.

Price of raw produce, how regulated, 201.
    and value, 269.
    defined, 271.
    generally equivalent to cost of production, 275.
    how affected by scarcity of money, 301.
    how affected by depreciation of money, 303.
    various circumstances affecting it, 305. 335.
    how regulated, 309.
    reduced by free competition of sellers, 378.
Prodigality, its pernicious effects, 425.
Production, cost of, 275.
Productive labourers, 92. 265.
Profits, derived from the employment of capital, 92.
    of capital, 115. 120.
    decrease with decrease of capital, 121. 258.
    tending to equality in all employments of capital, 182.
    proportioned to the degrees of risk, 185.
    circumstances which derange the equality of profits, 188.
    of agriculture diminish as inferior soils are culti-
    vated, 197.
    of the farmer, how calculated, 216.
    of mining, 242.
    a component part of cost of production, 276.
    great, of small dealers, 350.
Promissory notes, 327.
Property, security of, 36.
    in land, 37, 38.
    consequences of its establishment, 45.
    consequences of its insecurity, 49.
    in common, objections to it, 56.
    in land, effects of its extreme division, 231.

R

Rent, 189.
    effect of the high price of agricultural produce, 191.

INDEX. 461

Rent, derived from the surplus produce of agriculture, 194.
    why not paid in new settlements, 195.
    origin of, 197.
    definition of, 202.
    consequences of its abolition, 204, 5, 6, 7.
    rise positively, but not relatively, 205.
    of farms, 216.
    of mines, 241.
    of fisheries, 243.
    a component part of cost of production, 277.
Revenue, or income, origin of, 92, 93.
    modes of employing capital to produce it, 172.
    derived from property in land, 189.
    derived from cultivation of land, 213.
    of those who do not employ their capital themselves,
      245.
Rewards, advantages of, 169.
Riches, of what they consist, 24.
Rich and poor, distinction between, 82.
    contract between, 85.

S

Saving banks, 162.
Say's Political Economy, extract from, on the invention of
    printing, 111.
    on prohibitions in trade, 380.
Scarcity, its effect on wages, 125.
    its effect on price, 286.
Security, stimulus to industry, 63.
Skill, acquired by the division of labour, 66.
    higher wages paid for it, 134.
Slaves, fixed capital, 104.
Slavery, discouraging to industry, 105.
Smith, Adam, passage from, on the division of labour, 67, 68.
    on the pin manufacture, 71.

X 3

462   INDEX.

Smith, Adam, on forging nails, 73.
  on value, 270.
Soils of inferior quality increase the cost of production, 195.
Spain, her industry affected by the American mines, 316.
Spinning jennies, invention of, 109, 110.
Statute of labourers, 323.
Stockholders, fictitious capital of, 263.
  affected by variations in the value of money, 310.
Sumptuary laws, 429.
  effects of, 433.

T

Telemachus, passage from, on Salentum, 1.
  on Bœtica, 54.
Tenants at will, 219.
Townsend's Travels in Spain, passage from, on alms-giving, 167.
  on gentlemen farmers, 225.
  on farms held in administration, 228.
  on the influx of gold and silver in Spain, 417.
Trade, wholesale and retail, distinction of, 343.
  general advantages of, 344.
  wholesale, 345.
  retail, 349.
  home, 358, 359.
  policy of freedom of, 391.

U

Unproductive labourers, 265.
  how affected by fluctuations in the value of money, 308.
Usury, 259.
Utility considered as essential to value, 271. 276.

INDEX. 463

V

Value and price, 269.
    in exchange, 270. 286.
    its component parts, 276. 278.
    natural, 278. 286.
    and price, distinction between them, 303.
    no accurate measure of, 282.
Vineyards and olive-grounds, tenure of, 282.
Volney's Travels, passages from, on the effects of despotic
    governments, 48, 49, 50.

W

Wages, origin of, 85.
    of labour, their limits, 115.
    how regulated, 117. 137.
    increase with increase of capital, 121.
    decrease with increase of population, 123.
    diminish with diminution of capital, 124.
    impolicy of being fixed by law, 126.
    low in Ireland, 132.
    proportioned to skill, 134.
    to the severity and disagreeableness of the labour,
      134.
    how affected by scarcity, 125.
    high, not always accompanying great capital, 136.
    in China, 136.
    in America, 137.
    rise of, in England and Ireland, 144.
    high, encourage industry, 148.
    lowered by poor-rates, 164.
    component part of value, 276.
    affected by adulteration of the coin, 33, .
    effects of sudden increase of, 442.
Wealth, definition of, 25. 274.

464 INDEX.

Wealth, accumulation of, 83.
  reproduction of, 87. 92.
  incitements to increase it, 437. 443.
  effects of sudden increase of, 441.

Y

Yeomanry, 204.
Young, Arthur, travels in France,
  passage from, on the extreme division of landed property, 230.

Printed by A. Strahan,
Printers-Street, London.

For EU product safety concerns, contact us at Calle de José Abascal, 56–1°, 28003 Madrid, Spain or eugpsr@cambridge.org.

www.ingramcontent.com/pod-product-compliance
Ingram Content Group UK Ltd.
Pitfield, Milton Keynes, MK11 3LW, UK
UKHW010852060825
461487UK00012B/1085